ADVANCE PRAISE FOR
REFLECTIVE SUPERVISION AND LEADERSHIP
IN INFANT AND EARLY CHILDHOOD PROGRAMS

Thoughtful, thorough, appropriately complex yet practical, this welcome volume systematically addresses the nature and landscape of supervisory reflection. With a beginning insistence on the need for informed and steadfast institutional support, it undertakes the exploration of the skills and knowledge required of practitioners. The challenges and dilemmas necessarily encountered are vividly described and vignettes offer careful and illuminating illustrations of the many processes at work. Equally useful are the detailed tracking forms for supervisory development. Their widespread use would improve the overall level of supervision enormously. Overall, this is an extremely valuable contibution to the field.

— **Jeree Pawl, PhD**
Retired, former clinical professor, Department of Psychiatry, University of California at San Francisco
Director of Infant-Parent Program, San Francisco General Hospital

In this beautifully and skillfully written book, you will find your voice as a supervisor, discovering the words and the ways to bring out the best in your staff and yourself as a leader. A must for all front-line supervisors and their supervisors as well!

— **Linda Gilkerson, PhD**
Professor
Erikson Institute

Outstanding. A long awaited and necessary resource to the field. Reflective supervision has remained a bit of an enigma. Many professionals know the value of a reflective practice model but struggle to articulate it's complexity to funders and administrators. Heffron and Murch have done a marvelous job of defining and defending the importance of reflective supervision to grow and sustain a quality workforce. The resource available in the Appendixes are extremely helpful. The authors have also embraced the use of reflective supervision across a variety of disciplines. This text is a must-read for any supervisor or program manager.

— **Barbara Stroud, PhD**
Community Training Manager
Child Development Institute
Canoga Park, CA

Continued

Exceptional. This book on reflective supervision and leadership in infant and early childhood programs brings the Parallel Process to life "Do unto others as you would have others do unto others (Pawl & St. John, 1998)." Its richness comes from being applied and practical. Through the use of vignettes, it shows us how to connect theory and practice so supervisors and managers can support their staff so staff can support caregivers (or parents) in supporting their children even when coping with difficult circumstances. Similarly, through vignettes surrounding performance issues, it provides concrete tools for leaders, program managers and supervisors, to operate within the "blended" role of both being an administrator and supportive, reflective supervisor. The authors state, "Embrace complexity." They have done so here in a way that managers and supervisors can mindfully create a relationship-based program that prevents burnout and provides positive direction to staff so they can enjoy their rather than be overwhelmed by this most important, complex work.

— **Victor Bernstein, PhD**
Research Associate and Associate Professor
University of Chicago School of Social Work Administration

This book is an excellent resource to support ongoing professional development of practitioners working in a variety of settings with young children and their families. The authors provide current evidence based principles and strategies for building and maintaining reflectice practice and supervision of such practice. The vignettes are varied and useful to generate discussion in relationship based programs. The appendices with specific standards and forms for various program configurations add tremendously to the utility of this volume. I would definitely use this book with students as part of their supervised field work in early intervention and early childhood special education.

— **Maurine Ballard-Rosa, PhD**
Professor
Early Childhood Special Education
California State University Sacramento

REFLECTIVE SUPERVISION AND LEADERSHIP
IN INFANT AND EARLY CHILDHOOD PROGRAMS

Mary Claire Heffron and Trudi Murch

ZERO
TO
THREE®

National Center for Infants,
Toddlers, and Families

Washington, DC

National Center for Infants, Toddlers, and Families

Published by
ZERO TO THREE
Toll-free orders (800) 899-4301
Web: www.zerotothree.org

The mission of the ZERO TO THREE Press is to publish authoritative research, practical resources, and new ideas for those who work with and care about infants, toddlers, and their families. Books are selected for publication by an independent Editorial Board.

The views contained in this book are those of the authors and do not necessarily reflect those of ZERO TO THREE: National Center for Infants, Toddlers, and Families, Inc.

These materials are intended for education and training to help promote a high standard of care by professionals. Use of these materials is voluntary, and their use does not confer any professional credentials or qualification to take any registration, certification, board, or licensure examination, and neither confers nor infers competency to perform any related professional functions.

The user of these materials is solely responsible for compliance with all local, state, or federal rules, regulations, or licensing requirements. Despite efforts to ensure that these materials are consistent with acceptable practices, they are not intended to be used as a compliance guide and are not intended to supplant or to be used as a substitute for or in contravention of any applicable local, state, or federal rules, regulations, or licensing requirements. ZERO TO THREE expressly disclaims any liability arising from use of these materials in contravention of such rules, regulations, or licensing requirements.

The views expressed in these materials represent the opinions of the respective authors. Publication of these materials does not constitute an endorsement by ZERO TO THREE of any view expressed herein, and ZERO TO THREE expressly disclaims any liability arising from any inaccuracy or misstatement.

Cover and text design: Design Consultants

Cover art © Ruby Newman 2010. www.rubynewman.com

Library of Congress Cataloging-in-Publication Data

Heffron, Mary Claire.
    Reflective supervision and leadership for infant and early childhood programs / Mary Claire Heffron and Trudi Murch.
        p. cm.
ISBN 978-1-934019-90-0
1. Child welfare workers--Supervision of. 2. Child caregivers. I. Murch, Trudi. II. Title.
    HV713.H382 2010
    362.71068'3--dc22

                                                                                    2010040112

10 9 8 7 6 5 4 3 2

ISBN 0-978-1-934019-90-0

Printed in the United States of America

Suggested citation: Heffron, M. C., & Murch, T. (2010). *Reflective supervision and leadership in infant and early childhood programs*. Washington, DC: ZERO TO THREE.

DEDICATION

We dedicate this book to Emily Fenichel, who provided the original impetus for the development of this book. We treasure her support, inspiration, and friendship to this day.

TABLE OF CONTENTS

ACKNOWLEDGMENTS

We are grateful to many people for assisting and supporting us in writing this book.

Bill Issel was a tireless reader and commenter on multiple drafts. His clear thinking, writing skill, probing questions, support, and encouragement were invaluable.

Colleagues and friends at Children's Hospital and the wonderful infant mental health community in Northern California have inspired us with their commitment to reflective practice and supervision and their dedication to their craft of serving young children and families. Encouragement from colleagues around the country to expand on earlier articles to create a more comprehensive guide to reflective supervision has spurred us on.

We are thankful to Robert Murch for providing us with a quiet and beautiful place to work, write, and think. His confidence in us and his enthusiasm for the project helped to keep us going. Ginger Ward, CEO of Southwest Human Development, has encouraged and supported this endeavor since the very beginning. Her long-term and persistent commitment to the reflective supervision model has been a source of inspiration to us and taught us much about what it takes to do this work within the reality constraints of strained budgets, initial staff discomfort, and programmatic regulatory requirements. Jose Rojo provided us with ongoing support in producing the manuscript: We would have been lost without him.

Finally, we would like to express our gratitude to the colleagues and teachers who have helped us learn and think about our work with staff, families, and children. They include: Jeree Pawl, Judith Bertacchi, Audrey Holland, Rebecca Shahmoon Shanok, Linda Eggbeer, Linda Gilkerson, Lucia Milburn, Maria St. John, Barbara Ivins, Donna Davidovitz, and many others. They have guided us and given us comfort: We feel we are working together with them, shoulder to shoulder.

INTRODUCTION

This book is meant to be a hands-on resource for reflective supervision, program development, and leadership in programs for infants, toddlers, preschoolers, and their families. We have imagined it as an operating manual for reflective supervision and reflective practice that will illustrate the frameworks and foundations as well as the steps to support these practices in a wide range of environments. These various settings include early care and education, early intervention, child welfare, family support, and mental health programs. Throughout the book, we have given examples of the ways in which supervisors can be responsive to the diversity of experiences, beliefs, and perspectives that staff members bring to their work and that reflect factors such as their personal values or professional training. We introduce information and skills that will guide supervisors to address the range of roles and responsibilities encompassed in their positions.

When programs for infants, toddlers, and their families began to proliferate in the early 1990s, leaders in the field began to talk and write about the need for reflective supervision in a wide range of early childhood programs. ZERO TO THREE responded to this development by publishing *Learning Through Supervision and Mentorship to Support the Development of Infants, Toddlers and Their Families: A Source Book* (Fenichel, 1992). This slim collection quickly became known as the "Yellow Book" and soon became an indispensable resource for practitioners. Authors included Emily Fenichel, Rebecca Shahmoon Shanok, Linda Gilkerson, Judith Bertacchi, William Schafer, and others. This work helped practitioners to integrate reflective supervision more broadly and to extend the practice to non-mental health service delivery systems. This book inspired the next generation of authors and implementers—such as Deborah Weatherston, Brenda Jones Harden, Victor Bernstein, and the present authors—who have elaborated models of reflective supervision in numerous publications and in their teaching. As participants in this second wave, we have drawn on existing sources as well as our own personal experience as supervisors, program developers, teachers, and leaders to contribute to this vital and growing practice of reflective supervision.

Our work has also been inspired by writers from other fields who have contributed to the understanding of reflective supervision and practice. A major contributor is the philosopher Donald A. Schon, whose book *The Reflective Practitioner: How Professionals Think in Action* (1983) spans professions from science to mental health. More recently, researchers and teachers such as Jon Kabat-Zinn (1991, 2003) have demonstrated how mindfulness, a form of reflective practice often connected with meditation practice, reduces stress and increases the satisfaction of health care workers and others. In work that complements such studies, Daniel Siegel and his colleagues (Siegel, 2007, 2010; Siegel & Harzell, 2003) have begun to explore the links between neuroscience and mindful practices in their work at The Mindsight Institute, and these works have helped us integrate some of this understanding into our work on reflective supervision.

In writing this book we have used a broad and inclusive definition of reflective supervision. Our definition of the various roles a supervisor might play includes such activities as providing staff members a space for reflection and introspection, nurturing staff members' well-being, helping staff members understand the mission and values of the team and the organization, staff training, quality assurance, serving as an intermediary between direct service staff members and upper management, promoting change and innovation, and initiating community collaborations.

We have emphasized a blended model of supervision in this book because it is the most common—though in many ways the most challenging—approach to reflective supervision. The reflective supervisor is responsible for promoting staff members' growth and development and for providing opportunities to reflect on the work. At the same time, she holds administrative oversight—attending to the contractual, regulatory, and financial demands of the program. We recognize that in some settings, these core supervisory processes may be split apart: We will address the liabilities inherent in that approach and also discuss ways that a reflective stance can be integrated in all clinical and administrative activities.

In the writing process, we have examined our professional successes and missteps to provide examples, analyze dilemmas, and develop functional definitions. We use these to ground the theory of reflective supervision in the realities of day-to-day program practice. Throughout the book, we have used vignettes, examples of supervisory language, and guiding questions to assist readers in creatively implementing a reflective supervision model. We have used the feminine pronoun most of the time, as the majority of supervisors, direct service staff members, and program leaders in this field are female. Over time, we hope to see a better gender balance in programs serving young children and families.

The reflective supervision model is widely referenced, and programs such as Early Head Start and Healthy Families cite reflective supervision as best practice in their program guidelines. Infant and early childhood mental health treatment models that cite solid evidence for their outcomes—such as the Steps Toward Effective, Enjoyable Parenting (STEEP) program (Erickson, Egeland, Simon, & Rose, 2002) and Child–Parent Psychotherapy (Lieberman & Van Horn, 2008)—also describe regular reflective supervision as a must. Despite these widely accepted and promoted program practices and the availability of some excellent publications on reflective supervision, we feel there is a need for this amplified and functional handbook. However, this book is not and could not be prescriptive given the variations in program mission and populations, regional differences, discipline requirements, agency culture, staff, and resources.

This book has grown from deep personal commitment to work with infants, young children, and families, as well as a strong belief that reflective supervision is a foundational practice necessary for quality services and for sustaining the well-being of the staff members providing direct services. Our hope is that this guide will clarify the roles and functions of the reflective supervisor and describe in detail the skills, processes, training, and leadership required to effectively guide and support staff members from diverse disciplines, levels of experience, and education. In detailing the complexities, rewards, and pitfalls of reflective supervision, we address broad principles as well as specific practices of reflective supervision, such as team development and leadership. We have highlighted the strategic and potentially powerful position of the reflective supervisor as a link between direct services and program management. We intend the book to support reflective supervisors and other leaders responsible for the growth and well-being of staff members. We anticipate that it will also be helpful for teachers, trainers, consultants, program mentors, funders, and coordinators whose roles include teaching others about reflective practice and supervision. The book is intended to be a descriptive and practical set of operating instructions that will guide, but not restrict, the creativity and innovations of program staff members who want to shape their work through both a relational and reflective lenses.

REFERENCES

Erickson, M. F., Egeland, B., Simon, J., & Rose, T. (2002). *STEEP: Steps toward effective, enjoyable parenting.* Minneapolis: University of Minnesota, Irving B. Harris Training Center for Infant and Toddler Development.

Fenichel, E. (Ed.). (1992). *Learning through supervision and mentorship to support the development of infants, toddlers and their families: A source book.* Washington, DC: ZERO TO THREE.

Kabat-Zinn, J. (1991). *Full catastrophe living: Using the wisdom of your body and mind to face stress, pain, and illness.* New York: Dell.

Kabat-Zinn, J. (2003). Mindfulness-based interventions in context: Past, present, and future. *Clinical Psychology: Science and Practice, 10,* 144–156.

Lieberman, A. F., & Van Horn., P. (2008). *Psychotherapy with infants and young children: Repairing the effects of stress and trauma on early attachment.* New York: Guilford Press.

Schon, D. (1983). *The reflective practitioner: How professionals think in action.* London: Temple Smith.

Siegel, D. J. (2010). *Mindsight: The new science of transformation*. New York: Random House.

Siegel, D. J. (2007). *The mindful brain: Reflection and attunement in the cultivation of well-being*. New York: Norton.

Siegel, D., & Harzell, M. (2003). *Parenting from the inside out*. New York: Tarcher.

CHAPTER 1

WHAT IS REFLECTIVE SUPERVISION?

The practice of reflective supervision is sometimes referred to in ways that make it sound exceedingly simple or, alternately, overly mysterious. We have often seen the term used in passing as if readers would share and understand a precise and consistent definition. In the section below, we provide a concise working definition that is meant to guide and anchor the reader and expand understanding of this frequently used term.

A WORKING DEFINITION

Reflective supervision is a relationship-based supervisory approach that supports various models of relationship-based service delivery. The approach includes regular meetings, a collaborative relational approach, and an emphasis on reflection. Reflective supervision can be used across disciplines, systems of care, and service models for infants, young children, and families. These include infant and early childhood mental health, early intervention for children with disabilities, family support, community nursing, early care and education, and child welfare. Supervision provided in this model can be done on an individual basis or in a group.

In this model, the supervisor creates a safe and welcoming space for staff members to reflect on and learn from their own work with a trusted mentor/supervisor at their side. Caring for and understanding the supervisee is a primary aim of the supervisor. The reflective supervisor aspires to create a relationship with the supervisee marked by safety, containment, and mutual respect. This relationship in some ways can be a model for the desired working relationships with parents, children, and colleagues that create a ripple effect of collaboration and mutual respect throughout an agency. Reflective supervision provides an opportunity for relationship-based support and guidance that help staff members to foster meaningful and productive connections with parents, children, and colleagues. These enhanced connections lead to higher quality programs. If staff members are to be empathic, open-minded, collaborative, and respectful, they need a place to experience and learn about these kinds of relationships and interactions. Reflective supervision provides this opportunity.

REFLECTIVE PRACTICE

Reflective supervision builds staff members' skills in reflective practice. Reflective practice refers to a way of working that spans disciplines and encourages staff members to (a) consider the possible implications of their interventions while in the midst of their work; (b) slow down, filter their thoughts, and more wisely choose actions and words; (c) deepen their understanding of the contextual forces that affect their work; and (d) taketime afterward to consider their work and the related experiences in a way that influences their next steps.

A BLENDED MODEL OF SUPERVISION

Practitioners of reflective supervision often combine administrative and reflective supervisory functions to create a blended model of supervisory practice. This guides and monitors the structure and form of the work using a set of practices that invite ongoing growth through exploration and expansion of the supervisee's skills, knowledge, awareness, and intuition. Collaborative problem solving and support are fundamental hallmarks of this practice. The reflective supervisor is responsible for the work of the supervisee and for monitoring and supporting her overall job performance. The reflective supervisor has a role similar to that of a parent who needs to give her child varying doses of nurturing, teaching, and encouragement, as well as collaborative choices when appropriate. Rules and limitations are clarified. Although supervision is not parenting, this analogy is useful in describing the supervisor's overall responsibility for the quality of services, the protection of the children and families served, and the nurturing and development of the skills and abilities of the supervisee.

In this book, we describe and strongly support a blended model of reflective supervision. In day-to-day practice, management functions are hard to separate from educational and supportive functions. For example, a supervisor of a home visitor who persistently avoids writing up reports of home visits until they are overdue might treat that person simply as an employee who needs clarification of the rules and regulations. However, it might be more productive if the supervisor tempered her discussion with an exploration of the reasons for the employee's difficulty. Is the home visitor really a poor time manager? Does she need specific technical assistance with report writing? Or, is the avoidance of the task a way she is responding to difficulty she has in thinking about the content of the visits? A reflective approach fosters thinking about root causes of a problem and prompts the supervisor to work with the supervisee to tailor the kind of support that is most appropriate for each situation. The bottom line for the home visitor is that she will need to get better at getting reports in on time, but discussion of why this is hard may help her understand and move on from an unarticulated difficulty.

CORE OPERATING PRINCIPLES OF REFLECTIVE SUPERVISION

Three core principles of reflective supervision were first elaborated in *Learning Through Supervision and Mentorship* (Fenichel, 1992): regularity, collaboration, and reflection. These principles remain fundamental guideposts for the sound development of this supervisory process.

Regularity

Regular time/space

Reflective supervision should be scheduled in a regular and predictable manner, in contrast to supervision that is provided on an "as needed" basis or primarily in response to crisis situations. Regularity of supervision creates an opportunity for ongoing discussion of all aspects of the work, along with an expectation that the supervisor will know and understand the needs of each family in some detail. With this knowledge, the supervisor and supervisee can be proactive in anticipating and addressing potential challenges. This regularity offers the opportunity to reflect on the complexity of the work in a calm and thoughtful manner. Supervision that occurs regularly offers support to the staff person and at the same time builds accountability for the work. The reflective supervisor constructs her schedule so as to honor her commitment to the regular supervisory meetings. Changes to the agreed-upon schedule should be a rare exception. This concept of regularity helps define supervision as a predictable pause for staff members to be thoughtful about a dilemma or to celebrate a small success with a supervisor who shares responsibility for their ongoing work.

The frequency of supervision depends on factors such as staff members' experience, the nature of the work, and the available resources. For those providing in-home intervention services, reflective supervision would ideally happen once a week, with additional group opportunities for reflection built into the schedule and a clear plan for supervisory access. For staff members working with extremely high-risk populations or in crisis situations, more supervisory time may be needed, and it is imperative that the supervisees be able to reach their supervisor as needed. In early care and education settings, reflective supervision is no less valuable, but finding the time for it may be more difficult because of the continuing care needs of the children. Despite this formidable barrier, it is short-sighted and unrealistic to expect these providers to offer nurturing, relationship-based care to children and support to parents without opportunities for reflective supervision.

As programs are planned and reviewed, the cost of reflective supervision should be evaluated and factored into the budget. Although the costs may seem high, it is important to consider that the reflective supervisor is playing multiple roles as a teacher/mentor, source of motivation and support, quality assurance monitor, and team leader (see chapter 2 for a more complete discussion of supervisory roles). The payoff for a program with strong reflective supervision includes less staff turnover, stronger program outcomes, and continued professional growth.

Collaboration

In the reflective supervision model, the supervisor engages the supervisory partner in a way that respects that person's perspective, honors her work, and commits to thinking together to create more successful outcomes for the program. Reflective supervision is never "supervision by remote control" in which the supervisor directs the work from a distance, telling the supervisee what to do or even feel. Rather, it is a collaborative process, in which the supervisee is offered opportunities to work together with her supervisor to come up with approaches and strategies that draw on the experience, knowledge, and intuition of both partners. The collaborative principle implies that there is a kind of cocreation involved in supervision that draws on the resources of both the supervisor and supervisee. The amount and type of knowledge and expertise contributed by the supervisor will vary according to the needs and experience of the supervisee. However, the need for staff members to have opportunities to think together about the work and to examine alternative perspectives remains a constant even with the most experienced workers.

Reflection

The reflective supervisor pays particular attention to helping the supervisee develop and exercise her capacities to question her first impressions and to explore how the work she is doing is filtered through her own perspectives and those of the child, family, or colleague with whom she is interacting. Through the practice of reflection, supervisees learn that their internal experiences have meaning and that slowing down and considering these experiences from different angles will improve the quality of their work. Supervisees also must learn that the families, colleagues, and young children with whom they work have similar internal responses that are not always evident or understandable. A more detailed model of introducing and holding the reflective process will be introduced in chapter 4.

In any kind of work with children and families, there are many choices of what to say and do and a need to keep relationships central. The supervisor helps the supervisee move into this complex world and consider the effect and meaning of the available options. To do this reflective work, the supervisor must embrace a model that includes an awareness of personal perspectives of all involved and a set of skills to help the supervisee give full consideration to the multiple perspectives and possibilities.

REFLECTIVE SUPERVISION: THEORETICAL INFLUENCES AND DISTINGUISHING CHARACTERISTICS

A variety of theoretical influences distinguish reflective supervision from other supervisory approaches. These influences are briefly described below, with more extensive resources provided at the end of this chapter.

Relationship-Based

The study of relationships and attachment theory is a direct influence on the work of reflective supervision. The work of John Bowlby (1969, 1988), Alan Sroufe (Sroufe, Egeland, Carlson, & Collins, 2005), and others has exquisitely detailed how early relationships contribute to the shape and quality of later relationships as well as social and developmental outcomes. Early learning takes place in the context of relationships and is affected by the quality of those relationships. In many ways this is true for adults as well as children. Because supervision is understood to be a vehicle for promoting staff growth and development as well as a way of providing support and encouragement, close attention is paid to the quality of the relationship between supervisor and supervisee. The supervisor strives to create an atmosphere of trust, mutual respect, safety, and collegiality. These qualities permit the supervisee to feel heard and valued, which promotes learning and the exploration of complex issues.

Because reflective supervision is used with staff members who work with infants, young children, and families, and who are striving to support early relationships no matter what the specific content of their work might be, reflective supervision is a natural support for relationship-based approaches to service delivery. The supervisor creates a chance to experience and embody an attuned and responsive style that the supervisee can adopt in her work. The experience of this kind of supervision becomes a place to practice and hone the skills needed for successful application of relationship-based approaches in many different settings.

Parallel Process

Reflective supervision, as described here, is linked to a key concept usually referred to as the *parallel process*. This describes the ways in which the experiences that a staff person has with her supervisor can affect the way she interacts with a family. In turn the way the staff person interacts with a child, parent, or colleague can then positively spill over and influence the parent's relationship with her child.

The concept of parallel process is a foundational aspect of relationship-based work. Parallel process describes the interlocking network of relationships between supervisor, supervisees, families, and children. If, for example, the supervisor engages in a collaborative problem-solving process with her supervisee rather than telling her what to do, the supervisee is more likely to engage with a family in a similar way. The benefit of this approach for the supervisee is that the family or colleague will typically be more responsive to a style of respectful engagement than to rescue or direction.

Reflective Function

Arietta Slade (Slade, Sadler, & Mayes, 2005) and others have used the term "reflective function" to describe the importance of a parent's capacity to think and respond in a reflective manner rather than with projections, distortions, or premature conclusions when considering motives for children's behaviors. This capacity for reflection has been targeted as a focus of intervention, and the capacity for reflective functioning has been noted as a marker for more positive interactions between parents in children. Models of intervention such as Minding the Baby (Slade et al., 2005) actively seek to increase parent's ability to be reflective in their responses to infants and young children. Parents are encouraged to try to see the world through the eyes of their child: to observe and wonder about the meaning of the child's behavior rather than jumping to conclusions or making judgments.

In similar fashion, the reflective supervision model actively guides staff members to be more reflective in their work with children and families. Reflective supervision offers a protected time when staff members can explore a situation more broadly, striving to understand the meaning of the family's or child's behavior from both a cognitive and an affective perspective. Pausing also gives time for an awareness of the supervisee's own feelings and can help inhibit immediate and sometimes inappropriate reactions to a situation such as a disagreement with a colleague. Although most interventionists working with infants, young children, and families are likely to have a good capacity for reflective function to begin with, reflective supervision supports and expands these abilities.

Mindfulness Practice

Mindfulness refers to an acutely conscious awareness of the present moment and current situation. Mindfulness practices as described by Jon Kabat-Zinn (1991, 2003) and others are frequently incorporated into parenting and psychotherapy groups as a way to promote more reflective and attuned interactions. These practices include breathing techniques, relaxation, exercise, and other strategies designed to help reduce stress and increase awareness of self and others. Elements of these practices can be incorporated into reflective supervision to help increase awareness and infuse a sense of calm.

Ecological Perspective

"Things are not always what they seem to be" is an excellent motto for reflective supervisors. This simple phrase guides staff members to ponder and explore a wide array of seemingly unrelated possibilities with the supervisory partner before moving too quickly from a single vantage point. The supervisor realizes that the presenting problem, or question, is often only the tip of the iceberg and that there are always multiple contextual forces affecting any situation with parents and children. Taking the time to fully explore a situation often results in a very different understanding of the underlying issues and possible courses of action. To do this well, the reflective supervisor must cultivate a stance of curiosity and openness to new insights as she continues her own education so that she can bring new knowledge and information to this exploration. For example, a supervisor who has experience and training on sensory processing concerns will be able to help the supervisee do more refined observations and consider an alternative explanation for a child's aggression. That supervisor could guide her supervisee in differentiating sensory-seeking behaviors from those that are based in anger or hostility. Together, they might plan appropriate screening to figure out whether an occupational therapy referral might be needed.

Transactional Perspectives

Transactional systems theory informs an understanding of human development in important ways; it reflects the idea that all human development occurs in a nonlinear, dynamic manner. This is well illustrated by the notion of "goodness of fit" as first described by Thomas, Chess, Birch, Hertzig, and Korn in their book *Behavioral Individuality in Early Childhood* (1963). A baby with a quiet, slow-to-warm temperament might be frustrating to an active, on-the-go mother who wants her baby to show excitement and delight when presented with novelty. A parent whose temperament is also slow to warm might find this baby a better fit. For a reflective supervisor, it is often necessary to help supervisees think about the possibilities of how a variety of dynamic forces, and the goodness fit among the forces, may be affecting a classroom, child, family, or team.

Intersubjective Focus

The reflective supervision model is considered to be intersubjective in nature, meaning the supervisor and supervisee jointly share their thoughts, feelings, and reactions in order to reach a better understanding of the work and to collaborate more effectively. For example: *Supervisor: "I'm glad you brought up Clara and her mother today. When I hear you talking about them, I find myself feeling very anxious about this little girl's safety. But I am not sure why. There is nothing specific in what you have told me that would seem to put her in danger. Do you have any thoughts or feelings about this?"* Here the supervisor models the ways in which attending to internal experiences (in this case the supervisor's uneasy feeling) can lead to a better understanding of the work. The supervisor's attunement and sensitivity help the trainee regulate the many thoughts and emotions generated by working with infants, young children, and families. The supervisory experience should serve as a model for the approach that staff members then use with parents, children, and colleagues. With this intersubjective approach in supervision, staff members learn to explore the perspectives and motivations of others, consider how their own beliefs and experiences might be affecting their work and their clients, and become more comfortable with the array of feelings that can be stirred up when working with young children and families in classrooms, homes, and community settings.

Understanding the Effects of the Past

Past events lay down traces that can resurface in the present. Reflective supervisors acknowledge this by wondering about the ways past events may have shaped a family's behavior, feelings, or choices. These influences could occur in conscious or unconscious ways. On occasion supervisors may work with a staff person to explore issues from their own past that may be influencing their work.

As staff members grow in their appreciation of how the past may impact current situations and behavior, they should be supported in learning how to shape questions and build interventions that respect and do not intrude upon individual or family privacy. History is important, but the choice to revisit that past always remains with the parents. As supervisors work with staff members they should also consider the specific scope and purpose of the program well as the supervisee's skills, experience, and training. Often a supervisor will need to discuss a situation with a supervisee to figure out whether an issue from the past is something that can be worked with by the supervisee or whether a referral for another kind of treatment or support might be needed.

Consider this example: an infant mental health clinician is facilitating parent groups in an Early Head Start setting. A parent in the group has a history of trauma, and brings up details of her past experiences at each meeting. This often derails the intended discussion about parent–child interactions. This clinician may need help figuring out how to refer this parent for counseling services in a way that is not shaming or offensive. The clinician will also need support in deciding what to do during the group sessions when the needs of this traumatized parent begin to dominate the conversation. The supervisory space is the arena for thinking through these kinds of practice dilemmas that are related to the effects of the past on a family's or staff member's current experience.

Feelings Matter

Another organizing idea for reflective supervisors is that emotions matter: Neither staff members nor recipients of program services can be expected to simply "get over" the feelings they bring to an experience. The supervisor's job description thus implies an ability to tolerate strong affect, both negative and positive, and to appreciate the role that feelings play in both understanding behavior and planning interventions. The supervisor knows that the expression of feelings has different meanings for different people in different settings. She works to help the supervisee tolerate the strong feelings of others, as well as to express her own feelings in thoughtful and appropriate ways.

Bravery in the Face of Conflict

Reflective supervision involves not only support, listening, and encouragement but also analysis and evaluation of work performance, the setting of limits around personnel issues, and the occasional need to address legal and ethical concerns. The supervisor needs to be able to balance mentoring and monitoring functions. This requires tact and diplomacy as well as bravery in the face of conflict. Cultural or gender factors may exacerbate the difficulty of doing this, but the truly reflective supervisor is willing and able to deal with conflict and to discuss difficult topics even when she feels that she's being unkind or that the information might be hard for the supervisee to take. Through her willingness to address hard topics, the supervisor can also help supervisees address difficult topics in their work with children, families, and colleagues.

Strength-Based

Strength-based approaches are frequently misunderstood to imply that staff members should concentrate only on the positive aspects of a situation or characteristics of a child or family. In fact, a strength-based approach refers to an interest in uncovering and recognizing potential resources, personal characteristics, and relationships that can be mobilized to support the growth and development of a child or family. These resources can then become the base for interventions designed to address problems and challenges, often those identified by the family itself. The supervisor can help her staff members to discover these resources, which may be difficult to discern especially when working with families whose risks and difficulties seem overwhelming. A benefit of a strength-based approach is that it tends to reduce resistance to services and also allows those receiving the services to collaborate more actively in creating changes in their lives (Madsen, 1999).

Forgiveness and Acceptance

Given the inexact nature of human relationships, cultural differences, and the complexity of laws and regulations that govern work with parents and young children, it is inevitable that errors in judgment, mistakes, omissions, or overzealous actions will occur. Supervisees can feel frustrated that the forces of risk to which the families are exposed are overwhelming their well-intentioned efforts. Supervisees can feel guilty and overwhelmed when their work has not had the intended effect or has led to a complication for a child, family, colleagues, or the program. Supervisors can foster an atmosphere in which a supervisee can explore mistakes, ineffective choices, and misperceptions in a way that eventually leads from self-condemnation to self-forgiveness and acceptance. Through these experiences, supervisees realize that they can learn from mistakes but cannot always avoid them. Staff members who are helped to move from self-condemnation are also less likely to blame institutions, parents, or others in an attempt to alleviate their own distress.

The Relationship-Based Agency

Ideally, reflective supervision, program development, and leadership are program-wide practices that create a relationship-based service delivery system with chains of thoughtful dialogue that run throughout the organization. To create and nurture reflection at all levels, program leaders must not only champion these ideas but also practice them as they manage and guide the program. The practice increases respect for all voices by providing space and time for ideas to develop and be evaluated before implementation. Reflective supervision, program development, and leadership enhance communication within an agency, build skills, and promote relationship-based collaborations with other agencies and programs (Bertacchi, 1996).

Ripples of Reflection in the Agency

The ideal situation would be agency-wide acceptance of a reflective supervision model, along with the use of reflective practices in program development and leadership functions. However, some organizations may not be ready to retool their whole agency in this way. Nonetheless, it is possible to create pockets and programs where reflective program development and leadership can take root and flourish. Even in environments where reflective practice is not the norm, individual supervisors who consistently practice in a reflective manner will undoubtedly influence not only the staff members they supervise but also managers and others with whom they interact.

REFLECTIVE SUPERVISION: DISTINGUISHING CHARACTERISTICS AND PRACTICE DIFFERENCES

To fit the definition of "reflective supervision," certain approaches and practices need to be in place. For example, the supervisor must consistently offer opportunities to step back and reflect on the work; the relationship between supervisor and supervisee must be collaborative, respectful, and safe; supervision must be provided on a regular and predictable schedule; and a primary goal must be to provide staff members with an opportunity to learn and explore. However, the specific amount of time allotted for supervision can differ according to circumstances. The standard description of reflective supervision often advises or implies a once-a-week meeting in a private office and ongoing review of documentation in preparation for that meeting. Although this might be considered the gold standard, resources and needs vary. Consider these variations:

- A Head Start program coordinator provides reflective supervision groups for teachers and teacher assistants as part of a once-a-month staff meeting. The reflective supervision portion of the meeting is meant to help the staff members think together about their work and work more effectively as a team. The coordinator provides individual supervision quarterly with each staff person.

- Supervisors meet twice a month one-on-one with a senior supervisor to think about their work with newly hired family support staff members and to figure out best ways to help them manage their strong feelings about a new data entry system.

- A mental health provider working in a drug treatment facility calls her primary supervisor every day at 4:00 p.m. to get regrounded before she leaves for the day. She also meets for a weekly supervisory meeting.

- An infant mental health clinician working in a remote rural area meets with her supervisor monthly online using computers with built-in cameras. The supervisor has reviewed the tape of a session beforehand, and the two discuss ways that the clinician can help young parents engage their irritable infant. The supervisor has the taped session on her computer and midway through shows the supervisee a part of the tape in which she felt the intervention worked to support the parents and the child. E-mails are exchanged in the time between the regular online meetings.

- A social worker meets with a supervisor every time she completes a draft of a report for juvenile court. The supervisor uses a reflective approach to help the social worker realize and identify her biases toward a mother with a history of mental illness and figure out ways that she can work more effectively with the family and write the report in an unbiased manner.

- An intern in a community-based training program meets weekly with a supervisor to talk about a case on an ongoing basis so that the trainee can attain some of her learning objectives. Although the supervisor is not legally responsible for the work, she helps the trainee build her skills and has an agreement to send the trainee back to her program supervisor for the discussion of safety or ethical issues.

MISPERCEPTIONS ABOUT REFLECTIVE SUPERVISION

Staff members who are new to an agency with a reflective supervision model may need some time to adjust to and trust this very different approach. Individuals working in programs for infants, children, and families come from many different backgrounds: They often need to be educated about reflective supervision to offset any negative influence of supervisors in their previous work settings. If a working definition for a more reflective form of supervision is not clearly articulated, these "ghosts of supervisors past" may frame the expectation that staff members have for supervision. For example, a supervisee whose previous supervisor often criticized and shamed her in public is likely to react very quickly to any comment she perceives as criticism.

New staff members who have not previously experienced a reflective model are likely to need guidance and support to understand and trust a reflective supervisory process. Although reflective supervision does not erase differences in power or responsibility, the intent is far different than in other models. In those approaches, supervision can imply a hierarchical relationship in which one person directs and "bosses" a less experienced person. For some, the word "supervisor" conjures up images of someone who carries out disciplinary actions, or alternately a shadowy, mostly absent figure who appears at inconvenient times and focuses on an employee doing something wrong.

In addition to counteracting the influence of these previous supervisors, reflective supervisors may find themselves dealing with several other misperceptions, including the following:

Reflective supervision is "just listening"

A superficial understanding of reflective supervision can lead to a misconception that it is a time-consuming activity that involves "just listening" and rarely results in action. In fact, although listening is a core process, it is one part of an active dialogue between supervisor and supervisee. Listening provides an opportunity to identify concerns early, builds the competence of the supervisee, provides an ongoing platform for addressing issues related to quality assurance, and helps to prevent conceptual drift away from the core mission and values of the program's service delivery.

Reflective supervision is too much like therapy

Reflective supervision invites the participants to explore their thoughts and feelings, but only in the context of the work at hand. For example, a supervisor might think with a supervisee about why a particular parent is so difficult to engage. In listening to the supervisee, the supervisor might learn about the supervisee's individual background and beliefs, and the ways in which these factors might be affecting her ability to connect with this particular parent. The supervisor could carefully explore these possibilities with the supervisee, so that they could figure out ways of involving the reluctant parent. These explorations and the underlying atmosphere of trust and acceptance can help the supervisee start to feel understood. This is important because it will allow her to think more creatively and honestly about very complex situations—trusting that her supervisor will appreciate and respect her efforts. The supervisor can also help the supervisee frame the ways in which her own personal issues or circumstances may affect her work with the children and families. A home visitor who is herself pregnant may, for example, have special difficulty working with a pregnant teenager who smokes and fails to follow nutritional guidelines.

Given the atmosphere of personal trust and respect that is promoted in reflective supervision, a potential risk is that the supervisee will start to bring in problems from her own life that are not related to the work. Supervisors need to understand that the supervision is always about the work of the agency and is never a kind of individual therapy or counseling for the staff person. Supervisors need to know how to manage situations when the staff members' needs are persistently brought into the supervision time and dominate the session to such an extent that the needs of the children and families are not discussed. These necessary supervisory skills include knowing how to redirect, set limits, or suggest outside resources.

Experienced staff members don't need it

Some program managers have claimed that reflective supervision is not necessary if properly trained, empathic, respectful staff members are hired from the beginning. Program developers may also argue that reflective supervision is needed only at the beginning, and once a staff person is competent in relationship-based work she no longer needs the reflective supervision practice. However, these arguments do not take into account the ongoing need for staff members to work with ever-changing and difficult situations or to continue to develop their skills. Although the intensity of the supervisory needs may lessen, it remains true that this work is too important and too complex to do alone.

Reflective supervision requires a mental health background

In some circumstances, such as in mental health and social work, supervisors who are working with other social workers or mental health providers must be licensed in their field. Depending on the state in which they are working, they may have work experience and continuing education requirements related to supervision. However, staff members who are not trained mental health professionals can receive sufficient training in reflective supervision to be highly effective as reflective supervisors of staff members whose work they know and understand. The reflective supervisor needs to understand the work practiced by her supervisees. In addition, the supervisor needs training in providing supervision using a reflective model, plus ongoing opportunities for her own consultation and supervision. Ideally, a supervisor of home visitors will have had experience in delivering services in the home herself. If a supervisor has not done the specific job being carried out by her supervisees, it is essential that she have multiple opportunities for real-time observation of the work. She must also take responsibility for reviewing the regulations, laws, and ethics that are relevant to that position and discipline.

So, who can become a reflective supervisor? It depends, to an extent, on the work to be done and the resources available, but the most direct answer is that, for many jobs, an accomplished worker who has done the job, who is open and flexible, and who is willing to take on and learn a new set of reflective supervisory skills can become an effective supervisor. In some cases, limitations in the supervisor's background or the needs of staff members may mean that specialized consultation will also be needed to complement the work of the supervisor. For example, a supervisor in an early care and education setting such as Early Head Start with a background in early education could become an effective supervisor but would need mental health staff members for consultation. This supervisor would also need support and training to recognize where she might need to seek additional consultation. A supervisor with a background in mental health might also be effective in this setting, but would need to be certain she understood the goals of the work and how to engage staff working in a nonclinical setting.

EVIDENCE BASE FOR REFLECTIVE SUPERVISION

Reflective supervision is widely referenced as a necessary ingredient of quality services in almost every article, book, and presentation related to the infant–family field. Programs offering family support, comprehensive child development, early intervention, and infant mental health treatment often include reflective supervision as an essential part of quality service delivery. Some of these program descriptions are for services that are themselves well researched and evidence-based, such as the Nurse–Family Partnership (Olds, 2006), and child–parent psychotherapy (Lieberman & Van Horn, 2008). There are small studies on the effectiveness of reflective supervision in certain settings and disciplines. Yet, overall, there has been a lack of research on reflective supervision itself as defined in this publication. Happily, practitioners and researchers around the country are beginning to discuss this deficit and explore how the elements of reflective supervision in the infant and early childhood field that can be better understood through careful study and observation.

These additional studies will be necessary to affect policy and practice more fully and to help practitioners understand how to improve supervision practices. The studies will address important questions such as consideration of the personal qualities that affect supervision, dosage of supervision, effectiveness of supervision as a training strategy, and other questions that are now answered on the basis of experience, intuition, and collegial advice. It will also be helpful if the emergent studies look at the costs and effects that reflective supervision practices have on program quality.

In some fields such as nursing and early education, there are published studies that support the idea of a supportive and reflective approach to supervision. For example, a study by Howes, James, and Ritchie (2003) included reflective supervision as an important component of effective staff development for teachers in early care and education. Howes noted that participants who received reflective supervision, even those with less formal education than a bachelor of arts degree, were more responsive and more engaged with children than those who did not. The study also found a positive correlation between supervision and mentoring and staying in the field. Two newer studies (Amini Virmani & Ontai, 2010; McFarland, Saunders, & Allen, 2008) looked at how reflective approaches help practicum students in early education achieve more positive interactive capacities with young children. Finally, Geller and Foley (2009) suggested the valuable contribution of reflective supervision in speech–language therapy.

GUIDING QUESTIONS

1. How does the model of reflective supervision align with what I know about reflective supervision? Are there elements that I would like to explore more?

2. What questions does this overview raise for me? What have I experienced that seems similar to this model?

REFERENCES

Amini Virmani, E., & Ontai, L. L. (2010). Supervision and training in child care: Does reflective supervision foster caregiver insightfulness? *Infant Mental Health Journal, 31,*16–32.

Bertacchi, J. (1996). Relationship-based organizations. *Zero to Three, 17*(2), 1–7.

Bowlby, J. (1969). *Attachment and loss: Vol. 1. Attachment.* New York: Basic Books.

Bowlby, J. (1988). *A secure base: Parent-child attachment and healthy human development.* New York: Basic Books.

Fenichel, E. (Ed.). (1992). *Learning through supervision and mentorship to support the development of infants, toddlers and their families: A source book.* Washington, DC: ZERO TO THREE.

Geller, E., & Foley, G. M. (2009). Broadening the "ports of entry" for speech-language pathologists: A relational and reflective model for clinical supervision. *American Journal of Speech-Language Pathology, 18,* 22–41.

Howes, C., James, J., & Ritchie, S. (2003). Pathways to effective teaching. *Early Childhood Research Quarterly, 18,* 104–120.

Kabat-Zinn, J. (1991). *Full catastrophe living: Using the wisdom of your body and mind to face stress, pain, and illness.* New York: Dell.

Kabat-Zinn, J. (2003). Mindfulness-based interventions in context: Past, present, and future. *Clinical Psychology: Science and Practice, 10,* 144–156.

Lieberman, A., & Van Horn, P. (2008). *Psychotherapy with infants and young children: Repairing the effects of stress and trauma on attachment.* New York: Guilford Press.

Madsen, W. C. (1999). *Collaborative therapy with multi-stressed families—From old problems to new futures.* New York: Guilford Press.

McFarland, L., Saunders, R., & Allen, S. (2008). Learning and teaching positive guidance skills: Lessons from early childhood practicum students. *Journal of Early Childhood Teacher Education, 29,* 204–221.

Olds, D. (2006). The Nurse Family Partnership: An evidence based preventive intervention. *Infant Mental Health Journal, 27*(1), 5–25.

Slade, A., Sadler, L., & Mayes, L. C. (2005). Maternal reflective functioning: Enhancing parental reflective functioning in a nursing/mental health home visiting program. In L. Berlin, Y. Ziv, L. Amaya-Jackson, & M. Greenberg (Eds.), *Enhancing early attachments: Theory, research, intervention, and policy* (pp. 152–177). New York: Guilford Press.

Slade, A., Sadler, L., de Dos-Kenn, C., Webb, D., Zepchick, J., & Mayes, L. (2005). Minding the Baby: A reflective parenting program. *Psychoanalytic Study of the Child, 60,* 74–100.

Sroufe, L. A., Egeland, B., Carlson, E., & Collins, W. A. (2005). *The development of the person: The Minnesota study of risk, and adaptation from birth to childhood.* New York: Guilford Press.

Thomas, A., Chess, S., Birch, H. G., Hertzig, M. E., & Korn, S. (1963). *Behavioral individuality in early childhood.* New York: New York University Press.

FURTHER READINGS

Bulman, C., & Schutz, S. (Eds.). (2008). *Reflective practice in nursing* (4th ed.). New York: Wiley-Blackwell.

Dawley, K., Loch, J., & Bindrich, I. (2007). The nurse-family partnership. *American Journal of Nursing, 107*(11), 60–67.

Edelman, L. (2004). *A relationship-based approach to early intervention.* Retrieved May 12, 2009, from http://olms.cte.jhu.edu/olms/data/resource/1144/A%20Relationship-based%20Approach%20to%20Early%20Intervention.pdf

Germer, C. K. (2005). Mindfulness: What is it? What does it matter? In C. K. Germer, R. D. Siegel, & P. R. Fulton (Eds.), *Mindfulness and psychotherapy* (pp. 3–27). New York: Guilford Press.

Healthy Families America. (2008). *Healthy Families America self assessment tool 2008.* Retrieved March 2, 2010, from www.healthyfamiliesamerica.org/downloads/self_assessment_2008.pdf

Heffron, M. C. (2005). Reflective supervision in infant, toddler, and preschool work. In K. M. Finello (Ed.), *The handbook of training and practice in infant and preschool mental health* (pp. 114–136). San Francisco: Jossey-Bass.

Johns, C. (2008). *Becoming a reflective practitioner* (2nd ed.). Oxford, England: Blackwell.

Parlakian, R. (2001). *Look, listen, and learn: Reflective supervision and relationship-based work.* Washington, DC: ZERO TO THREE.

Pawl, J. H. (1994). On supervision. *Zero to Three, 15*(3), 21–29.

Pflieger, J. (2002). Reflective supervision. *Head Start Bulletin, 73,* 34–36.

Schafer, W. (2007). Models and domains of supervision and their relationship to professional development. *Zero to Three, 28*(2), 10–22.

Schon, D. (1987). *Educating the reflective practitioner.* San Francisco: Jossey-Bass.

Shahmoon-Shanok, R. (1992). The supervisory relationship: Integrator, resource, and guide. In E. Fenichel (Ed.), *Learning through supervision and mentorship to support the development of infants, toddlers and their families: A sourcebook* (pp. 37–41). Washington, DC: ZERO TO THREE.

Shahmoon-Shanok, R. (2006). Reflective supervision for an integrated model: What, why, and how? In G. Foley & J. Hochman (Eds.), *Mental health in early intervention: Achieving unity in principles and practice* (pp. 343–381). San Francisco: Jossey-Bass.

Siegel, D. J. (2007). *The mindful brain: Reflection and attunement in the cultivation of well-being.* New York: Norton.

Siegel, D., & Harzell, M. (2003). *Parenting from the inside out.* New York: Tarcher.

Stern, D. N. (1985). *The interpersonal world of the infant.* New York: Basic Books.

Stern, D. N. (2004). *The present moment in psychotherapy and everyday life.* New York: W.W. Norton.

Weigand, R. F. (2007). Reflective supervision in child care: The discoveries of an accidental tourist. *Zero to Three, 28*(2), 17–22.

CHAPTER 2

"Caps for Sale": Roles of the Reflective Supervisor

Like the peddler in the much-loved children's book *Caps for Sale* (Slobodkina, 1968), supervisors wear many hats, and often all at the same time. At any given moment, one supervisory role may be more prominent or have a higher priority than the others, but it helps to have an overarching framework that encompasses them all. Such a framework will help the supervisor maintain balance and perspective when she is pulled too strongly in one direction or another and will prevent any one role from dominating. It will also help make the supervisor less vulnerable to her own blind spots and keep her from sticking to roles that are more comfortable or interesting to her.

This chapter provides a description of five key supervisory roles, with some discussion of the specific skills needed to perform each one and an overview of useful strategies and related techniques. Some roles are discussed in detail; others are outlined and then explored at greater length in subsequent chapters. Our hope is that by better understanding each role, it will be easier to blend and integrate them as needed to meet the complex demands of real-life supervision.

The five key supervisory roles are as follows:

1. Supporting staff members' development

2. Providing a "secure base" where staff members can safely explore the meaning of their work

3. Maintaining program ideals and standards, quality assurance, and safety

4. Facilitating open communication and effective team functioning

5. Providing program leadership

The vignette below illustrates these roles, how they can be blended, and the thoughtfulness required to set priorities reflective of individual and program needs:

> *Lisa is supervising a young home visitor in the Early Head Start program. During her weekly meeting, she asks how things are going with Stephan and his family. Stephan is a 10-month-old who has recently been diagnosed with a type of seizure disorder which has a very poor prognosis. Lisa discovers, after some probing, that*

the home visitor has not actually visited the family in the last month—since the diagnosis was made. As the supervisor, Lisa has a number of choices based on the supervisory roles described above. She can:

- **Help the home visitor build her professional skills**—*to learn more about this disability condition or to increase her knowledge about how to access services for children with disabilities.*

- **Provide a safe place for the home visitor to explore her feelings about working with this particular family**—*hopelessness in the face of a life-threatening medical condition, fear about working with a family who is expressing intense grief and anger about their child's illness, or incompetence or confusion regarding her role in this situation.*

- **Maintain the ideals and standards set by the program, agency, and contract**—*including the expectations for making regular home visits and the consequences for not carrying out the responsibilities of the job.*

- **Support open communication and collaboration with team members**—*in this case by asking what the home visitor has learned from the physical therapist who is also seeing the family, and then suggesting a joint visit with her.*

Ideally, the supervisor, like the peddler, is able to balance all of these hats to keep them from tumbling in disarray. If the supervisor oversimplifies a situation—in this example, by focusing on the home visitor's discomfort or, alternately, on the possible need for disciplinary action—she loses the opportunity to help the home visitor grow and develop and for the family to receive high-quality services. The reflective supervision model helps the supervisor avoid getting stuck in one role. It helps her find a way to both support the home visitor and to draw attention to the consequences of failing to provide contracted services. To use this model, the supervisor must keep all the roles in mind while carefully and thoughtfully choosing where to begin and what tone to set. Here is a sample of how the conversation with Lisa might begin:

Supervisor: I'm glad you are sharing the information about Stephan and his family, but I'm a bit worried. I know you know this—but you can't decide on your own not to visit a family. That is something we would need to talk about together in order to make a plan. I can imagine that it might be difficult to sit with this family, now that they have received this news. But I wonder what has gotten in the way of making the visits.

> *Supervisee: I think I just haven't known what to do. I was so surprised about this diagnosis and so sad. It seemed like they didn't really want me there, and I could not think of any way I could really help.*
>
> *Supervisor: I can imagine this was hard, and I'm glad we are talking now. How can I help you to regain contact with the family so we can ensure that this family does receive services and explore the support they may need even though the picture has changed recently?*

In this model, and in the example above, where clinical and administrative supervisory responsibilities are blended, the supervisor attends to all aspects of her staff's work:

- The knowledge, skills, and expertise related to working with children and families;

- The ability to form therapeutic* relationships with families and build collaborative partnerships with team members;

- The self-awareness about the effect of one's own feelings, experiences, beliefs, and values; and

- The need to meet billing requirements, ensure timeliness of reports and paperwork, and the importance of compliance with various program requirements.

In addition to the key roles described, supervisors also often participate in program development and leadership activities, help build community partnerships, and engage in advocacy activities that relate to improved services for children and families. Individual programs and agencies will differ in the degree to which supervisors have responsibility for particular aspects of staff members' performance, but in most cases the roles delineated in this chapter will all be assumed. Job titles may also differ (director, supervisor, program manager, or site manager), and in some instances certain roles may be given more emphasis, but most often these positions cover a similar range of roles and responsibilities.

ROLE 1: HELPING INDIVIDUAL STAFF MEMBERS/TEAMS GROW AND DEVELOP—SUPERVISION AS A RELATIONSHIP FOR LEARNING

> *It was Jamie's first day on the job as a mental health consultant to the Wee Round-Up child care center. Jim, her supervisor, had been a part of the interview team when she was hired, and he had been impressed with her academic credentials in the area of family systems, family development, and family counseling. She had*

---

* *Here as elsewhere in this text, the term* therapeutic *refers to any kind of curative or healing effect. It does not necessarily refer specifically to mental health treatment.*

glowing recommendations from her internship supervisors, all praising her wonderful skills as a team member and her ability to apply academic principles in a real-life setting. As he prepared for his meeting with her, Jim reminded himself that he had much to learn about Jamie to know how best to support her. He recalled another supervisee, new to the field, who had come in with a very strong resume. He had found himself becoming impatient at times when she didn't catch on as quickly as he had assumed she would. Later, when they had been able to talk about it, the staff person had said that she had come to feel like an impostor, since she didn't actually have all the skills Jim had believed her to have. Jim resolved to be more careful with Jamie and to spend more time finding out about her strengths and needs.

The supervisor has a primary responsibility for supporting the growth and development of the supervisee. This plays itself out in different ways depending on the developmental stage of the supervisee, but it always remains a central focus. Why is this role so critical?

Many professionals come to programs for young children and families with some but not all of the skills, knowledge, and expertise needed to do their jobs well. (See chapter 4 for an extensive discussion of the skills and competencies critical to this work.) There are several reasons why staff members may not be fully prepared to address the complex needs of the children and families on their caseload.

First, preservice programs often do not address one or more major areas important for the infant and early childhood field. For example, special education programs often do not focus on the clinical skills needed for work with families, and clinical or social work programs may leave out more recent theoretical knowledge about child development. Some staff members have more expertise in working with adults but need help in learning about infants and very young children. Some may have worked with preschoolers but never infants or toddlers. Some are highly skilled in the technical aspects of their individual disciplines—for example, a speech–language pathologist who knows a great deal about pediatric feeding disorders and how to treat them—but are less knowledgeable about adult learning strategies or how to work with multistressed families when promotion of child development may not be the parents' top priority. Staff members with a strong background in counseling or mental health may be comfortable with the degree of self-reflection and awareness needed in infant–family work, whereas others may be less so. The field is enormously complex and transdisciplinary in nature. Although each discipline has its specific focus and expertise, there are large areas of shared knowledge and skills. A holistic approach to the child and family as well as an understanding of the transactional nature of child development and an appreciation that the child develops through interactions with his or her environment and primary caregivers are necessary foundations for all practitioners.

Second, many programs hire staff members who do not have degrees but bring skills and knowledge they have learned working in other, similar programs. In some locations where it is difficult to find trained staff members, individuals with a strong interest in working with children and families may be hired even though they lack the recommended academic background. In these cases, there must be a commitment to provide these staff members with ongoing professional development opportunities. There may be a need for staff members with specific cultural and linguistic skills. If there is a shortage of credentialed workers who possess these qualifications, an agency may choose to hire staff members who do have these skills and then provide them with additional training support. In addition, many programs such as Head Start and the social welfare system have made a commitment to hire and train former recipients of services or individuals with particular linguistic skills for outreach, advocacy, and case management positions.

Third, while preservice course work and in-service workshop training can be highly effective in presenting conceptual frameworks, research findings, key concepts, and strategies, most staff members require support to integrate this information into their daily practice. Often, agencies and programs devote considerable resources to sending staff members to training conferences, only to find that there is little actual effect on professional practice. This is due, in part, to a lack of time and attention devoted to follow-up activities that would support implementation of training content.

Fourth, all staff members, no matter what their level of training or experience, require support to learn to understand their clinical experiences through the lens of their personal experiences, cultural background, and education.

Finally, the field of infant and early childhood practice is in constant flux. Practitioners who were fully proficient in established service delivery models at one time may find themselves in the position of needing to learn new ways of delivering their services—or, in fact, undergoing a major reorganization or reconceptualization of their job. For example, providers of early intervention services for infants and toddlers with disabilities have, in recent years, moved from clinic-based to home-based services; they have also learned to work with the family as their primary client, rather than interacting mainly with the child, and accommodate a variety of multidisciplinary team models that are very different from the more traditional "lone ranger" approach. Child and family mental health providers who have begun to work with very young children and their families have had to learn a new subspecialty in their work even though they have years of experience and are fully credentialed. Nurses and therapists proficient in their fields have come to realize that their expertise is more likely to be beneficial for infants, young children, and families if they become proficient in a variety of family-centered practices such as developing collaborative problem-solving skills and forming a therapeutic alliance with parents on behalf of their children.

For all these reasons, on-the-job training and technical assistance provided through regular reflective supervision are important for improving the quality of services provided to children and families. Reflective supervision has been demonstrated to be an effective vehicle for promoting ongoing staff development. Supervision is an important tool for learning because the relationship between the supervisor and the supervisee encourages the supervisee to honestly examine her needs in an open and sometimes vulnerable way, knowing that her supervisor will be a trustworthy companion on the learning journey.

The supervisor's role as a teacher and mentor is most effective when it is tailored to meet the needs of the individual supervisee. The better the supervisor knows the staff person, the more helpful she can be. Some information about the individual staff person is gathered during the initial job interview, hiring, and orientation period, but ideally this is seen as just the beginning of the process of getting to know the supervisee. In reality, one is likely to know very little about the full range of a new person's knowledge, skills, expertise, and actual practice in spite of interviews, reference checks, and reviews by former supervisors. It behooves the supervisor to actively seek an understanding of how the supervisee approaches all aspects of her work. Too often, this process is abandoned after the initial interview and job orientation period until specific performance concerns surface, a crisis occurs, or the staff person leaves for another job.

When bringing on a new staff member, the supervisor should acknowledge, right from the start, that together they will be exploring which aspects of the work are most comfortable and what the supervisee's professional development goals will be. If the staff person knows that this is an expectation for all members of the staff, and not an indication of concerns or doubts about her particular skill level, she is more likely to actively participate in an ongoing assessment of her own strengths and needs. When professional goals are functional, specific, and frequently referenced (not just during the annual performance review), they can become a central focus of the supervisory process.

Consider this example in which the supervisor (Jan) is working with a new speech therapist in the program:

> **Supervisee:** Hi, Jan. I was thinking about our supervision today and wondered if you could help me think about my work with Joey. I am feeling kind of frustrated, since I'm not sure how I can help him with his speech when he won't even look at me—let alone talk with me—when I come to his house. All he seems interested in is playing with his mom!
>
> **Jan:** Great question! I can certainly imagine that might be frustrating and even a little disappointing since you have had so much direct experience doing therapy with children this age. Could you tell me a little more about how things go when he and

his mom are playing together? How they are communicating with each other, and if they seem to understand each other? I'm thinking about the professional development plan we worked on last week—when we were talking about figuring out how to focus on increasing parents' ability to support their child's development. This might be an excellent opportunity to think about that goal. We could talk about how to help Mrs. Adams learn to give Joey language models that will be useful to him. After all, in the end I guess the most important thing will be for Joey and his mom to understand each other. I know that working with parents and kids together is a new model for you, and I wonder if you are missing some of the direct feedback from him. Given Joey's age, it is not too unusual for him to be a little shy, and his interest in playing with his mom provides a good way to get at his language needs since our program really focuses on parental involvement.

Creating and using staff development plans are crucial for effective supervision with both new and continuing staff members. Individual goals in the plans are based on supervisees' self-assessment, in conjunction with supervisory input. This input is based on the many opportunities the supervisor has for observing and interacting with her supervisee. In our experience, it requires some discipline and effort to actively engage in this process of ongoing observation and assessment, because of the many other demands being made on the supervisory partners such as pressing needs of children and families, administrative requirements, and team issues. Nonetheless, the process deserves to have priority. One of the challenges inherent in being a supervisor is being able to stay objective, continually gathering information about staff members' skills and needs.

Opportunities for Ongoing Assessment of Staff Skills

Individual supervisory sessions are ideally suited for this purpose. Ongoing conversations about a staff person's adjustment to the job and her vulnerabilities and needs are essential. Every discussion about a specific child and family or group situation provides an occasion for knowing more about how the staff person sees and understands her work both from a technical, discipline-specific perspective and from a relationship-based point of view.

Direct observation of the supervisee's work, when it is purposeful and done over time, will also be valuable for helping the supervisor to understand the supervisee's skills and needs. Joint home visits, review of case reports, observation of the discussion taking place in team meetings, and videotapes of sessions with children and families are all informative and necessary for the supervisor. Time available will influence how much direct observation of the supervisee is feasible, but it should be seen as an essential for new and experienced staff members.

Formal inventories of key skills and competencies—such as the California Infant-Family and Early Childhood Mental Health Workforce Competencies (n. d.) and Michigan Association for Infant Mental Health's (n. d.) Endorsement. Typically the supervisor and supervisee both review the assessment material and then come together to discuss their thoughts and impressions.

It is critical that staff members understand right from the start that their growth and professional development are a primary focus of supervision. Supervisors should acknowledge that the work is complex and that no professional ever masters all the skills she needs for the job. The supervisor should remind the supervisee that new ideas and information are always becoming available and that the expectation is for each staff person to actively seek ways of enhancing her practice.

This approach also builds in the idea that there is room for growth in an agency or a profession. Some staff members may be more ambitious or have more personal space to be thinking about their career path, and some may be less interested. In either case, a focus on continued development of skills and expertise leads to more dynamic and effective service programs.

No one should feel overscrutinized or that a supervisor is somehow trying to "catch" her making a mistake. Because many professionals will never have experienced an approach to supervision that emphasizes personal and professional growth, they may at first feel quite vulnerable and may interpret any suggestion as a criticism. Supervisors can help reassure their staff members by statements that:

- Acknowledge their own learning curve: "When we went to that autism conference, I was a little confused by the distinction the speaker made between sensory problems and regulatory problems. Let's try to think about that when we go on a home visit to the Jones family next week."

- Solicit feedback about how comfortable the supervisee feels about an issue in a way that normalizes "not knowing": "You mentioned that this mom is worried about her baby's feeding and wondering if she is ready to start table foods. Is that an area that you have had a chance to explore, or would you like me to help you find someone to go with you on the next visit? I realize that this is something you may not have had the opportunity to learn about in your speech internships."

- Indicate a willingness to share responsibility for any difficulties: "Mrs. Jones called me to complain about her early intervention services. I'd really like to get your point of view. I assured her I would discuss it with you and that we would try to figure out a better approach for her child. Let's talk about what happened at that last home visit so we can figure out what got her so upset and how we can address her concerns."

The supervisor should clearly communicate that she and the supervisee may need to seek outside resources to address questions that arise in discussing their work. She should also acknowledge that solutions and new formulations will typically be developed through a collaborative process.

There are numerous naturally occurring opportunities for staff members to learn and grow through supervision. As noted above, material to prompt staff members' growth and development can come from individual supervision meetings, joint home visits, program visits, review of case notes and reports, videotapes of sessions, and team meetings. The supervisor begins by inviting the supervisee to talk about a problem or to bring up a specific issue. This becomes a teachable moment that is further amplified through discussion and reflection. The supervisor may tentatively suggest possible ways of articulating a concern to a parent or team member, tying the current situation back to a theoretical concept and engaging in collaborative problem solving. Again, the critical element is the supervisor's continual alertness to potential teachable moments—which must be balanced against the equally important need to be fully present, listening with an open mind and without an overarching agenda, to the supervisee's discussion of her work.

This juggling is a true art: to be fully engaged in the supervisory conversation and at the same time thinking about what it means for the supervisee and what she might learn from it. In fact, it is quite likely that a supervisee will be most creative, insightful, and receptive to a new perspective or idea when she knows the supervisor is most fully engaged and trying hard to understand her experience and point of view. Learning is most likely to take place when staff members feel supported, respected, and contained, and when they believe they are receiving the gift of the supervisor's near perfect attention.

Attending special conferences or workshops can be worthwhile for supervisees if the event is linked into the ongoing supervisory experience. This linkage and the value of such experiences will be greatly increased by (a) purposeful selection of the workshop—discussed ahead of time, with specific articulation of what the supervisee hopes to learn and what specific child or family issues might be relevant to the content; (b) attending the training with staff members, so as to have a shared experience and shared language about the topic; (c) a follow-up conversation in supervision or in a team meeting or both about key concepts, how they apply to the caseload, and how they relate to current program practices or other recent training content; and (d) periodic reference to workshop content in the course of ongoing supervision or team discussion. If possible, it is beneficial for the supervisor to communicate with the presenter, letting her know of the specific interests, level of sophistication, and concerns of staff members who are attending the conference.

Reflective Supervision: A Relationship for Learning

The supervisor's first role is to use the many ways outlined in this section to help the supervisee "metabolize" new ideas so they can be applied in a meaningful and functional way. Experience, mediated by supervisory conversations, can help staff members understand and articulate new content. It is also important for the supervisor to have a good grasp of available resources and additional readings and be available for follow-up discussions. Reflective supervision has been called a "relationship for learning" (Fenichel, 1992). As described throughout this text, staff members will learn best when this relationship is characterized by safety, trust, respect, clarity as to roles and responsibilities, willingness to address difficulties, collaboration, and mutuality. A tall order!

Content Areas: Potential Priorities for Staff Members' Growth and Development

The following are important content areas that, depending on the professional discipline, may not be included fully in preservice training programs. This is not an exhaustive list, and it will change as the field (and each specialty area within the field) develops. Each program would also need to consider the specific demands of their work setting, region, clientele, and specific job responsibilities to determine staff development priorities. For example, professionals working in group child care, a neonatal intensive care unit, or a substance abuse program would require specialized training related to each of those programs and targeted populations, in addition to the foundational knowledge and skills described below. Expectations will vary depending on the individual staff person's discipline, role, and work setting. For example, the Early Head Start home visitor needs to have a good basic understanding of the importance of early parent–child relationships and an ability to support positive interactions. She would not, however, be expected to provide infant–parent psychotherapy. Conversely, the infant–parent psychotherapist should be knowledgeable about working with multistressed families living in poverty but would not need to know the details of federal Head Start regulations (although over time she should become familiar with them).

Current approaches to child development

Staff members may have had course work in child development, but it is important to explore with them the specific content of that course work. They may have learned about the traditional "ages and stages" of different developmental domains—a series of milestones linked to a chronological age expectation (e.g., pulling to stand at 9 months, first words at 1 year, stranger anxiety at 18 months). However, they may not have studied or understood theories related to the transactional and integrated nature of development—that is, the ways in which each developmental domain influences and parallels the others, the continual interplay between the child's environment and experience and his constitution, and the effect of experience on brain structure and function.

Unless an individual has specialized in the study of developmental psychology or infant mental health, she may have relatively little knowledge or understanding about early social–emotional development, its important role as an organizer of overall development, the importance and developmental course of self-regulatory skills and executive function, or the importance and developmental course of attachment in young children. Other important areas of child development include understanding sensory development, early coping skills, and the social–emotional foundations of early communication development.

How culture and context shape development and guide intervention

It is important for professionals in the infant–family and early childhood fields to realize how cultural and contextual perspectives shape an understanding of child and family development. Different parental beliefs, perceptions, resources, values, and priorities will influence how parents are with their children and what and how they teach them. Developmental expectations and interpretations of children's behavior will vary, as will a parent's concept of what is a problem, what characteristics or aspects of a child's development are valued and attended to, what kind of assistance is sought or accepted, and what kinds of relationships they might seek to have with an early intervention professional. All these factors will directly affect assessment, intervention planning, and service delivery activities as the practitioner and family work together to form a collaborative partnership. The following examples illustrate how culture and context shape parents' view of a concern and how parents' experience and beliefs must be factored in to shape an appropriate intervention. In reading these, imagine what an interventionist would need to know in order to work with the families.

Rashid is a 3-year-old whose parents are recent refugees from the Middle East. Both parents value learning a great deal and are confused by the play-based curriculum in the Head Start program. They want Rashid to be learning letters and numbers.

***

Kylie is a 2-year-old girl who is living with her mother in a homeless shelter. Because the family has been on the move for many months, Kylie's mom is impatient with the family support worker who suggests that Kylie may need extra cuddling because of the instability. Mom expects Kylie to adapt to their lifestyle and thinks that the family support worker's advice will lead to trouble.

Family development, family systems, and community resources

Knowledge and understanding of an ecological approach to working with young children at risk and their families is an essential but sometimes unfamiliar area for some practitioners. Practitioners can be more helpful if they understand the context within which the parent and child are living and the many factors that influence their day-to-day life. These factors include discovering who is part of the family, what roles each member has, and how decisions are made. Practitioners will need to learn about working with teen parents, same-sex couples, grandparents who are taking the primary caregiver role, and recently immigrated families. For example, families who are recent immigrants may have chosen to come to their new home eagerly or may have been forced to leave by harsh political or economic realities. A teenage pregnancy can be accepted and supported or can cause major family conflicts. Practitioners will need to understand how cultural and religious beliefs shape what seems right and wrong to families. Even more important than detailed knowledge about the particular culture is having the ability to approach and engage families to talk about these issues. This requires a set of skills that promote interpersonal sensitivity and cultural responsiveness. Staff members will need to learn that there are always multiple perspectives on any concern and that it is essential to take the time to understand and be open to the variety of needs that families present.

Jorge is an 18-month-old being raised by his 17-year-old mother and her boyfriend. The couple and child live with the mother's godparents, and everyone seems supportive and happy. However, after a few weeks, the mom reveals that she is living with the godparents because her own family refused help because of her "bad decisions." While mom appreciates the godparents, she misses her home and her siblings and worries all the time that Jorge is missing out on his grandparents' love.

***

Lorna, a social worker, is delighted that she has found a good adoptive home for Carla, a 9-month-old whose mother has lost her parental rights. However, she is confused when the elderly great-grandparents appear and protest the fact that Carla is going to be adopted by a same-sex couple. The great-grandparents have decided that they want to take Carla in despite their health problems.

Importance of caregiver–child relationships and interactions

All infant–family professionals need to have a basic appreciation of the fact that learning takes place in the context of relationships and is critically affected by those relationships.

This means that no matter what discipline a professional is in, a top priority is the promotion of positive caregiver–child relationships and interactions. Key skills are the ability to observe those interactions and to help parents or teachers engage with the child in ways that will support the development of a secure attachment. All practitioners should be aware of the red flags that signal the possibility of a caregiver–child relationship at significant risk, and professionals need to know when to refer for mental health services. This entails knowing what community resources are available and how to introduce and describe these services.

Professional use of self

This content area encompasses all the ways in which the quality of the professional's interactions with the client can influence the intervention outcomes. As Jeree Pawl, one of the leaders in the field of infant mental health, so elegantly stated, "How you are is as important as what you do" (Pawl, 1994). The practitioner's technical and discipline-specific expertise is, of course, critical; however, it is not the only factor in determining how helpful the services offered will be. Professionals with a background in counseling or mental health will have studied the ways in which the caregiver–professional relationship can either support or interfere with effective intervention. Others will need specific instruction to understand this critical area. Specific skills related to "use of self" include the ability to:

- Form a therapeutic alliance with a family on behalf of the child;

- Consider a range of possible interpretations of the behaviors of another person by inquiring about or imagining the perspective of that other person;

- Empathize with another person's experience while maintaining objectivity;

- Resist becoming overwhelmed and engulfed by the feelings of others;

- Use partnering communication strategies as alternatives to direct or didactic instruction (e.g., collaborative problem-solving techniques);

- Understand the importance of self-awareness—monitoring one's own thoughts and feelings in the moment and appreciating the effect of one's own past experiences, values, beliefs, and culture on the work;

- Consider all the ways in which role, age, gender, ethnicity, race, class, and context can have an effect on families;

- Appreciate the ways in which a family's past experience can affect them and how they relate to service providers or a service delivery system;

- Understand the importance of boundaries—the ability to maintain a distinction between personal and professional relationships;

- Recognize how our history, values, culture, privilege, and discipline-specific training can lead us to have specific biases or "triggers" when we do our work; and

- Use self-disclosure to model ways of using self-awareness to understand another person and situation more fully.

The supervisor's own use of self within the supervisory relationship is a powerful way to teach the supervisee professional use of self. In the example below, the supervisor models emotional availability to a supervisee who seems to have distanced herself from her feelings about a child and family:

> **Supervisor:** *As I listen to you, I find myself feeling very sad for little Joshua and worried that we might not be able to really help him. What comes up for you as you work with the family? I'm wondering how you feel when you are with them.*

Standards of best practice for developmental assessment, intervention planning, and service delivery for very young children

Best practices for developmental assessment involve principles such as those described by Meisels and Fenichel (1996):

- Families help to plan and carry out assessments as full partners in the assessment team and are fully involved in discussions about the results and implications for treatment and services.

- Children are assessed in the context of interactions with familiar caregivers. Relationship assessment may be a part of this in some settings and, if so, should be carefully planned and carried out so that the parent feels supported and understood.

- Assessment involves multiple observations, at multiple times, and in different settings, such as at home, in centers, and in the community. Information is gathered from multiple sources (multidisciplinary assessment team).

- Young children should not be assessed by someone they don't know, and a parent or primary caregiver should accompany them while they are being evaluated.

- Evaluation and assessment instruments are used for the purpose for which they were designed and with the population for whom they were designed.

- Assessment is ongoing and reciprocal with intervention—it is a dynamic process (i.e., it generates questions to be explored and is the basis of program design, and progress is continually assessed so as to generate new questions and new plans).

These concepts are relevant to all infant and early childhood professionals, regardless of their specific discipline or program assignment. Likewise, professionals in the infant–family field ought to be able to write integrated developmental assessment summaries, which include input from the multidisciplinary team, and paint a holistic picture of the child in the context of his family and daily life. It is important for practitioners to be knowledgeable about the development of functional goals, which are meaningful in the context of every-day family routines and activities, and which are reflective of family priorities, resources, and concerns. These are in contrast to goals that focus on splinter skills (e.g., "name four foods" or "stack three blocks") or those that are so vague as to be difficult to address or measure. Examples of functional goals include *Cora will ask for help when a task is too difficult* or *Mom will be able to change Janey's diaper without Janey having a temper tantrum.*

As direct service providers, all staff members need to be able to function as part of an integrated service delivery team. (In some cases, the "team" may be members of different agencies providing a variety of services not available through one agency.) This collaboration requires team members to develop an integrated, holistic approach to working with a family. It involves listening carefully to one another so as to understand how each person's observations and insights contribute to a coherent understanding of the child and family. It also requires developing strategies that are useful across domains and stated in language understandable to everyone on the team, including family members. The supervisor has responsibility for teaching new staff members about the role of the team and for setting the tone for positive, collaborative relationships. She should also help the team develop guidelines for working together that support positive communication. Ideally, every staff member will feel responsible for maintaining good communication with her team members and will take the initiative to do so. However, when communication breaks down, the supervisor's role is to work with team members to understand the situation and repair communications as necessary.

In summary, in the reflective supervision model, the supervisor has a primary responsibility for assessing her supervisees' knowledge and expertise in a wide range of content and skills areas and then overseeing their professional growth and development in these areas. A number of key content areas have been described that are important for all early childhood professionals and that often are not included in preservice professional training programs. Of course, each professional is also responsible for mastery of essential discipline-specific knowledge. A supervisor may have a different professional background than her staff member (e.g., an infant mental health specialist who supervises a speech–language pathologist). If together they identify a need for supervisory support that is specifically related to that discipline (e.g., selecting a specific feeding therapy protocol), the supervisor will assist in finding an appropriate resource.

ROLE 2: PROVIDING A "SECURE BASE"

In the reflective supervision model, staff members are offered a safe, protected space to come back to: a place where they can explore and experience the meaning of the work. When appropriate, the supervisor encourages her staff members to venture into new territory while providing assurance that they will have guidance and support as they go. At other times, the supervisor may figuratively pull the supervisee away from a precipice. The supervisor uses some or all of the following approaches to establish and maintain this "secure base" (Bowlby, 1988).

Commitment to Regular Meetings

To fulfill this role, supervisory time must be regular and protected. The supervisee should always know when the next meeting will be, and there must be a joint commitment to keeping this time available. This is in contrast to supervisory situations in which meetings take place only in times of crisis, at which point people tend to be more reactive than reflective. Ideally, this commitment is honored within the agency as a whole, so that supervisors are not asked to cancel supervision to attend to other agency business. Because supervision is protected and regular, there is an opportunity to be creative and proactive in thinking about the work. The supervisor can help slow things down enough so that staff members can experiment, make connections, try out new ideas, and pay attention to details or information that at first might seem only marginally relevant.

Providing a Holding Environment

The notion of a holding environment was originally discussed by Donald Winnicott as he described the parent's ability to create a sense of containment and safety for the child (Winnicott, 1965). We use the term here to describe a critical supervisory function. To create a holding environment, the supervisor makes it clear by her words and actions that she will stand by her supervisee even when the supervisee is angry, upset, scared, or worried, or has made a mistake. She will stay calm, so as to help the supervisee become calm herself and thus able to think more clearly. The supervisor will listen to and empathize with her staff person's concerns, so that together they can move forward in understanding the situation better, and when possible they will start to make a plan to address any problems or difficulties. She will make it clear that she is a partner, that difficulties are shared difficulties, and that the supervisee will not need to make hard decisions alone. Supervisors need to pay close attention to the language they use if they wish to maintain a safe holding environment. Consider the difference in these two statements from a supervisor: "That certainly is a tough situation. What do you think you will do about it?" versus "That certainly is a tough situation. Let's think about how we might handle it."

Tolerate Ambiguity and Embrace Complexity

The reflective supervisor helps her supervisee tolerate the ambiguity frequently encountered in work with infants and young children by at least naming the dilemma so that there is a starting place or focus for their energies, as in the following scenario:

> *The toddler playgroup staff members are upset because when Jessica and her mother, Jenny, come to the group, the maternal grandmother comes too and keeps jumping in and telling Jenny how to play with her daughter. The playgroup staff members understand that one of their primary goals is to support positive, responsive interactions between Jessica and her mom. Grandmother seems like a barrier to this. They come to their supervisor to ask for help in "getting Grandma out of the way."*
>
> *The supervisor listens to this story, empathizes with the staff members' frustration, and asks some questions to further understand the situation. In sharing information, the team discovers that (a) the grandmother provides housing, food, transportation, and stable caregiving for Jessica and her mom, and (b) the grandmother has expressed a great deal of worry about her ability to provide the support her daughter and granddaughter need. At this point, the staff members start to have a better appreciation of the complexity of the situation, and realize that their dilemma is finding a way to support everyone (Jessica, Jenny, and Grandma). Although this may turn out to be a difficult task, staff members feel they have made a great deal of progress by coming to this way of understanding their work with this family.*

The mantras "Embrace complexity" and "Tolerate ambiguity" are central to the reflective supervision process.

Containment

Staff members can be overwhelmed, and almost paralyzed, by the enormity of the problems facing their client's families. One of the ways a supervisor can help them to contain their anxiety, be calm, and stay focused is to assist in defining a reasonable focus for their work with each individual family. This includes exploring the strong feelings aroused, setting manageable goals, establishing priorities, and analyzing problems so as to break them down into more manageable and understandable parts.

Containment also applies to the notion of programmatic change. Some changes are reflective of new developments in the infant–family field, while other changes are driven by budgetary concerns caused by cuts or available funding. As a consequence, staff members are frequently asked to adapt to changes: to take on a new service delivery contract, to adopt a new model of practice, to learn a new set of skills, or to conform to new policies and regulatory requirements. Often these changes come unexpectedly and without adequate time to plan or adjust. This can be stressful to the program as a whole and more so for some staff members in particular. At these times, the supervisor's ability to "contain"—to provide a base of security for staff members—is especially important. She can do this by:

- Providing up-to-date information to all team members;

- Allowing adequate time for exploring the anticipated difficulties;

- Guiding the discussion back to a consideration of what the effect will be for children and families;

- Reflecting on other changes that have occurred and what strategies might have been helpful at those times;

- Relating new practices to familiar, established practices—so they seem less challenging;

- Pointing out when negativity seems to be wearing the staff person down and diminishing her sense of optimism and hope; and

- Using humor to brighten the mood and communicate a more positive outlook.

Bearing Witness

At times, the supervisor provides invaluable support simply by listening, being there for her staff person, and acknowledging the sadness and pain she has witnessed with a family. The supervisor can highlight that what is sharable is made more bearable (Siegel, 2010), and she can help staff members see how this kind of bearing witness with a family can be a support even if no problems are solved or resources offered.

Motivating and Inspiring

Infant–family work can be extremely rewarding, but it also is likely to expose staff members to many very sad, worrisome, and distressing situations. Service delivery systems are often poorly organized and frustrating to work with, and regulatory demands can be high and seem quite capricious. Resources are generally inadequate. Finally, as noted before, the field is constantly changing, and workers are frequently in the position of being responsible for changing contract demands. Under these circumstances, the supervisor plays a vital role in helping to motivate and inspire staff members. She can support a supervisee who is feeling hopeless, overwhelmed, and sad in part by providing a holding environment, as described above: giving time and opportunity for talking about these stresses, and empathizing with the feelings expressed. The supervisor helps her supervisee to stay hopeful, without denying the difficulties and challenges of the situation. She does this by guiding the staff person to acknowledge the progress that has occurred (which is sometimes overlooked in the midst of dire circumstances), appreciate what is going well, identify the strengths and resources available (including her own), and set reasonable priorities. She works with her supervisee to analyze a complex situation, and break it down into smaller, more manageable issues or tasks. At times, the supervisor simply bears witness and helps her staff members move toward acceptance of great sadness. She can also hold out the possibility that something good will come from a situation that they don't yet understand.

The supervisor can articulate and reinforce the importance of the work, reference the mission and core values of the program, and suggest that staff members see their efforts as part of a broader context—such as helping to build a coordinated care system or promoting social justice. She can help staff members learn how to talk about their work, be explicit about why and how they do what they do, and why it matters. When staff members are struggling to cope with program or practice changes, the supervisor can inspire and motivate by articulating the potential gains for children and families. She can provide encouragement by recalling other times when change was handled effectively and identifying the ways in which what staff members are already doing has laid a solid foundation for new efforts. The reflective supervisor offers staff members reassurance that they are not starting from scratch but in fact already have many of the requisite skills and processes in place. Supervisors can also help staff members recognize that they are not solely responsible for child and family outcomes. Intervention and therapeutic work is always a collaborative effort between professionals and families, and there are times when they must realize that there is nothing more to be done and that it is all right to let go.

This is often easier said than done. Staff members usually have a strong commitment to the families they work with and may experience strong feelings of failure and even incompetence when the family does not participate or fully engage in the services offered. The supervisor should be prepared for the fact that her supervisee may need to work hard and over a long period of time to recover from this experience.

Exploring

Exploration is at the heart of the reflective supervision model. It is one of the qualities that most distinguishes it from other approaches in which there is more of an emphasis on administrative matters and in which the supervisor tends to take on a more directive role. In the reflective model, supervisory time is protected as an opportunity for slowing down, stepping back, and trying to think more broadly and at greater depth about the complex situations that inevitably arise in work with young children and families. With assistance from her supervisor, the practitioner can go back and reexperience specific moments and interactions with a family to understand them better. She can acknowledge and explore her own thoughts and feelings—and reflect on how these may be affecting her understanding of a situation and her responses to it. Supervisees will also learn that their own reactions can be a valuable source of information that will help guide the work ("You mentioned that you are always happy when this family cancels. Any idea what that is about?"). Supervision provides an opportunity to explore different perspectives ("Do you have any thoughts about what the mom might have been feeling at that time? How about the baby? Would having this information help us understand any better why they acted the way they did?"). The art of structuring these questions will be explored in more depth in chapter 4.

Using collaborative problem-solving techniques, the supervisor will first empathize with whatever the staff person is feeling about a difficult matter and then start to explore the issue. This can be done by asking a variety of questions that often provide information about the history, meaning, context, importance, and possible solutions.

- How long has this been going on?

- Do you think the family has any concerns about your role in the home?

- Why do you think she might have said that?

- Have there been any recent changes in the family?

- What do you think might happen next? Any ideas about our choices at this point?

Other strategies, such as commenting on observed patterns of behavior, reframing an issue so as to offer a different perspective, or offering interpretations, can be part of this process (Doan-Sampon, Wollenburg, Campbell, & Portage Project Staff, 1999):

> *In the past you have talked about how you wish this dad could start to be a little more assertive in seeking the care his baby needs; maybe at this visit he was just trying it out on you—and it came off as a little harsh. Any chance that was what was going on?*

Through these kinds of discussions, the supervisor and supervisee are likely to come up with a much richer understanding of the situation (the presenting problem is often only the tip of the iceberg), and from there they can at least tentatively formulate a hypothesis about what is going on and make a plan for possible next steps. Questioning and collaborative problem solving are effective when and only if the supervisor is genuinely open and attentive to the perspective brought by the supervisee. If questions and collaborative problem solving are only a prelude to the supervisor dictating what to do, it is likely that the supervisee's willingness to explore and creativity will diminish over time.

Through the exploration process, the reflective supervisor helps to open up a space around a problem, to allow it to be seen in a different context, from multiple perspectives. One of the most important roles of the supervisor is to help supervisees avoid "hydroplaning": jumping too quickly to conclusions, making interpretations without fully exploring a situation, and acting hastily. The continuity of regular supervision is an asset here. It makes it easier for the supervisor to be the "historian" of the work with each client and thus to keep a good perspective on new situations or crises as they arise.

Successful implementation of this supervisory role depends on the supervisor establishing a strong relationship with her supervisee—that is, a relationship in which there is enough safety for the supervisee to explore freely, without fear of revealing her mistakes or lack of skill. There needs to be enough trust that staff members can address sensitive issues such as those related to professional boundaries, the possible effect of the practitioner's and the family's past experiences on the working relationship, and the part that differences related to culture, power, race, and class may play. The supervisor can hold up a mirror for the supervisee so that she understands better how she is perceived by others and how she may affect others and they her. The supervisee can experience firsthand the ways in which a relationship can be a vehicle for learning, intervention, and change. Please see chapter 4 for a more in-depth discussion of these strategies, skills, and attributes.

ROLE 3: MAINTAINING IDEALS AND STANDARDS, QUALITY ASSURANCE, AND SAFETY

In this blended model of supervision, the supervisor is responsible for all the administrative aspects of her supervisee's work (e.g., paperwork, meeting billing standards, and adherence to regulatory standards and requirements), as well as for ensuring the overall quality of the program. At the same time, she provides supervisory support in difficult situations and promotes staff members' development. This inevitably entails a dynamic tension between mentoring and monitoring functions. As noted in chapter 1, it may help to think of supervision as analogous to parenting, where the need to protect, nurture, teach, set limits, and clarify expectations must be balanced and integrated. The reflective supervisor seeks to provide a safe environment for learning while at the same time holding the supervisee accountable for the quality of the work.

Avoiding Conceptual Drift

The supervisor can serve as navigator, keeping the program on course while using the mission, core values, and standards of best practice as guiding stars and as an anchor if needed. In this way, the supervisor keeps a collective focus on the reasons for doing this work, what the work is really about, and why the way it is done is critical. When staff members are trying to make difficult decisions, she can invoke these principles and core values as a way of helping them to find their way, as in the following example:

> *The staff members of an early intervention program were at first hesitant to start including parents in their toddler playgroups. They preferred the old way, where parents just dropped the children off and then picked them up at the end of group. This arrangement was easier, because staff members were in control of the situation and could follow their intended lesson plans. Having parents stay and participate introduced all kinds of variables, and the sessions were much more difficult to structure. The supervisor, by calling attention to core principles and established best practices, was able to help the staff members realize the benefits of this change. They readily acknowledged that toddlers learn best in the context of relationships with the people most important to them and that the parents were in the best position to support their child's growth and development. Shifting the program focus to promoting the caregivers' ability to do this made sense and helped staff members tolerate the change in program format.*

It is the supervisor's responsibility to keep the big picture in mind, to consider the effect of program practices on children and families, and to encourage everyone else to do the same. The supervisor can do this by pivoting back to the work and asking, "How will this decision affect the children and families?" The supervisor can lead by example—practicing and exemplifying core values and principles of the agency, keeping up with recent research, bringing in new information to share with staff members, and supporting and participating in ongoing training opportunities.

Integrating Performance Standards and Administrative Requirements Into Daily Program Routines

All programs operate under a set of defining guidelines and requirements related to ensuring program quality. In many cases, there are multiple standards—those established by the individual agency (e.g., billing expectations), the local or state governing entity (e.g., the state's system for gathering demographic information about children served under the federal Individuals With Disabilities Education Act), and the federal government (e.g., the detailed and complex Head Start performance standards). These often require extensive documentation. Direct service providers (home visitors, classroom teachers, and therapists) may find adherence to program policies and procedures a burden, particularly in regard to accurate and timely completion of required paperwork. They may see these tasks as less important parts of their job, particularly in the face of the intense needs of their clients. For example, if an Early Head Start home visitor feels she has to choose between spending an extra half-hour talking with a distraught parent and completing her home visit log, she is likely to put the documentation off until another day. Supervisors can easily find themselves in the position of taking on the primary responsibility for adherence to the sometimes overwhelming, and constantly changing, program standards and requirements. As one frustrated supervisor put it: "I feel like I am always nagging my staff members about cleaning up their room!" No one wants to be in this position, and it is not helpful to the supervisor or employees.

The supervisor's challenge is to help staff members understand the meaning and purpose of the standards (if possible!) and to develop a sense of shared ownership for the responsibility of meeting them. Strategies for accomplishing this include the following:

- *Preview and review guidelines and standards regularly—and include opportunities for discussion of the meaning or function of individual items* (e.g., the Head Start standard about displaying children's work in the classroom). Staff members should be aware of the process as a whole and be informed about timelines and deadlines well in advance. It helps if they can have a sense of how individual monitoring items reflect core values of the program—for example, to realize that audits of a child's file are designed so as to ensure that children receive services in a timely manner, that the services are developed in collaboration with families, and that child outcomes are functional for everyday life. Professionals all understand that these are critically important goals and that it requires real effort and focused attention to achieve them.

- *Involve staff members in monitoring and quality assurance activities, so that all monitoring has a self-assessment component.* This might involve periodic quality assurance through record reviews, observations of programs, and so on. Ask staff members to report back to the team about the results of their findings, their interpretation of what they found, and what actions they intend to take as a result.

- *Build regular opportunities for assessing program quality and adherence to established standards into ongoing program and supervisory routines.* Simple examples include agreeing to review billing as a standard part of a monthly supervision session, with the staff person asked to assess whether targets were met, to interpret what actually occurred, and to share what the plan is for the coming month. This is in contrast to a common pattern of announcing expectations, having the supervisor (as opposed to the staff person) monitor them sporadically, and waiting until there has been a period of failure to meet these standards before bringing it up as an area of concern. File reviews can be included as part of regular team meetings, with staff members taking responsibility for presenting their findings and the supervisor setting the tone for a constructive discussion of the results. Supervisors who regularly read progress reports, intervention log notes, and evaluation reports, and who accompany staff members on home visits, will have many opportunities to discuss qualitative aspects of service delivery as part of the ongoing supervisory process. Again, this can be done in a reflective, respectful, and collaborative manner.

To the greatest extent possible, quality assurance activities should be part of the everyday program routine, rather than a sporadic, stressful, and disruptive event. In some instances, the supervisor will have to work hard to avoid this occurring, as for example in Head Start, where an outside review team from the national Office of Head Start conducts an intensive, overall program review on a regular basis. This review is a high-stakes process, as it can result in program sanctions. By using the strategies outlined above, the effect on staff members will be minimized and the results of the review are likely to be positive.

Overseeing and Carrying Out Recruitment: Interviewing, Hiring, and Orienting New Staff Members

One of the most effective ways of ensuring program quality is to hire employees whose knowledge, skills, beliefs, and values closely align with the program or agency and with the specific demands of the job. Staff recruitment is often identified as one of the most challenging supervisory/administrative tasks, especially for those jobs that involve home visiting with high-stress, multirisk families. There is a shortage of well-trained professionals in most of the early childhood fields, and so it can be tempting to hire anyone with the requisite background and credentials. However, experience (usually painful!) indicates that it is far better to spend the time looking for a well-qualified candidate. It is critically important to clearly articulate the program's mission and core values, the service delivery model, and specific job expectations during the interview process. These can also be explicitly stated in the job description. In addition to attending to the concrete tasks and discipline-specific expectations, there should be a focus on aspects of the work such as:

- Reflective practice and supervision;
- Relationship-based work;
- Ability to work as part of a team;

- The importance of coordinated and integrated services;

- Ability to form a therapeutic alliance with families on behalf of children;

- Understanding of current information about child development (beyond "ages and stages");

- Collaborative problem-solving strategies;

- Professional use of self;

- The importance of self-awareness of one's own culture, beliefs, and values;

- Ability to take, or think about, the perspective of another (e.g., a parent, child, or team member);

- Good communication skills—active listening and respectful, clear expression; and

- Organizational capabilities and the ability to handle multiple priorities.

See Appendix 4 for a sample job description that includes these kinds of job expectations.

When these issues are discussed and explored during the interview process, there is a higher likelihood of recruiting staff members who are well-suited for the work. An applicant's skills in these areas can be assessed through interpretation of case scenarios, by asking for examples from their past experience that relate to these aspects of the job, and through reference checks. Some useful interview questions might include:

- *How do you feel the worker's relationship with the family affects program services?*

- *How would you think about a situation where there appeared to be a conflict or misunderstanding with a family? How do you think you might eventually handle something like this?*

- *Given our job description and what we talked about in this job, how would you explain your role to a new family, teachers, or social workers?*

Once a new staff person has been hired, the orientation period offers valuable opportunities for laying the foundations for successful employment. Establishing a positive supervisory relationship is an important part of this process; this is discussed in detail in chapter 6. The supervisor can make clear, right from the start, that both the clinical and administrative aspects of the job are important and that there will be an ongoing focus on the quality of the work with children and families. This can be done in the context of a collaborative, supportive, and respectful relationship, so that the supervisee really understands that her supervisor is there to help her do her very best work. We have often found it valuable to spend extra time with a new staff person, including time for less formal, more spontaneous interactions. "Front-loading" supervisory support pays off in the long run. When we look back on our more difficult supervisory situations, we realize that there were often early signs of problems, misunderstandings, or a mismatch in philosophy or skills. It is best for everyone if these issues can be addressed early and directly.

Conducting Regular Performance Reviews, and Assisting Staff Members in Formulating a Professional Development Plan

Most programs have some kind of system in place for carrying out regular performance reviews. These reviews can be extremely productive and helpful—but often are not. Ways that a supervisor and agency can get the most out of the process include the following:

• Design the performance review form so as to mirror the job description. Assuming that the job description includes all the important aspects of the work—such as interpersonal skills, ability to work as part of a team, the quality of relationships with families, and engagement in and use of supervision—the stage will be set for a meaningful and in-depth review. Ideally, the initial interview questions, job description, and performance review all reflect a consistent and coherent picture of the work responsibilities and program values.

• Make self-assessment a central part of the performance review process. Each staff person is given the performance review form in advance so that she can think about and assess her work over the past year.

• Ensure that the annual performance review is respectful, reflective, and collaborative in nature—that both the staff person and the supervisor come prepared to think about what has happened during the year. Together they can formulate a series of statements about what has been accomplished thus far and what should be worked on in the future. This is an opportunity to slow down, step back from the day-to-day concerns related to individual children and families, and identify themes, underlying issues, and long-term goals. The performance review should reflect and build on all the supervisory conversations of the past year. If these have been well documented, the supervisor will be able to review her notes so as to identify themes and trends and to include specific examples of past performance in the discussion. It is essential that any concerns about the supervisee's job performance have already been addressed clearly and directly prior to the performance review: There should be no surprises. Once staff members trust that this process is constructive and see that it is part of the ongoing supervisory dialogue, they are more likely to actively engage in an honest appraisal of their skills and achievements.

• If at all possible, avoid assignment of numerical values to staff members' performance, and avoid use of rating scales (e.g., "meets expectations," "exceeds expectations," or "fails to meet expectations"). In our experience, staff members then tend to focus exclusively on the "grade" received. They are less likely to join with their supervisor in assessing their performance and thinking about how they would like to do their work in the future. In addition, use of numbers, grades, or rating scales gives the false impression of objectivity or being "scientific." To a large extent, ratings are based on the supervisor's judgment, rather than on any clearly measurable standards, and so they are actually quite subjective and easy to dispute or dismiss. This approach undermines the notion of supervision as a mutual and collaborative process, as it is the supervisor who ultimately determines the rating.

• Commit to clearly and directly addressing any concerns related to staff members' performance. As noted previously, these should already have been discussed during regular supervisory sessions, but they must also be reflected in the annual review. These include issues that may be difficult to articulate, such as interpersonal skills, team participation, and cultural responsiveness. If there are disagreements between staff members and the supervisor, these can also be included in the performance review summary.

• Include a professional development plan in the performance review process. This plan builds on the performance review and provides a guide for the coming year. Together, the supervisor and staff person reflect on the issues they have identified during the review process (including areas of special interest to the staff person and performance concerns). They then select three or four goals to focus on in the professional development plan. For each goal, they develop specific objectives, strategies, sources of support, and criteria for success. These goals are mutually negotiated, with both the supervisor and supervisee able to select outcomes that are high priorities for them. (See Appendixes 5 and 6 for sample performance review and professional development plan forms, respectively.)

Addressing Supervisee Performance Issues

For many supervisors, dealing with conflict and talking to staff members about poor performance rank as among the most challenging of their responsibilities. There are a host of reasons, including a personal history of avoiding conflict; fear of backlash from the team; fear that staff members will not like them; discomfort with strong affect (staff members might cry or get angry); concern for legal repercussions; lack of adequate documentation; and lack of skill in articulating concerns, particularly in the area of communication, team work, interpersonal relationships, boundaries, countertransference, and cultural diversity.

In fact, supervisors often shy away from having these difficult conversations. This can have negative consequences for the program and for the services delivered to children and families. These costs should be kept clearly in mind, as they can be a powerful motivator in helping supervisors summon the courage to do what at first may seem too difficult. When supervisors fail to address staff members' performance concerns, the following occurs:

- The problem generally does not resolve on its own. Things typically get worse!

- Team functioning can suffer, as can staff members' morale. The supervisor may lose credibility with other staff members.

- The problem is not explored, and therefore there is no opportunity to gain additional information or insight into the situation. Assumptions can't be challenged.

- The supervisor does not receive valuable feedback as to her own contribution or other mitigating factors.

- The staff person in question does not have the opportunity to learn, grow, change, and do better work.

- A great deal of time and psychological energy can be spent (and wasted) in worrying about and reacting to the staff person who is causing problems.

- We forgo the possibility of having a more capable and effective person in the job.

- The program or agency is put at risk (financially, legally, or in terms of community respect).

- Most important, services to the children and family suffer, and clients are denied the possibility of receiving high-quality services from a well-functioning team.

Having enumerated the possible, even likely, results of failing to address poor job performance, we must also acknowledge the fact that many supervisors need help in learning how to do so effectively and in a manner consistent with the principles of reflective supervision. Some key skills and strategies are described below:

- *Preview your concerns with a peer or your own supervisor.* This will help you articulate precisely the nature of the problem(s) and the effect of these problems on teammates, the agency, children, and families; it also allows you to provide concrete, recent examples illustrative of your concerns.

- *Explore the history of the problem.* Determine how long it has been going on, the possible meaning of the staff person's behavior, and any instances of self-awareness or improvement in the area of concern. Through this discussion, you may discover that there really is no significant effect on the team or services, that you do not have enough specific examples available, or that there is a very plausible explanation for what is going on. As a result of this conversation, you may decide to simply wait and see how things develop over time, rather than addressing the topic directly with your staff person.

If you decide to go ahead, you could consider role-playing the upcoming supervisory conversation to practice what you actually want to say.

- *Choose your time and place.* Of course, any difficult supervisory conversation should take place in private, with adequate time available. If you anticipate that this will be a distressing experience for you or for the staff person, you may wish to schedule it for the end of the day.

- *When meeting with the supervisee, use "spotlighting" techniques.* Focus on one or two issues; state your concern simply, calmly, and clearly, emphasizing the effect on the work; ask for your staff person's thoughts on the matter; and then listen to what she says.

- *Avoid the "spotlighting sandwich"* of stating multiple positive things about the staff person, inserting a spotlighted concern, and then finishing with more praise or an apology.

- *Pivot back to the work.* If the staff person starts to talk about all the personal reasons she is having difficulty doing her job, refocus the discussion by comments such as: "I can understand how your obligations at home are making it difficult for you to get all your home visits done. Do you have any thoughts about how you are going to be able to address this? Given everything you are dealing with—do you think it is realistic for you to be working full-time right now? Should we think about giving you a reduced schedule?"

- *Keep your focus.* If your supervisee responds by bringing up other issues that seem to be diversionary (e.g., how other staff members are upset, or things you have done that are of concern to her), stay on track by saying something such as: "I will think about what you have said, but right now let's refocus on this issue of how you are interacting with your teammates during our team meetings."

- *Summarize and make a plan.* At the end of the meeting, ask your supervisee to think about what she will do to address the concerns, and how you can help her to succeed. Then agree to meet again soon to formulate a plan.

- *Keep good documentation of all supervisory conversations.* This is absolutely critical and an area of needed improvement for many supervisors—even the most experienced.

Some supervisors will use team meetings to focus on problematic areas of documentation or billing, because they do not like to bring the issues up with an individual. This can be demoralizing to the team members who are meeting requirements, and in general a much better approach is for the supervisor to work directly with staff members who are struggling.

As difficult as it may be to have these conversations, the ability to do so is an absolutely critical supervisory role and skill. Anyone who has ever come into a new supervisory position and had to inherit staff members whose poor performance was not addressed by the previous supervisor can testify to the problems this creates.

ROLE 4: FACILITATING OPEN COMMUNICATION AND EFFECTIVE TEAM FUNCTIONING

Supervisors often find themselves in the position of being the leader of a team. As such, they are in a position to support positive and constructive communication between team members. They also have a primary responsibility to ensure that all staff members have equal and timely access to important information.

Team Leader

Work with infants, toddlers, and their families is multidisciplinary in nature. Unfortunately, most professional training programs are not. In addition, there are often administrative and systems issues (e.g., billing forms, assessment and report-writing processes, and discipline-specific treatment plans) that support a fragmented approach to service delivery. Much of this work is done through home visiting, which involves staff members working by themselves during much of the day. For all these reasons, it can be quite challenging to implement a real team approach and to ensure open and clear communication between team members. The supervisor has an important leadership role in creating and supporting effective team work, which is discussed at greater length in chapter 5.

Basic supervisory responsibilities include:

- Helping staff members realize that they do not work in isolation;

- Fostering an understanding of the child and family as a whole—rather than as a collection of separate areas of need (e.g., speech, mental health difficulties, occupational therapy, resource needs, and parenting education);

- Setting the expectation that team members will collaborate to develop an integrated approach to working with a family (including team assessment, goal development, and ongoing intervention and treatment);

- Overseeing and facilitating regular meetings of staff and team members, with the expectation of respectful communication (including listening!), balanced contributions, ability to tolerate differences, and the ability to explore broadly and then to come to a decision, make a plan, and follow through on it;

- Helping the team develop and identify as a team (including an understanding of their purpose and mission) and maintain cohesion while addressing difficult issues; and

- Acknowledging and celebrating the successes of the team.

Team leadership is a critical function, especially in a field where teamwork is so essential; staff members often work on their own, out in the community, where standards and conditions of practice are continually changing. Please see chapter 5 for a more in-depth discussion of this aspect of supervision.

Facilitating Open and Clear Communication

The supervisor is in a position to facilitate communication at all levels and in many different ways. First, and very powerfully, the supervisor can model respectful and empowering communication. By adopting a responsive and reflective style, she will set the tone (and an example) for communication throughout the program. She is in a position to draw attention to the ways individual staff members do or do not practice consideration for each other and support a spirit of collaboration. She can help staff members learn to be brave in the face of conflict: to express their concerns clearly and directly to one another. By discouraging triangulation (when A complains to B about C) and resisting the temptation to be drawn into struggles between team members or other colleagues, she can help staff members develop better problem-solving skills. If staff members are able to talk about their work clearly and concisely with each other, they will be more capable of communicating effectively with families. If they learn how to have difficult conversations with each other (in which staff members disagree and express concerns), they will be better prepared to have these kinds of discussions with families.

Second, the supervisor is in an excellent position to attend to the information being given to staff members and at the same time to ensure that staff members have the opportunity to express themselves and be heard. She can see that all staff members have equal access to the same information in a timely manner, as well as equal opportunity to be part of the decision-making process. During times of program and policy changes, it is essential for the supervisor to describe these changes clearly. She must give information about the purpose and goals, the timing, the ways in which each individual will be affected, and the possibilities for giving input. At the same time, the supervisor can function as an advocate for her staff members and team: finding ways of expressing their input, suggestions, and concerns to those at a higher level of decision making. If staff members trust that she can and will act on their behalf, they will be more open to hearing about and accepting programmatic change.

Finally, an important role for the supervisor is to help staff members understand the big picture: to see their program in a broader context (as part of an agency, state, or national system). She can help them appreciate the ways in which outside constraints or demands may be affecting their day-to-day work.

ROLE 5: PROVIDING PROGRAM LEADERSHIP

The reflective supervisor's opportunities to take on leadership roles will vary from program to program, depending on the individual's specific position and abilities, as well as the agency size and culture. Leadership is a critical aspect of supervision that encompasses and goes beyond the job functions already described (promoting staff members' development, being a source of inspiration and support, ensuring program quality, maintaining good communication, and building strong teams).

Supervisors are often seen as leaders because of the authority they have, their experience and expertise, and their access to those in top management who are in a position to make key decisions. In the field of early childhood, supervisors have frequently been promoted from direct service positions and have longevity within their particular organization. They may, therefore, be very familiar with the particular culture of the program and be in a good position to help others learn the informal yet powerful rules, customs, and values that govern the everyday workings of the organization. Supervisors who have been at an agency for a long time will also have a historical perspective, which will put them in a position to help others understand current policies, practices, and priorities. This historical connection can also be a liability, as these supervisors may be overly attached to the old ways (e.g., "the way we do things around here…") and reluctant to accept new leadership, processes, and practices. In these instances, supervisors may actually function as saboteurs, who are able to be quite effective due to the power they have within the organization. Ideally, the supervisor uses her influence and authority in a positive and constructive manner that benefits the program as a whole.   Specific leadership functions include program oversight, program development, community collaborations and partnerships, and advocacy.

Program Oversight

As mentioned previously in this chapter, the supervisor is often responsible for the overall health and well-being of her part of a program (e.g., balancing mentoring and monitoring activities, making sure that budget expectations are met, implementation of program policies and procedures, and hiring and training staff members).

A supervisor may function as a site manager, ensuring that the office and work space is maintained appropriately. She may be in charge of developing a plan for implementation of a new program initiative or responding to a contracting agency's requests for data or other information. A supervisor is likely to supervise clerical staff as well as clinical staff, and she will need to be attuned to the administrative functions needed to support the direct services.

Program Development

The early childhood field is in a constant state of flux. New research provides support for evolving standards of best practice (consider the shift from center-based to home-based service, or the growing appreciation of the importance of early social–emotional development). Changes in political and economic conditions have a significant effect on the service delivery system. Early childhood programs, if they are to thrive, need to adapt. Supervisors, as program leaders, play an important role in this process. Depending on the individual responsibilities and organizational structures, supervisors are often in a position to suggest new ideas for needed services, lead teams figuring out how to respond to changing community needs, and give critical feedback to top management about the challenges experienced by direct service staff.

Community Collaborations and Partnerships

In most communities, there is a network of agencies and programs charged with providing a wide range of services and supports to young children and families. Typically, their needs exceed the resources available. In addition, there is much to be gained by a coordinated, integrated approach, so that the various service providers work together on behalf of the family. No individual practitioner or agency can afford to work in isolation and still hope to provide the best services for the children and families in their care. However, it is often extremely difficult to find ways of forming effective community partnerships and supporting real care coordination. It falls to those in leadership positions, including supervisors, to initiate and maintain effective community collaborations and partnerships. There are many different ways a supervisor can do this:

- Become well-informed about other agencies' services, eligibility criteria, and referral processes.

- Pass this information along to staff members, so that they can help families to access these resources.

- Establish a personal connection with key individuals in partner agencies: This will be very valuable when problems need to be addressed and solved.

- Make it clear to staff members that it is each person's responsibility to reach out to community partners. Pick up the phone! Don't just wait to be called.

- Establish processes that support collaboration: regular staffings, cross-agency communication forms, and joint planning sessions with families.

- Resist the temptation to create an "us against them" mentality; staff members will take their cue from the supervisor. If she speaks respectfully and empathically about the efforts of community partners—referencing the constraints they may have in doing their work—supervisees will be more open-minded and tolerant in their own interactions with that agency's staff members.

These strategies require time, effort, and real commitment but can result in dramatically improved services for children and families.

Advocacy

Early childhood programs are, by nature, designed to meet the needs of some of the most vulnerable and least powerful people in society (e.g., very young children, minorities, families living in poverty with limited education, and those experiencing stresses such as domestic violence or substance abuse). These populations have difficulty advocating effectively on their own behalf. It is the responsibility of early childhood programs and professionals to advocate for them and to help them find a voice that can be heard. Supervisors, as program leaders, can be part of local and regional committees that serve in an advisory capacity to policy makers. Through their professional organizations they can advocate for implementation of best practices in service delivery. They can, for example, help mobilize families to attend legislative hearings where important issues are being discussed.

SUMMARY

The intent of this chapter is to provide an overview of the many different roles and responsibilities of the reflective supervisor. Subsequent chapters are devoted to a more intensive consideration of various aspects of this model: We wanted to begin by offering a holistic picture that would illuminate the core principles and key practices.

Amy has just been offered a promotion from home visitor to supervisor in the Rattlesnake Junction Healthy Families program. She is excited and a little nervous at the prospect; after all, she remembers how she felt when she first started 5 years ago and was told that reflective supervision was an important part of the program. She would be meeting with her supervisor every week. Amy recalls her first reaction: "Every week! What on earth will we find to talk about? Those management types—all they ever do is sit in their office, push papers around, and make trouble for those of us who actually do the work!"

Now that she has had a chance to be part of this supervision and was so lucky to have Mary as her supervisor, she wonders how she could ever manage to do the job. She appreciates that Mary somehow managed to support her and at the same time challenge her to grow and learn. Mary helped her pay attention to all the important details (including getting her billing in on time) and at the same time made sure there were lots of opportunities for slowing down and thinking carefully about complicated and even scary situations.

Amy had to think long and hard about whether she could wear all these hats and play all these roles. At the end of the day, she realized that one of Mary's greatest gifts was in helping her know herself well enough to feel that she was up to the challenge.

SUPPLEMENTARY EXERCISE FOR SUPERVISORS

Consider the key supervisory roles described in this chapter:

1. Supporting staff development

2. Providing a "secure base" where staff members can safely explore the meaning of their work

3. Maintaining program ideals and standards, quality assurance, and safety

4. Facilitating open communication and effective team functioning

5. Providing program leadership

Make a pie chart that reflects a recent supervisory session you had with a supervisee. Divide your pie into pieces that reflect how much time you devoted to each key role. As you look at your chart, ask yourself why certain sections of your pie might be bigger or smaller. Consider how the experience level of the staff members may affect the shape of your pie chart. Monitor to make sure that "providing a secure base" is a prominent piece of your pie; if it is very small, ask yourself how it might be enlarged. Consider any other imbalances and how they might be addressed.

Advanced practice. Videotape a supervision session and review it with the five roles in mind.

REFERENCES

Bowlby, J. (1988). *A secure base: Parent-child attachment and healthy human development.* New York: Basic Books.

California Infant-Family and Early Childhood Mental Health Workforce Competencies. (n.d.). Retrieved April 19, 2010, from www.ecmhtraining-ca.org

Doan-Sampon, M. A., Wollenburg, K., Campbell, A., & Portage Project Staff. (1999). *Growing: Birth to three—Revised.* Portage, WI: Portage Project.

Fenichel, E. (Ed.)(1992). *Learning through supervision and mentorship to support the development of infants, toddlers and their families: A source book.* Washington, DC: ZERO TO THREE.

Meisels, S. J., & Fenichel, E. (Eds.). (1996). *New visions for the developmental assessment of infants and young children.* Washington, DC: ZERO TO THREE.

Michigan Association for Infant Mental Health. (n.d.). *MI-AIMH Endorsement: Overview.* Retrieved April 19, 2010, from www.mi-aimh.org/endorsements_overview.php

Pawl J. H. (1994). On supervision. *Zero to Three, 15*(3), 21–29.

Siegel, D. (Speaker). (2010). The neurobiology of "we": How relationships, the mind and the brain interact to shape who we are. (Audio recording no. ISBN 159179949x.) Los Angeles: Mindsight Institute.

Slobodkina, E. (1968). *Caps for sale: A tale of a peddler, some monkeys and their monkey business.* New York: HarperTrophy.

Winnicott, D. W. (1965). *The maturational processes and the facilitating environment: Studies in the theory of emotional development.* New York: International Universities Press.

Further Readings

Bertacchi, J., & Coplon, J. (1992). The professional use of self in prevention. In E. Fenichel (Ed.), *Learning through supervision and mentorship to support the development of infants, toddlers and their families: A source book* (pp. 84–90). Washington, DC: ZERO TO THREE.

Bertacchi, J., & Gilkerson, L. (2009). How can administrative and reflective supervision be combined? In S. S. Heller & L. Gilkerson (Eds.), *A practical guide to reflective supervision* (pp. 121–134). Washington, DC: ZERO TO THREE.

Bertacchi, J., & Norman-Murch, T. (1999). Implementing reflective supervision in non-clinical settings: Challenges to practice. *Zero to Three, 20*(1), 18–23.

Bowlby, J. (1999). *Attachment and loss: Attachment* (2nd ed., Vol. 1). New York: Basic Books.

Cox, E. (2005). Adult learners learning from experience: Using a reflective practice model to support work-based learning. *Reflective Practice, 6,* 459–472.

Heffron, M. C., Grunstein, S., & Tilmon, S. (2007). Exploring diversity in supervision and practice. *Zero to Three, 28*(2), 34–38.

Howes, C., & Ritchie, S. (2002). *A matter of trust: Connecting teachers and learners in the early childhood classroom.* New York: Teachers College Press.

Kalmanson, B., & Seligman, S. (1992). Family-provider relationships: The basis of all interventions. *Infants and Young Children, 4*(4), 46–52.

Norman-Murch, T. (2005). Keeping our balance on a slippery slope: Training and supporting infant/family specialists within an organizational context. *Infants and Young Children, 18*(4), 308–322.

Parlakian, R., & Seibel, N. (2001). *Being in charge: Reflective leadership in infant–family programs.* Washington, DC: ZERO TO THREE.

Siegel, D., & Hartzell, M. (2003). *Parenting from the inside out.* New York: Tarcher.

CHAPTER 3

"It's in the Bricks and Mortar!": Organizational Supports for Reflective Supervision

Reflective practice in support of relationship-based work is a core value, and its full promise will best be realized when an agency builds its principles into the "bricks and mortar" of its everyday work at all staff levels. Once an agency makes the commitment to implement reflective supervision, it is likely to take several years for the ideas to be fully realized, and planning, patience, and persistence are essential. The following are administrative practices and strategies that are helpful when planning to implement reflective supervision at an organizational level.

Available to All

Ideally, reflective supervision is available to everyone within an organization, including clerical, administrative, information technology, and accounting staff members; direct service providers; and supervisors and directors. All staff members then get the benefit of slowing down, stepping back, and reflecting on their work. This gives them the opportunity to explore complex issues, to understand the larger context, and to understand their own reactions and responses. Supervisory conversations offer the chance to be proactive in addressing upcoming challenges and to plan ahead for future projects and activities. This gives supervisors and supervisees a calm and protected time to think carefully and creatively even when the work is stressful or overwhelming.

This supervision model is based on the idea that the quality of relationships and interactions, in this case between staff members and their supervisor, affects what they learn, accomplish, and are able to cope with. It follows then that all agency staff members benefit from and deserve supervisory support and attention.

The "dosage" of supervision (i.e., how much and how often) may vary depending on staff members' position, with clerical staff members likely to receive less than those who are working directly with children and families. These direct service providers, who are often working off-site and in families' homes, can be exposed to demands and situations that are extremely complex, evoke strong and contradictory emotions, and constitute real threats to the family's or their own well-being. Direct service staff members will therefore typically receive more frequent and more intensive support (e.g., individual supervision, team meetings, and case review). But the principles are the same—the supervisee should feel well understood and supported by her supervisor. They should work together to solve problems, in an atmosphere of trust and respect. Job expectations should be made clear, and concerns addressed directly. It will help if written job descriptions are clear and if there can be clarifying conversations when job expectations shift because of changes in funding or program direction.

Cost is often raised as a barrier when thinking about providing reflective supervision to a team, program, or an agency. Although there may indeed be initial costs that could seem a barrier to this new approach, planners should consider that supervision time is a built-in time that serves many functions, including training, support, quality assurance, and reduction of staff turnover. In addition, staff members whose jobs and responsibilities are known by a supervisor can be covered more easily when illness pulls them out of the workforce. Thus, the actual time costs may be less than for agencies that provide supervision on an as–needed or crisis basis, which often results in decreased productivity, poorly served families, lost clients, compassion fatigue, chaotic classrooms, and burnout. Although additional studies are needed to track how regular reflective supervision mitigates these barriers to program quality, there is ample clinical evidence and some solid research that points to reflective supervision as a cost-effective practice (Geller & Foley, 2009; Howes, James, & Ritchie, 2003; McFarland, Saunders, & Allen, 2008).

SUPERVISION FOR THE SUPERVISORS

Supervisors need their own reflective supervisory support if they are to be effective and continue to develop their skills. The power of the parallel process is that supervisors are then better able to provide this kind of support to their staff members, who in turn can implement these reflective practices in their work with families. Of course, it is important to realize that parallel process can and sometimes does work to negatively affect the work. For example, stress tends to be contagious. The supervisor who is very concerned about budgetary and billing problems may overemphasize this aspect of the work in conversations with staff members, thereby neglecting or minimizing the clinical aspects of the work. The result may be a supervisee who becomes very anxious about meeting productivity expectations. She could then become critical or judgmental of the families on her caseload who have difficulty keeping appointments, without trying to understand the underlying reasons for the poor attendance.

Supervisors may need to seek out their own supervision if it is not available within their organization. This could be provided by colleagues from other agencies who are in similar positions or by peers within their program. It should have the same key characteristics of being regular, reflective, and collaborative. Everyone involved in infant and early childhood practice needs and deserves a support system and the opportunity for exploration and honest self-reflection. For those who obtain supervision from outside their agency, it is critical to get permission from their manager. The arrangement should be formalized, as best as possible, by contracting and clarifying the parameters of the discussions. This will help protect against possible conflicts of interest, violations of confidentiality, and boundary problems. It is helpful to establish a set schedule because explicit commitments are more likely to be honored than informal, ad hoc plans. See chapter 7 for a more in-depth discussion of this topic.

EVALUATION OF THE SUPERVISORS

Supervisors benefit from feedback and evaluation by their supervisees done in a manner that protects staff members' confidentiality. If the agency has a 360–degree evaluation process, supervisors should be included in it. This 360–degree evaluation process is an approach in which performance reviews are at least partially based on input from multiple sources, including team members, administrative support staff members, supervisors, and supervisees. See Appendixes 7 and 8 for sample evaluation formats suitable to be included in a 360–degree evaluation.

ADEQUATE RESOURCES

Implementation of reflective supervision within an organization requires dedication of adequate time and resources to support the practice. Although these will vary greatly depending on the individual needs of the agency, staff members' background and expertise, the nature of the work performed, and the available funding, resource allocation must be addressed directly and honestly. Time for individual supervision, team meetings, and participation in professional development activities is essential and must be protected. Program managers who cut into regularly scheduled supervision time by engaging supervisors in other administrative activities often notice a significant downward shift in program quality and staff members' satisfaction with their work.

BUFFERING AND THE TRICKLE-UP THEORY

In reality, the actions and style of individuals in top management positions may not always be consistent with the principles of reflective practice and relationship-based work, even when in theory they support reflective supervision. This is understandable when there are strong financial, political, and regulatory pressures, or when the agency is undergoing major changes. Individuals who are successful in heading up a program or agency may be more action-oriented, adventurous, and entrepreneurial risk takers. These are qualities that are very important for their trailblazer role but may result in their being less practiced at slowing down, stepping back, monitoring their own reactions and responses, and wondering about the meaning of the behavior of others. In these instances, the reflective supervisor or program manager needs to learn how to stay calm, focused, and well-regulated, even when her own manager may seem not to be.

Supervisors are often caught in the middle. There is an art to maintaining the reflective stance even when under pressure. The goal is to represent the needs and point of view of direct service staff members to upper management, while at the same time not being so protective of those staff members as to lose perspective about the needs of the agency as a whole or to be unable to see the need for change even when it will be difficult. Ideally, an effort should be made to engage the manager/director in a collaborative problem-solving process and hope for a trickle-up effect of reflective practice. This effort requires preparation, gathering adequate information about the issue ahead of time, staying calm and focused, and being open to a different perspective and point of view. It is very possible that there are policy, financial, or administrative considerations that the manager/director must consider but are not known to midlevel supervisors.

A CORE PRINCIPLE AND KEY PRACTICE

The role of supervision should be stressed from the moment an individual first approaches the agency and seeks a position there. It can be included in job descriptions, discussed in job interviews, and addressed in performance reviews. During an interview, the applicant could be asked to describe the kind of supervision she is looking for and the times when supervision has been especially helpful to her. A person who is quick to say, "Oh, I am very capable of figuring things out on my own—I usually don't need any help" might raise a red flag. The interviewer would want to follow up with some careful exploration to discover whether that person simply had not had any other kinds of opportunity for supervisory support and felt that a competent professional should express a high level of independence. If, however, she seemed actively resistant to sharing and discussing her work on an ongoing basis, she might not be a good fit for the staff position.

When expectations for supervisees are clearly spelled out in job descriptions, performance review forms, and supervision agreements, the supervisor has the responsibility to discuss them in detail with a new staff member. The following is an example of the way supervisory expectations might be represented on a performance evaluation form.

Competency:

Uses supervision effectively, takes initiative to secure professional development opportunities, and applies relevant information in the work setting.

Indicators:

- *Actively participates in supervision that is regular, reflective, and collaborative in nature.*

- *As appropriate, takes the initiative to seek supervisory input.*

- *Accurately identifies areas of mastery and areas targeted for personal growth and development.*

- *Seeks assistance and guidance when needed.*

- *Incorporates constructive direction from supervisor to improve job performance.*

- *Accepts responsibility for the quality of job performance and makes changes as needed.*

- *Maintains awareness of current professional information in the fields of activity. Undertakes regular and ongoing efforts to maintain competencies in the skills used and incorporates new knowledge and skills on the job.*

- *Shares pertinent information with supervisor and team members regarding work progress, successes, barriers, concerns, and other information that may have an effect on the department's service or image.*

An introduction to reflective supervision should be included in every new staff member's orientation, so that supervisees can begin to understand the process, expectations, and benefits. New staff members will then understand that this is a core value and practice for everyone. This is especially important for those who are just entering the workforce or who are coming from other organizations with a different approach to supervision and have not had experience with reflective supervision. These staff members might otherwise perceive the focus on supervision as an indication of lack of trust in them as a professional or as implied criticism.

After new staff members have been briefed about reflective supervision, it is helpful for supervisors to review and discuss a written reflective supervision agreement. Many agencies use such an agreement as a short introductory form to review important responsibilities of both the supervisor and the supervisee. This form can include such things as how to prepare questions and topics for discussion, the importance of bringing up interpersonal issues such as those related to professional boundaries or tensions reflective of cultural differences, and the way in which the supervisor will provide time to evaluate the quality of the supervision sessions. See chapter 6 for more detail on beginning supervision and Appendix 2 for a sample supervision agreement.

ATTENTION TO EXTERNAL PARTNERSHIPS AND RELATIONSHIPS

Infant and early childhood work is likely to involve working with other agencies and community providers, government agencies, funders, and others, whether as joint service provider, contractor, contractee, recipient of funding, or collaborative partner. This work can be time-consuming, difficult, and at times frustrating. It is easy to begin to see the outside agency as the "other" and the source of problems. Although there is a natural tendency to engage in black-and-white thinking (i.e., "They are bad. We are good"), it is not likely to be productive, and it rarely leads to constructive solutions. In fact, it is more likely to simply increase frustration and impede progress because of lost opportunities for problem solving. Therefore, it is important for supervisors and management staff members to implement the principles of reflective practice and relationship-based work in interactions with these other programs and agencies. Supervisors can encourage exploration of challenging issues with the goal of trying to understand the other agency's perspective and underlying reasons for their actions. Supervisors can initiate outreach to community partners and can seek to establish personal relationships with peers within those organizations. These may serve as a foundation for more successful collaboration in the future. Here are two examples of cross-agency work in which a supervisor uses reflective supervision techniques to address black-and-white thinking and support better services:

Holly is the site manager and supervisor of an Early Head Start program. Jesse, one of the children in the program, was removed from his home because he was seriously scalded in a bathtub. Scott is the teacher for the toddler.

Scott: *Holly, I am so upset—that Child Protective Services worker is just out of her mind. She has recommended that Jesse go back home. They are going to take him out of that nice foster home and send him back there with those parents. I don't get why they are so lax.*

Holly: *Scott, I hear that this is worrisome to you, but I wonder if they have information we might not have access to that might support their decision. Do we know anything about how they made their decision? Have you been able to talk to the worker?*

Scott: *She called, but I haven't called her back. You know they have never listened to us in the past....*

Holly: *What if we asked for a meeting to talk together about Jesse's welfare and how we can support his needs? That way we can listen to them, and they can hear some of your worries.*

***

Eva, a teacher in the local Head Start, is working to create a developmental playgroup in the local YMCA for children on their waiting list. She approaches her supervisor with concerns:

Eva: *I don't know how I agreed to do this. Those people don't know the first thing about kids. You should have heard her talking about the ditto sheets for quiet time. They have all sorts of them about exercise and diet. Awful, it was our first meeting, but nothing got accomplished.*

Supervisor: *I wonder if it might be a good idea to back up a little and explore more what they would like to gain in doing this and what experience they have had with playgroups.*

USING CONSULTANTS AND TRAINERS WISELY

When working with consultants from another program or agency, supervisors should take the initiative to orient the consultants to their staff members and program as well as to the agency's commitment to reflective practice. There should be clearly established lines of communication and shared expectations as to how to work together. A collaborative stance will help the agency staff members explore and explain their needs and help the consultants understand what the agency would like to accomplish. Supervisors are responsible for helping consultants develop good working relationships with program staff members and for helping them address any challenges that may arise. Ideally, the supervisors from both agencies (the ones providing and receiving the consultation) should be in regular contact regarding the status of the work. If there is a strong, collaborative relationship at the supervisory level, the interactions between the program staff members and the consultants are likely to be more positive and constructive.

GUIDING QUESTIONS

Review the organizational supports for reflective supervision as outlined in this chapter. Consider how your agency addresses each of these.

- Is there some area in which your agency is particularly strong?
- What do you think is the effect or impact of this strength?
- Is there an area in which your agency might need improvement?
- Why might this be important?

Think about possible resources or first steps in helping to build support in this area and what results you might hope to see after doing so.

REFERENCES

Geller, E., & Foley, G. M. (2009). Broadening the "ports of entry" for speech-language pathologists: A relational and reflective model for clinical supervision. *American Journal of Speech-Language Pathology, 18*, 22–41.

Howes, C., James, J., & Ritchie, S. (2003). Pathways to effective teaching. *Early Childhood Research Quarterly, 18*, 104–120.

McFarland, L., Saunders, R., & Allen, S. (2008). Learning and teaching positive guidance skills: Lessons from early childhood practicum students. *Journal of Early Childhood Teacher Education, 29*, 204–221.

FURTHER READINGS

Bertacchi, J. (1996). Relationship-based organizations. *Zero to Three, 17*(2), 1–7.

Copa, A., Lucinski, L., Olsen, E., & Wollenburg K. (1999). Promoting professional and organizational development: A reflective practice model. *Zero to Three, 20*(1), 3–9.

Jones Harden, B. (2009). Beyond reflective supervision: How can my organization support well-being? In S. S. Heller & L. Gilkerson (Eds.), *A practical guide to reflective supervision* (pp. 135–148). Washington, DC: ZERO TO THREE.

Norman-Murch, T. (1996). Reflective supervision as a vehicle for individual and organizational development. *Zero to Three, 17*(2), 16–20.

Norman-Murch, T., & Ward, G. (1999). First steps in establishing reflective practice and supervision: Organizational issues and strategies. *Zero to Three, 20*(1), 10–14.

Weston, D., Ivins, B., Heffron, M., & Sweet, N. (1997). Formulating the centrality of relationships in early intervention: An organizational perspective. *Infants and Young Children, 9*(3), 1–12.

ESSENTIALS FOR SUPERVISORS:
KNOWLEDGE AND SKILLS NEEDED
FOR REFLECTIVE SUPERVISION

Often, staff members are promoted to supervisory positions on the basis of their outstanding performance as direct service providers. This chapter addresses the new knowledge and skills that must be considered as the individual moves into her new role as reflective supervisor. Experienced supervisors will also benefit from this elaboration of what else is needed to provide reflective supervision as they seek to sharpen their skills, deepen their understanding, and increase their comfort level.

Reflective supervision is an imperfect art. The goal is the full engagement of the participants in a reciprocal process aimed at understanding the many variables that shape program services. Below are explanations and examples of the necessary knowledge and essential skills that the reflective supervisor will aspire to master over time.

NECESSARY KNOWLEDGE

The list of what a reflective supervisor needs to know is long and open to amendment depending on the kinds of work involved. Each supervisor needs either to have a base of knowledge and experience that grounds her in the work she is supervising or to be willing to build that base through experience, observation, and training. If a person has been promoted out of a direct service role, it is important that she have opportunities to broaden her range of knowledge and experience, and that she is able to appreciate and accept perspectives and ways of intervening other than her own. (See chapter 2 for a description of the basic content knowledge that grounds work with infants and toddlers and their families.)

The categories below outline the "what else"—in addition to the knowledge related to direct service—that program developers should consider as they hire and train new supervisors or continue the development of an existing supervisory team. Training should be ongoing and reinforced by opportunities for the supervisor to learn through her own supervision and consultation. (One of the skills a reflective supervisor needs—how to conduct team meetings and, in some cases, small group supervisions—is addressed in chapter 5.)

Knowledge About Relationship-Based Work

The supervisor must help her supervisees to understand that the relationships they build with parents, children, and colleagues become the medium for their service delivery. Their knowledge of children and families will be best deployed when staff members engage children, families, and colleagues effectively. Supervisors must successfully communicate to supervisees that the quality of relationships will greatly affect the usefulness and the impact of the services delivered. Verbal descriptions and formal training on relationship-based work will take on greater meaning when positive supervisory relationships provide the foundation.

Relationship-based work stresses collaboration and engagement with others that goes beyond a teaching/telling approach. Because of this focus on working actively together, rather than in a top-down "do as I say" approach, reflective supervisors must also have a good sense of the difference between professional and personal relationships. In a parallel fashion, supervisors will need to know how to help supervisees define, frame, and hold appropriate rational boundaries in the face of pulls from families or children. (Please refer to chapter 2 for an outline of the essential roles of the supervisor.)

Specialized Knowledge of Child and Family Development Pertinent to the Service Population and Setting

Reflective supervisors require additional grounding in the content and practices specific to settings or populations. For example, a supervisor practicing in a residential drug treatment setting for families needs to understand the kinds of treatment parents are receiving as well as know how stages of recovery might affect parenting. A reflective supervisor working with premature babies and their families needs to be aware of the medical conditions related to prematurity as well as the stressors that a premature birth puts on parents. Supervisors also need to have a sense of the various systems that affect the families and children of the staff members they are supervising. For example, supervisors of home visitors who work with families involved in the child welfare system must have a solid understanding of how that system works so that they can support their staff members. An understanding that different systems may have different priorities can help supervisee's negotiate collaborative working arrangements more easily.

Creating a Shared Framework and Expectations for Supervision

Supervisors need to know how to create both a shared framework for supervision and clear agreements about the process of reflective supervision. Supervision sessions are most effective when the supervisee and the supervisor come prepared. Preparation might include review of home visit logs, charts, Individualized Family Service Plans, reports, classroom observation notes, videotapes, and notes from prior supervision sessions by the supervisor and development of questions and priorities for discussion by the supervisee.

Supervisors may find it helpful to follow a sequence for their one-on-one supervision meetings. This sequence could include:

1. Greeting and checking in on any immediate needs,

2. Observing the supervisee's general mood and tone,

3. Recapping the discussion from the last session, and

4. Jointly setting an agenda for the time available during this current session.

The agenda should be mutually negotiated, with both parties indicating their individual priorities. The supervisor may want to bring in administrative topics or protect time for a follow-up on prior sessions. It is important for supervisors to document their work with supervisees and to consider what kinds of information should be included. These notes can be used to help the supervisor link supervisory sessions and identify overarching themes or recurring concerns. It is helpful for supervisors to pay attention to their internal responses during supervision and to note times when they feel unsure about how to proceed. These points can be brought into their own supervision. A sample supervisory log form for documenting supervision sessions is included in Appendix 3. (See chapter 6 for a step-by-step process of beginning new supervisory relationships, and see Appendix 2 for a sample supervision agreement which covers the key points that should be covered in first sessions with new supervisees.)

Use of Media

Research on supervision in human services has shown that use of video to review the "real-time" work of staff members is useful for their professional development. The review process can help staff members grasp subtle aspects of their work such as pacing, attunement to the other, and choice of interventions. Incorporating media into supervision requires (a) knowing how to help staff members set up and use media in their work settings, (b) paying attention to confidentiality issues related to use of media such as use of appropriate releases and secure storage, and (c) learning how to apply reflective supervision strategies while reviewing a videotaped session. See Edelman (2009) for an excellent technical guide and Bernstein (2002–2003), Wajda-Johnston (2005), and Starting Early Starting Smart (2003) for information on using video reviews as a supervisory strategy.

Organizational, Time Management, and Human Resource Skills

Supervisors must know how to access data, information, and specialized resources for the benefit of their staff members. Many supervisors will need to enhance their program development skills, such as data management, program planning, and grant and report writing. Mentoring and specialized training in these areas should be made available as needed so that the supervisor can do her work as efficiently as possible. Supervisors will often face competing priorities and need to make appropriate choices to allocate time as effectively as possible.

The reflective supervisor also needs to know the lines of authority in her agency related to human resource functions. In most agencies, the supervisor should have at least a basic understanding of personnel and human resource functions, such as employment laws, sexual harassment guidelines, and agency policies on leave and vacation time, as well as her responsibilities for these areas within the agency. If the supervisor participates in hiring new staff members, she will need to have information about the kind of questions that can be asked and acceptable interview procedures.

Knowledge About Adult Growth and Development

Supervisors are often responsible for structuring learning and training experiences for their staff members. Some supervisors may take on direct training responsibilities, but even if they do not, an understanding of the ways adults learn will be helpful in working with others to plan learning experiences for staff members.

ESSENTIAL SKILLS

This section extends the discussion about supervisory roles begun in chapter 2 and introduces detailed descriptions of important skills. Mastery of this material should be seen as aspirational rather than a "must have" set of competencies that would require either sainthood or a lifetime of practice. Some skills may be as natural as breathing, but they can be deepened through awareness and practice. Some may be harder to come by and may take years to develop, requiring both new knowledge, self-awareness, and rigorous practice. Individual differences and baseline abilities also factor into acquisition of these knowledge and skills. Experience, practice, and sensitivity will help supervisors learn to select the right skills, appropriate context, and timing for their use.

There is no final endpoint in the development of this skill set, but hopefully supervisors will always achieve forward momentum leading to a higher level of competence.

Knowing When to "Zoom Out" and "Zoom In"

The supervisor needs at least two interchangeable lenses for her work. The first provides a broad-angle view that can capture a vision of the big picture: the program, the team, the mission of the program, and the community. Conversely, the supervisor needs to have a close-up lens that focuses on the nuanced details which often are the nexus for change within a child, family, or organization. In the following example, note how the supervisor, Peter, moves from one view to another when needed:

Emily is a skilled social worker who does home studies for an adoption unit. Her supervisor, Peter, has discovered in working with Emily that she is concerned about the rapid transitions that children are now required to make from foster care to adoptive homes. Emily is perplexed about the new transition policy and sad because she has seen several children suffer as a result of a lack of planning. Peter supports her feelings and works with her on strategies for helping the children and families on her caseload manage transitions, given these shortened time periods. Switching to a broad-angle lens, Peter reviews charts from the past 6 months and notices that other workers are also working with shorter transition periods. After consulting with others in his agency, Peter organizes the data and requests a meeting with the unit director for adoptions in the county social service agency to discuss these trends. Peter's ability to work with his supervisees on the important fine details of their work while at the same time attending to the big picture and the larger systems issues makes him an effective supervisor. Eventually, his advocacy proves useful, prompting a change in the time frames for adoption transitions, thereby speaking to the needs of the many children in the foster care system.

Empathizing With the Feelings and Experiences of Others

One of the most critical supervisory skills is to be able to connect and communicate in such a way that the supervisee feels understood, appreciated, empowered, and supported. This can happen only when the supervisee knows that she is being heard and that the supervisor is fully present and attempting to understand her feelings and experiences. Empathy should be offered without the supervisor trying to distance herself from her staff member, change the subject, dismiss the concern, or fix the problem prematurely. Even though the supervisor may feel that she is being pulled in these directions, offering the opportunity for staff members to verbalize strong feelings often allows these feelings to shift and change. In exploration, the supervisor may also assist the supervisee to develop more empathy for the perspective and experiences of others. This is central in work with young children and families, as there is frequently an inclination to identify with one person, often the child, and demonize a parent, teacher, or colleague.

The supervisor must know how to contain and hold these feelings simultaneously, maintaining a focus on the big picture—including needs of children, families, and the agency—as well as the realistic constraints of budget, time, and regulations. The supervisor must remain grounded and as objective as possible even while identifying with and feeling empathy for the supervisee. She must resist being swept away by another's feelings: This ability to remain open and receptive to feelings without being bowled over is critical. Only then can the supervisor help the supervisee contain and organize her own feelings and responses. The supervisor must also understand that an empathic stance does not lessen the need to hold the supervisee accountable for her work, as in the following example:

> *Rhonda, a supervisor in a Healthy Steps program, meets with her supervisee, Celina, who provides developmental guidance and support to parents and young children in a medical clinic setting. Celina comes to the supervision session in a somber mood. She recounts how, during a routine well-child exam, a parent had described in detail her child's abuse by a babysitter. Rhonda listens and then quietly says to Celina, "I feel so concerned about the pressure you were feeling. I also feel so sad for this parent as I hear you. It sounds like this was a conversation where we may need to follow up with a child abuse report." Celina blurts out her confusion about what she should have done, and slowly she and Rhonda go over the encounter, carefully sorting out feelings and determining exactly what was said. Then they are able to plan their next steps and decide what actions they should take.*

Promoting Sociocultural Awareness

Racial, class, cultural, linguistic, educational, and gender differences affect staff members' relationships and the delivery of services. It is essential that the supervisor is skilled in raising questions and making comments that address the ways in which differences can factor into relationships and program services. The supervisor needs to provide opportunities for staff members to talk about differences in a sensitive and responsive manner that supports the growth of self-knowledge and enhances the quality of services. A supervisor must find the skill and sometimes the courage to bring up the differential treatment of clients or colleagues based on race, gender, or sexual preference; unintended slights; or unexamined negative assumptions about another person's background. Self-awareness and a stance of respect and inclusion will assist the reflective supervisor to work with staff members from many backgrounds and perspectives. This self-awareness begins with the supervisor's understanding of how her unique characteristics (e.g., race, culture, religion, privilege, age, and gender) have shaped her and might affect others. The supervisor should also take into account the complex arc of racial and social justice in her service population and community. The reflective supervisor realizes there is always more than one way to adapt to the needs of the diverse families and children served. She understands that specific service approaches do not always work with every population. Below are examples that show how a supervisor can support awareness of diversity and in doing so promote service delivery that is respectful and effective:

Veronica is a well-educated African American speech therapist who grew up in a working class family. In her work, she encounters many African American families who have had less opportunity than she has had. Veronica finds that many families respond to her with caution, and she has used her supervision time to think about her own feelings about these reactions. Veronica initially had not thought about the ways in which her education might affect her ability to engage with her clients. She was hurt when a parent told her she was acting "too White." Sujata, her supervisor, has helped her to begin to understand her feelings and explore the perceptions of the parents. Through her supervision, she has figured out ways to open a dialogue with families that allowed room to talk about perceived differences in class and what this means to their work together. As Veronica tried out different ways to engage and talk about the family's perceptions, her background, and what the family really wanted from the program, she grew more confident and had fewer families drop out of her caseload.

***

Angela is a team leader and supervisor for a group of community home visitors on an Early Head Start team. She notices that the staff members who are Spanish-speaking do not talk at the team meetings but are very open during individual supervision. She worries that their knowledge about the community and the culture of the immigrant families served is not being shared with others on the team. In a team meeting, Angela asks what conditions would make it easier for everyone on the team to be heard. After a lively discussion, one of the team members speaks up and says that she wonders if she is talking too much, making it harder for others to bring things up. Angela thanks her for her insight and invites the team to keep looking at this so everyone's voice can be heard.

***

Brenda is a supervisor for an all female group of nurses providing a community-based program. Jake has just been hired to join the group. In group supervision before Jake started working, one of the nurses quips that Jake is the sheik the harem has been waiting for. After the laughter calms down, Brenda notes:

"I wonder if we need to talk together about what it will be like to have Jake on the team. This is the first time a man has been on the team. What do you think this experience will be for him? How do you think we can help him feel welcome?"

Giving the Gift of Near Perfect Attention

The ability to pay close attention to another person, to listen attentively and respectfully, and to resonate with that person's internal and external experiences is essential for providing reflective supervision. The supervisor must be able to tune in to individual supervisees as well as to groups in team meetings. This attunement allows the supervisor to recognize the cues and responses of the other and adapt her internal state or behavior in a way that encourages ongoing communication. This kind of listening involves paying attention to details and remaining open-minded and tentative (see more on this below in the Slowing Down or "Negative Capability" section on p. 84) even though the situation seems familiar and clear. While the supervisor hears what is being said, she should also be asking herself what the effect of the information might be on the supervisee, family, or child. When the supervisor does this, the information shared retains a kind of freshness, and the supervisor stays open to the collaborative process rather than taking on the stance of an expert instructing a less-knowledgeable staff person.

Having a supervisor who listens so closely, and pays such close attention, may lead some supervisees to believe or wish that their supervisor will be fully accessible at all times. Therefore, the supervisor will also need to help staff members understand that she may not always be immediately available but will keep them informed as to when and how they can reach her, and she will leave a backup plan for handling crisis situations when she is gone. The following are examples of supervising with near perfect attention:

Shana, the supervisor, is conducting a staff meeting during which she wants to present some of the data from program outcome measures. She notices the staff members' flat facial expressions and their gaze avoidance. She says, "I know we had agreed to talk about this material, but I am getting the feeling that there is something else on your mind. Perhaps you would like to discuss it. Let's take 15 minutes to open up the discussion before we get back to the outcome data."

***

Tala approaches her supervisor, Ellen, hesitantly because she sees she is going into a meeting with the program managers. Ellen asks her if the matter can wait for an hour when she will be finished with the meeting. Tala says she can wait, and Ellen tells her she will see her then. Ellen emphasizes that at that time she will be able to really listen to all the details and give the matter her full attention so that together they can figure out what to do.

Looking Within

Supervisors need to be aware of their own style and struggles and be willing to wrestle with their personal demons as they appear. For example, a supervisor might have a tendency to take things personally or to become irritable in the face of the support needs of a particular staff member. Other difficulties might include the desire to rescue or take over or a discomfort with difficult supervisory conversations. Some supervisors may even experience a strong physical response each time there is a need to be direct with an employee about issues such as incomplete documentation or failure to follow through on job responsibilities. Supervisory introspection includes developing an understanding about what comes easily and which areas are avoided or struggled with. This awareness can lead in turn to an identification of the supervisor's professional development needs and the support she might need from her own supervisor, as in the following example:

Patti is a supervisor who runs a small Healthy Families team. She works hard to create a healthy and cohesive atmosphere, and is very proud of the work the team does. The program is respected in the community and within the larger program. Things went well for Patti until the program expanded and two new staff members were added. These staff members did not seem to have the same work ethic and commitment to the families. Patty felt as if these newer staff members were intruders to their well-functioning group. Patti became aware of her difficulty in addressing the performance issues with these staff members. She realized that she was afraid of her own growing anger at these new people, who seemed to be threatening the reputation of her program. Her fear of exploding paralyzed her until her program manager helped her identify what was keeping her from talking to them. She came to realize that she needed to build her skill at being able to directly address conflict. She also began to realize that she had a certain resentment of having to work harder to accommodate and train the less skilled staff members. Once Patti had located her own demons, she was able to begin to grapple with the situation. Patti's program manager said she would be very glad to help Patti work on this, starting with these concerns about the new staff members.

Summoning Patience

> *Do you have the patience to wait till your mud settles and the water is clear?*
>
> —*Lao-tzu, 1988, p.15*

Patience helps the supervisor appreciate that each person's skill level, learning style, and time needed to process a concern or grasp a needed skill is likely to be different. Patience also helps the supervisor accept that the information she has may be incomplete or that the situation may have shifted and that, if she can wait and remain alert, more is likely to be revealed.

> *Ellie is an infant mental health specialist who gets into the same situations time and again with her clients: She gets overextended and makes poor judgments about boundaries. Her supervisor, Rosario, feels that she has tried in many ways to help Ellie understand how this occurs. Rosario feels a bit irritated, but before meeting with Ellie she decides to review her last few months of notes from supervision. In doing this, Rosario realizes that although these situations continue, they are less frequent, and Ellie is beginning to "get" it and raise questions about boundaries herself.*

Learning to Not Know

In time, supervisors learn that there is usually more to an issue than what is initially presented or what seems obvious. The supervisor must learn to remain curious and stay open-minded, while helping to uncover nuances and details. She can help the supervisee explore a situation more fully using questions to encourage thinking about alternative perspectives and interpretations. The supervisor can also raise questions that help identify what else would need to be known to build an intervention plan. She can help her supervisee remember that different people will have different feelings and reactions in response to the same event. This stance involves a certain amount of "not knowing" or reminding oneself that even though an issue seems clear-cut, there is probably more to it than first meets the eye. As the supervisee learns to tolerate this state of "not knowing" she will be able to continue to explore and to try to learn more. She will be able to resist the tendency to act before having a more complete understanding of the situation at hand.

Practicing Diplomacy and Transparency

Reflective supervision requires diplomacy as well as the ability to address concerns honestly and transparently without generating a strong defensive reaction. Holding back information for too long can be destructive of the trust that individuals and the team have in the supervisor. Reference to one's own feelings can sometimes be useful in situations where transparency is needed. This works best when it seems as if an expression of the supervisor's feelings will help the supervisee be more candid herself. The capacity to be diplomatic and transparent is critical, both when it comes to talking with the supervisee about her work with children and families and for addressing administrative concerns.

> *Aquila supervises Janice, an early childhood classroom teacher. Aquila has been concerned about the low turnout at Janice's family play days. She tells Janice: "I worried about how to bring this up to you because I know you have worked hard on this, but I am wondering if you have any sense of why the turnout is so low at these groups? We need to address this, and I wanted to get your take on it."*
>
> ***
>
> *Tina, a supervisor of a group of nurses providing postnatal home-visiting services for high-risk babies, receives the news that the contract for her program is going to be changed and reduced in the coming year. She does not know the details about what the changes will be or how deep the cuts will be. She feels worried but reasonably confident that the services will be continued. She waits for a staff meeting time and says that she needs 15 minutes to address a programmatic issue. She assures the staff members that their services are valued and that recent evaluations have been glowing. She informs them that the contract will be altered in the coming year but admits that she does not know exactly what that will mean. She promises that she will give them relevant information as it becomes available. She also assures them that if there are reductions, the agency will work to absorb them into other services. She invites people who need more information or a chance to discuss this to see her individually.*

Tolerating Conflict and Strong Affect

Strong feelings and occasional conflict are the daily bread of the reflective supervisor. Some supervisors may need to fortify their ability to be in the midst of conflict and strong emotions without becoming overwhelmed or swept away. Some supervisors deal with this by using an imaging strategy. They imagine that the strong affect coming toward them is being collected in a sturdy container that they are holding. With the strong feelings safely enclosed, the supervisor can examine and reflect on the contents without being engulfed by the wave of fast-moving feelings. With the feelings contained, she is also better able to resist the impulse to rush in to fix the situation or to flee the scene. She is then more likely to be able to carefully choose a response and a course of action."

> *Frieda, the supervisor/manager of a large child development center, receives a call from a teacher saying that a parent is in her classroom screaming and angry because her child was hurt on the playground the previous day. The teacher has assured the parent that the child is now okay, with just some minor scrapes. The teacher is worried because the parent is frightening the other children. She cannot manage the situation and asks that Frieda come immediately.*
>
> *Frieda brings the parent into her office and listens to her tell the story of how her child was hurt. The parent's feelings are still intense, but Frieda keeps holding the image of the slightly injured child, wondering to herself what the situation had meant to the parent. Frieda acknowledges to the parent how frightening it must have been to hear that her child had fallen off the slide. She listens as the parent insults the program, the teacher, and her own leadership. Frieda notes the anger and says she understands it, but she asks that the parent talk with her without insults and in just a little lower tone because of the children. She emphasizes that she wants to understand what happened and wants to be useful in helping the family and child. The parent explains that she was most upset because when she got the call her health insurance had lapsed, and she felt that she would not be able to pay for any needed medical care.*
>
> *Throughout the episode, Frieda's own heart has been racing. She was worried that the whole center would be upset by the mother's screams. She felt like screaming back at the mother, but she used her own skills to stop herself and focus on trying to offer understanding and support. She resists the urge to remind the mother that her child is fine; instead, she focuses on repeating, "How frightening that must have been to drive over not knowing exactly how your little boy had been hurt." At the end of the conversation, she asks the parent if the program might be able to help her figure out how the insurance had lapsed and work with her to get it back.*

Conflict between staff members on a team or within an agency can be perplexing for supervisors. They may worry about how the tension caused by conflict is affecting direct services, or they may try to make everything right for everyone.

Supervisors often receive complaints from their supervisees about colleagues who are not pulling their weight or who have done something that seems unacceptable by program standards. It is tempting to intervene directly, and at times it may be necessary. However, a first step when staff members report conflict with a colleague is always to use reflective exploration to help the staff member figure out the perspective of the person and any personal contributions to the troubles. The next step is to help the individual figure out ways to address the issue herself. This approach builds staff members' confidence in addressing difficulties directly with colleagues. When intrastaff irritations, conflicts, and disagreements are addressed, splits and long-lasting hostilities can be avoided or minimized. Unaddressed intrastaff discord can last for months or years, seriously affecting program quality.

A child care team was talking about a recently held holiday party for parents and children. Iris, one of the teachers who had a key role in the party, had failed to show up, and the postmortem of the party included several sarcastic remarks about her absence. The head teacher has asked to meet with the site supervisor, Kalene, to figure out how to handle the conflict. Iris has stopped talking to the two people who made the rude remarks, and tension in the classroom is rising.

Kalene is tempted to pull everybody together but wants to build support for the head teacher to be able to handle the conflict. She asks her for details and discusses what it felt like when the rude remarks started coming. She also asks if the head teacher had known about Iris' absence, and the head teacher admits she had not known until the event. Kalene asks the head teacher what she might want to do about that and realizes that the whole subject has not yet been touched. She asks what might diffuse the tension. Together, they plan that the head teacher will meet with Iris and explore the absence and take responsibility for not discussing this sooner. Then they figure out that it would be important to have the teachers who were making the rude remarks meet with her and Iris. The head teacher can again apologize for not being more direct in the meeting and explore the issue of what happened but also remind them that questions and information-seeking are different than sarcasm. Kalene offers to be a support at that meeting if the head teacher feels it would help, but she adds that she does not want to take the lead.

Avoiding the Jump to Conclusions

Moving toward a quick fix without adequate thought is problematic. Supervisors can be led to do this if they forget that their role is to promote critical reflective thinking, not to provide solutions and strategies. The supervisor who can avoid reflexive inclinations to tell or proclaim "the right way" creates a kind of "waiting room" in her mind. Over time, she adds bits and pieces of information, issues, concerns, worries, and possible action items through her active wondering with the supervisee. The room is visited often and is large enough to take in new details and observations. If there is no acute danger, the supervisor waits and continues with a reflective approach until the supervisee begins to make a needed shift, or when she feels that she must use the accumulated information to make a more direct intervention in order to help the supervisee get on a more productive path.

> *Monica, a supervisor, has just begun to work with Roseanne, a bilingual home visitor in an early intervention program. Roseanne is a recent graduate from a child development program and is eager to learn. She has made several comments about family culture implying that the families are not interested in their children's learning. Exploration of these comments and suggestions for alternative approaches have not changed Roseanne's basic frustration with families who just won't play with their kids. Monica is beginning to feel her own irritation with Roseanne and has concerns and doubts about Roseanne's suitability to the program. She stores her feelings in her mental "waiting room" and continues to try supportive interventions with Roseanne. She uses questions to help Roseanne realize that there is more than one way of playing with children and that there might be deeper cultural differences between her and her families, which she may not fully understand despite her bilingual abilities. She invites Roseanne to observe these parents and children carefully, looking for times when the interaction is rich and there is delight and mutual attention.*
>
> *After some time has passed without much shift in Roseanne's views of the families, Monica revisits her concerns and has a careful discussion with Roseanne about her judgmental attitudes toward some families. Roseanne becomes tearful and talks about her feelings of inadequacy and sadness when she visits these homes. Together, the home visitor and the supervisor make a plan to strengthen Roseanne's knowledge of cultural differences in child rearing and discuss ways for her to plan activities that will be more likely to engage families effectively.*

Remaining Tentative

For the reflective supervisor, remaining tentative entails making it clear that many options are on the table, that no specific hypothesis or interpretation has been made, and that there are many avenues to explore. If the supervisor wants to offer an opinion or suggestion, she does so in a tentative manner: "I wonder what would happen if…" or "I'm not sure what to think about this, but perhaps…." Taking a tentative approach helps prevent defensive reactions and provides space for the supervisee to bring in new information or consider novel ideas. Remaining tentative supports the notion that the work is co-created and constructed, and that the supervisor is not telling or ordering particular responses. It is reflected in language such as: "I don't know if this would work here, but let's explore this together. I'd like to hear more about your ideas of how to do this. Let's imagine how this might play out over time." Below is a supervisory interaction where this approach is used effectively:

> *Tara is a supervisor for Stacey, who is a mental health consultant to child care programs and is just beginning to work with a new site. Stacey walks into supervision somewhat distraught and asks, "Tara, just tell me what to do to keep myself from screaming in this classroom. The teachers are mean to the kids, and the director never comes out of her office. I am at my wit's end." Tara's first instinct is to rescue Stacey by describing interventions she has used in similar situations and suggesting that Stacey follow suit. She suppresses this urge and instead responds, "It sounds so hard." After inquiring about the details of the situation, Tara begins to offer some ideas: "I am not sure this would work, but what do you think about the idea of beginning by trying to get an appointment with the director to talk about what she was hoping for by bringing in a consultant? She had this conversation with the previous consultant, but I think it would be important to work on getting to know her yourself and figuring out why she is so distant from the classroom." By demonstrating a tentative approach, the supervisor is opening up some possibilities for Stacey and suggesting that it might help to understand more about the situation. Tara does this without being directive or prescriptive but rather by supportively proposing a different angle of approach.*

Bearing Witness

Staff members who work in programs for infants, young children, and families at risk for social, developmental, and medical reasons are likely to encounter sadness, fear, and helplessness from time to time. They will come across children with health and developmental problems, families that are falling apart, and, sometimes, domestic or community violence. They may feel a strong pull to help, to problem solve, and in general to remove all impediments to a happy childhood. Staff members sometimes find themselves in situations where all efforts have failed or where no more can be done for a child or a family. At these times, the reflective supervisor's main job is to bear witness with the staff person, who in turn is bearing witness with the parents or other colleagues. The supervisor helps her supervisee recognize and hold hopelessness, grief, and disappointment. She supports her staff members by standing by and being somebody who can raise the possibility of next steps, when and if the time is right to move on. However, just being present and sharing in the unimaginable sadness of a child's or parent's illness, abandonment, abuse, or death is often the best and only intervention. The supervisor needs to remind herself and her staff members that what is shareable becomes more bearable.

Communicating Confidence, High Expectations, and Belief in the Supervisee's Value

A supervisee does best when her supervisor conveys a sense of confidence in her unique talents and her ability to think clearly, make good judgments, and ask for support when needed. A supervisee who feels appreciated for the particular strengths she brings to the work is more likely to feel safe enough to discuss areas in which she is less confident. A supervisee's willingness to share her struggles then presents an opportunity for a discussion about the possibility of trying out a different approach or building her skills. Supervisors who communicate the message that the supervisee should "be like me" miss the point of reflective supervision.

Slowing Down or "Negative Capability"

Deliberately slowing down and not reacting when there are powerful impulses to respond or act quickly requires intent and awareness that has been termed *negative capability* (Simpson & French, 2006). This skill creates more time for the supervisor to reflect. While the supervisor is outwardly quiet, there is usually a beehive of internal activity. Negative capability also opens a space during supervisory sessions for the supervisee to enter with her ideas and feelings rather than being overly influenced by the supervisor's suggestions.

In addition, negative capability builds the supervisor's ability to tolerate brief periods of silence in the supervisory session. The following vignettes provide two examples of negative capability. In each, the supervisor creates a space for thinking. In the second vignette, the supervisor helps the supervisee focus on the complexity of the situation, rather than immediately moving toward the most obvious path.

Cherene, a supervisor in a program for foster children and their caregivers, receives a call from Janelle, one of the home visitors in the program. Janelle says she will be late for supervision because of traffic. Cherene finds herself irritated because this is a frequent pattern. She takes a breath and thanks Janelle for checking in, and then adds, "Let's talk more when you get here." When Janelle arrives, Cherene says to her, "I really appreciated the call, and I wonder if we can talk a bit about how this happens so often."

***

Amber is a young home visitor in a Head Start program. She is very confused by a family who appears to want her assistance in obtaining treatment for their son Kahil's asthma. However, when she begins to take steps to implement a plan they have developed together, the parents act as if they don't need the services and hadn't asked for them in the first place. At times they have even seemed offended that Amber has followed up on something they requested.

In beginning the supervision, Carlos, the supervisor, listens carefully, empathizes with Amber, and then begins to develop a hunch that he hopes will expand Amber's critical thinking about this case. He asks, "What are some of the ways the family let you know they wanted help with Kahil's asthma?" As she asks this question, Carlos is working hard not to tell Amber what he thinks has happened just to save time.

Carlos again listens as Amber tells her how she has brought in information about asthma based on the child's health information form and really praised the special asthma clinic in the community. Carlos remarks to Amber, "It seems logical that they would want to do this, right?" Amber agrees and then adds that the family had also told her that the doctor had said Kahil could outgrow the asthma. Carlos asks Amber if she felt the specialized treatment might be more important than the family thought it was. Amber replies, "Absolutely, and hmmm… I wonder if I have been a little pushy." Carlos said, "What would it look like if you were being pushy?" Amber replied, "I guess I would forget everything else, kind of the way that I did." At this point in the conversation, Carlos wondered with Amber about what feelings her eagerness to talk about the asthma might have brought up for the family. Later, they thought together about how she could continue to address the concerns about the child's asthma without being so directive with the family and setting off their defenses. Amber asked Carlos if he thought it would be good to talk about what it was like for the family to have the doctor say one thing and then Amber push the treatment on them. Carlos, demonstrating his negative capability, said, "I am not sure—let's think a little more about that." Carlos's negative capability supports Amber's thinking process. Moving too quickly to agree with a potentially good intervention closes off a fuller consideration of the service dilemma. In a few minutes, Amber and Carlos settle on what Amber will say to the family, and Carlos validates Amber's willingness to struggle with an important intervention.

Using Questions—Gentle Inquiry

Skillful use of questions and a stance of open-minded inquiry are crucial for the reflective supervisor. Questions are useful during supervision sessions, as they slow down the problem-solving process and invite reflection, information sharing, perspective taking, and critical thinking. Questions can expand the space around a dilemma so that it can be seen from different angles. However, questions must be used gently, so that the supervisee does not feel like she is under interrogation from some sort of grand inquisitor. The image of a spacious house is a helpful metaphor for complex situations encountered by staff members as they work with children and families. If one stays in only one room of the house, the room where the difficulty resides, the situation can seem overwhelming or confusing. Taking time to visit the other rooms and finding out what else is going on brings up other possibilities of what to do. Space then flows around the problem, diminishing its size and often creating a partial or even total reappraisal of the problem. Careful use of questions shapes what should be considered by the staff person. Using questions skillfully is an art. It involves the adjustment of follow-up questions by observing the responses and pace of the supervisee and monitoring one's own internal responses. This gentle and thoughtful form of inquiry promotes a trusting relationship and a fluid exchange of information and feelings between supervisor and supervisee. In contrast, poorly chosen questions can seem intrusive, off the point, critical, or even attacking. Asking too many questions doesn't give a supervisee time to think. If the questions are not carefully chosen, they can feel random, as if the questioner is not paying attention. It is important for the supervisor to craft and sequence her questions carefully. See Appendix 10 for a list of sample questions. The following steps are guidelines to help sequence questions:

- Always start with broad, open-ended questions, such as: "Can you tell me a little bit more about what happened?" or "What do you think could be behind this shift in attitude?"

- Listen carefully and choose aspects of the supervisee's response to follow up on. This should be based on an appraisal of what would be most useful and would not feel too intrusive or presumptuous. Follow-up questions fall into different categories. Content questions ask for more information about an aspect of the situation. Alternately, process questions might be about the feelings of the supervisee, children, or parents.

- Try to consider how the potential response to a question could lead to broader understanding. Sometimes, the supervisor's questions seem to come out of the blue. In fact, these are often based on prior knowledge about the situation or an intuition, based on experience, about an important underlying issue and careful listening to the supervisee.

- Ask questions that are relevant and helpful. For example, a supervisor is listening to a perinatal home visitor who works with teen parents. She is telling the supervisor about a new client. He asks which school the client is attending. At this point in the supervision, this question is relevant to service delivery, as some schools have child care resources that might be needed. In another situation, the question might have less importance or have been a complete distraction.

This idea of relevance is essential when supervisors go after specific information. Why might this information be important? If there is no specific reason to ask a narrow question, it might be best to continue to ask more open-ended questions or to offer comments that are an invitation to continue (e.g., "I don't quite think I understand this situation. Could you tell me a little more?"). Sometimes an open-ended question can illuminate a particular aspect of the work that seems to be overlooked. For example, after a long explanation about a teen mother's problems, the supervisor might respond, "I'm hearing so much about the parents, but I'm wondering about the baby's responses to this change." Supervisors also should use questions to explore the supervisee's feelings, which are critical aspects of understanding the full picture (e.g., "As I listen to you describe this child, many feelings come up for me. How is this for you?").

Questions can be directed at aspects of what was said or not said by the supervisee, or sometimes at aspects of the supervisor's own responses to the material (e.g., "I wonder what it means for you that this case has raised so many worries for me about safety?"). Questions can also be directed toward nonverbal somatic or body-based responses (e.g., "I see you withdrawing a bit as I talked about the need to report this family to child protective services. Is this something that is hard to consider?"). The following vignette illustrates the skill of sequencing questions:

> *Laila is a reflective supervisor working with Brooke, a social worker whose job involves helping foster children and their families make positive adjustments. Brooke has just told Laila about her afternoon with Michael, a 9-month-old foster child who had to be moved to a new home because his former foster mother had a heart attack. Brooke is very upset because Michael cried a great deal and seemed very confused by the move. Laila talks with Brooke, helping her explore her own feelings about these events and trying to assist her in moving toward thinking about what can be done to support Michael in this new placement:*
>
> **Laila:** *What was it like to hear about Mrs. Johnson?*
>
> **Brooke:** *I was devastated. I had worked so hard to help Mrs. Johnson build a*

supportive relationship with Michael. It just seems unfair to everybody that he has to be moved. Mrs. Johnson is going to be devastated by this. She just loves that little boy.

Laila responds empathically that Brooke has worked very hard and been quite successful with Michael and Mrs. Johnson.

Laila: *What do you know about the future for them?*

Brooke: *She'll be in the hospital for a few days, but the doctor says she just can't handle the stress of an active baby and that she should not keep caring for him if she values her health.*

Laila: *It's hard to think about how difficult this will be for her or what she will do to stay connected, but what do you think would help Michael at this point?*

Brooke: *It is just so hard to think about him crying so pathetically.*

Laila: *He is missing Mrs. Johnson and has no way of understanding where she has gone. Can you imagine what might help him feel safe?*

Brooke: *Maybe some of his stuff. I could see if Mrs. Johnson's daughter would let me bring over a few of his familiar things like his binky, his teddy bear, and that music box he likes. When I saw him today, none of that was there.*

Laila: *That's a great idea. Do you think she would let you have a picture of Mrs. Johnson and Michael?*

The following sequence indicates how the use of carefully crafted questions fits into the overall process of collaborative problem solving:

- Empathize.

- Explore.

- Use a variety of questions from open-ended to more narrowly focused.

- Embrace complexity.

- Tolerate ambiguity.

- Name the dilemma—open a space where the issues can really be seen.

- Accept the feelings and normalize.

- Whenever possible, ask, don't tell.

- Summarize to move forward in the discussion.

Promoting Reflection

Learning to think, feel, and act in a reflective manner is cultivated over time in many different ways. Supervisors benefit from a coherent approach to promote reflection in supervision sessions. It is common for supervisees to think that they need to bring all of the details of all of the events of the past week into one session. This can lead to an overload of information and an absence of true reflection. The following steps adapted from the work of Christopher Johns (2008) can be used within the broader framework of supervision sessions to build the capacity to remember details and work the "reflective muscles" needed in day-to-day work:

1. Begin by helping your supervisee or group slow down and bring the mind home. This can be a greeting followed by few seconds of silence, offering a cup of tea, or any reminder that we are here together for a specific purpose. The supervisor might introduce this more reflective part of the session by saying something like, "Let's take a few minutes to really dig into what is going on with Jamal and his dad."

2. Alternately, you might request a description of an experience that seems significant or important in some way for the supervisee: "Let's talk a little more about what happened at the end of the playgroup last week."

3. Ask: "What seems most significant about this? What do you find yourself wondering about? Were there things that were confusing or mysterious?"

4. Ask: "How do you imagine the child, parent, or colleague was feeling and what do you think made the person feel that way? How were you feeling? What do you think made you feel that way? What factors or pressures were influencing your thinking or feeling? Do you have a sense of what you were you really trying to do in this moment? Did you feel effective in that moment? What was the effect of what you did or said on the child, parent, or colleague? What did you notice?"

5. Ask: "What sort of ideas or information guided you, or what information or skill did you feel you needed? Do you feel you understood the context and what was going on with the people involved and the situation?"

6. Ask: "Did you feel understood? How did you think you were seen?"

7. Explore: "If you could replay this scene, are there things you might want to do differently? Why do you think you would do it this way? How do you think this might play out?"

8. Summarize and reflect: "Thinking back on what happened in this meeting, are there things you understand in a different way now than when we started this conversation? Do you think this will change the way you work with this family or child the next time?"

This framework has several critical components: calming the mind and relaxing, selection of some specific event or scene from the supervisee's work, and analyzing and examining the event from multiple perspectives. It is not meant to be a series of questions always asked in the same sequence. It is not necessary or recommended to ask all of these questions during any one conversation. Rather, they are offered as ways to help guide an exploration and take it in a number of different directions. Supervisors should find words and pacing that are comfortable for them. The goal is to slow down the process, remember more clearly and in greater detail, and let new insights develop along the way.

Solving Problems the Collaborative Way

Collaborative problem solving is important because it is the approach we as supervisors want our staff members to use with families and colleagues. Even if the reflective supervisor feels certain about what action should be taken or how a situation should be interpreted, she takes a collaborative approach. She is careful, at the same time, to remain honest and authentic with her supervisee, asking real questions and making comments without having a hidden agenda. The supervisor solicits information and reflections from the supervisee but also contributes ideas and thoughts. The supervisor will use partnering strategies such as reframing, commenting, observing, and scaffolding to engage in a joint problem-solving process with her supervisee. In the following vignette, Alma, an experienced classroom teacher, is meeting with her supervisor, Claudine, in their regular monthly meeting. Claudine has been alerted by e-mail that Alma needs to talk about a new teacher assistant (TA) who is perpetually late for work:

Claudine: *Alma, I could tell by the tone of your e-mail that you were a bit frustrated. Tell me a little about what you have tried with the TA to help her see how important this is.*

Alma: *Well, I told her I couldn't really handle all the kids without her there.*

Claudine: *Did that make any difference?*

Alma: *She was apologetic, and the next day she was on time, but after that it was back to the same thing.*

Claudine: *Did you talk to her again?*

Alma: *No, she can tell how I feel.*

Claudine: *If I read you right, you are pretty annoyed. What do you think would happen if you asked her what made it so hard to get here?*

Alma: *I just feel she should take responsibility, or I should do something.*

Claudine: *What do you think you should do?*

Alma: *I have been thinking maybe I should start documenting and move toward firing her.*

Claudine: *How is the rest of her work?*

Alma: *That's the problem. She is the best assistant I have had for years except she just can't get here on time.*

Claudine: *What a dilemma. She is making you furious, and yet you value her work.*

Alma: *That's it—I just don't know if I can make it through another week.*

Claudine: *Can you imagine what you would say to her if you sat down to talk about this problem?*

Alma: *I'm afraid I am too mad.*

Claudine: *What would happen if you let her know that you value her work but that it is hard for you and you are getting very annoyed?*

Alma: *She knows that; she is now avoiding me. I have been giving her hard looks.*

Claudine: *Would you be willing to give it a try or do you think it would be better to move ahead with personnel actions?*

Alma: *I'll try it, but could you help me figure out what to say? I am worried I might get emotional and blow it.*

Claudine: *Let's practice now.*

Filtering and Focusing

The reflective supervisor is often bombarded with needs and reactions from supervisees. The ability to name and frame concerns and then record, remember, and return to them requires sorting out what is the highest priority in a conversation. Filtering is the skill of taking it all in and then in a subtle or more direct way focusing on the needs that require the most attention in the moment. In using the skill of filtering and focusing, the supervisor is attempting to hold onto important details while not losing track of the big picture or other less pressing details that may need to be returned to at a later time.

Harriet is a reflective supervisor working with Anton, a speech therapist. Anton is struggling with a family whose child has a serious language delay. He has just been told that the parents are divorcing. Anton, who has recently been through a breakup with his own partner, is overwhelmed by the situation. The dialogue below illustrates filter and focus skills used by Harriet. She alternates use of empathy with a set of statements that help Anton come back to the compelling issues that have been overlooked because of his surprise and his reactions to a situation that was similar to his personal experience:

Harriet: *This breakup seems to have caught you by surprise.*

Anton: *Yeah, it is just like what happened to me when Gwen left. I didn't see it coming. I just found myself overwhelmed and sad as they told me.*

Harriet: *It sounds like it brought back all those feelings with Gwen. In the midst of it all, I wonder if you had a chance to talk with them about their arrangements for their child or what this will mean to the little guy.*

Anton: *Honestly, I think I just blanked out about the child.*

Harriet: *I can see that this was tough coming on the heels of your own breakup. I don't know if this is the right time, but at some point soon I wonder what would be a way to focus on the topic of next steps, and how you might be able to help the child with the changes in the family?*

Spotlighting

There are times when a supervisor needs to address an issue very directly. The technique known as spotlighting can be very effective in these situations when other, less-direct approaches have not worked. The approach is respectful of the staff person and offers her an opportunity to give information, reflect, and respond. In spotlighting, the supervisor (a) uses her own feelings as an avenue to bring up the situation, (b) states clearly and specifically the nature of the concern, (c) limits herself to one issue and ideally to one incident or one moment, (d) articulates the effect or consequence of the worry while stating why it matters to the work, and (e) invites the supervisee to explore the issue with her rather than demanding any specific action. This technique can be used when there is a serious job performance concern; when the supervisee is having significant interpersonal difficulties with children, families, or team members; when there are questions about a child's immediate safety; or when a staff person's action has legal or regulatory implications. It can also be used when the supervisor finds that the more indirect approaches have not been effective in focusing the supervisee's attention on an important matter.

The vignette below illustrates spotlighting:

> *Andrea, a home visitor, and her supervisor, Stella, are looking at a videotape of a home visit with a young family and their prematurely born baby who is now 2 months old. In the videotape, the baby's bottle is propped while the mother and the home visitor talk intently. For a moment, Andrea looks perplexed, but she continues to talk with the mother about a matter unrelated to the baby. Stella asks a series of questions, including "What do you think made the mother prop the bottle?" Andrea's answers do not demonstrate much insight or even worry about the situation. After these questions, Andrea switches the subject to a technical question about a report she is completing.*
>
> *After helping Andrea with the report, Stella spotlights the situation: "I find myself coming back to the videotape of the baby's feeding and feeling a little anxious. I noticed that you looked a little worried at that moment in the tape when mom propped the bottle, and I was concerned that it seemed hard for you to make an intervention about the bottle-propping that might have helped the mom and the baby. Could we look at that part of the tape again and think together if there might have been a way to engage mom in a discussion about the feeding?"*

The vignette below illustrates how spotlighting can be used to address an administrative issue:

> *Jamilla, a supervisor in an infant mental health program, has just discovered that her supervisee, Thalia, has been negligent in completing her billing paperwork for the third month in a row. Because of these delays, the agency was unable to bill for the work she had done that month. Jamilla's first reaction is to be furious. Her whole department is under some scrutiny about billing, and Thalia's lateness only highlights this difficulty. In thinking about this situation, Jamilla realizes that her reaction is heightened by her own anxiety stemming from these organizational pressures. She realizes that Thalia's late billing is not the only thing she is worried about. Jamilla, aware of her irritation and the complexity of the situation, does not contact Thalia right away but instead waits until their regular supervisory meeting the next day.*
>
> ***Jamilla:*** *Thalia, I got our billing statistics yesterday and noted that there was nothing listed for you because the bills had been turned in late. I wasn't sure if*

there was something happening that I had missed or if they had made a mistake in the billing office. I wanted to get your perspective on what happened.

Thalia: *I know, I blew it again. That part just seems to get away from me. Last week, when I planned to do my billing, my kid got sick and I had to take the afternoon off. I always feel like I just have too much to do.*

Jamilla: *I know you have a lot of complex cases, and emergencies do come up, but do you mean that you save all your billing to do at once?*

Thalia: *I do, it just seems more efficient.*

Jamilla: *In a way I can see your point of view, but I am worried because you've been late with your billing before. Have you considered trying a different way to get it done?*

Thalia: *Well, I have always done it at the end of the month, and it is just lately it's not worked out so well. I always do get them in eventually.*

Jamilla: *I appreciate that, but the late billing means extra work for the billing staff, and it also makes our department statistics look like we are not working as hard as we really are.*

Thalia: *I'm not going to do it again…*

Jamilla: *I can see you don't want this to be a problem, but it's hard to control for emergencies. Why don't we see if we can come up with a way to build in some time for billing on a weekly basis?*

Thalia: *I think it will eat into my home visit time, but I will give it a try.*

Jamilla: *Thank you. I wanted to be sure that you understood how important this is, and that from now on you will meet our deadlines. As a team, we need to make sure we get our billing numbers up, and addressing any late billing will really make a difference. I appreciate your being willing to make the change.*

Refocusing and Balancing of Attention to a Variety of Needs

The reflective supervisor must maintain a balance between attending to administrative responsibilities and the needs of staff members, children, and parents. Staff members may, for example, have strong emotional reactions to a child's distress that cause them to lose sight of the mother's perspective. In this case, the supervisor will acknowledge their intense feelings and try to help contain those feelings so as to refocus on the needs of the family as a whole. The reflective supervisor must often make choices about how to balance her attention effectively. This refocusing and balancing require being able to interrupt, redirect, and comment in a sensitive manner and to reintroduce conversational strands that have gotten lost or been forgotten. The following vignette illustrates refocusing and balancing; it involves Carmela, a supervisor of a Head Start program, who is meeting with Laquita, a teacher. Laquita is distressed about parents who are not following through on treatment for their child's medical needs:

Laquita: *You wouldn't believe it. The kid is wheezing so bad we can't even let him run on the playground. The mom is just out to lunch. I have told her a hundred times about this, and they took him to the doctor once. The health coordinator says we shouldn't even take him in the classroom, but I can only imagine how bad things might be at home if they neglect his basic medical needs. They were supposed to go back to the doctor, and I am not sure what happened. I think the kid has some kind of allergy, and we don't know what it is. Every time he takes a bite of lunch I'm worried he is going to go into anaphylactic shock.*

Carmela: *You seem pretty worried about this; I wonder what the parent understood from the doctor's visit?*

Laquita: *Who knows? She doesn't seem worried.*

Carmela: *I wonder what would happen if you asked to speak to her about how the wheezing gets in the way of his experience in Head Start.*

As this conversation continues, Carmela realizes that she has not addressed the teacher's disrespectful way of talking about the parent.

Carmela: *I am glad we are talking about this parent, and I can see how worried you are about the child.*

Laquita: *I find myself waking up at night worrying that he is not getting his treatments.*

Carmela: *Do you think that being angry at these parents could be affecting your work with them? Sometimes being upset like this can make it hard to even believe that they could be helpful to their son.*

Laquita: *Well, I need to let off steam about her; isn't that what I am supposed to do in supervision?*

Carmela: *You are supposed to do that, but I hear that you are really fed up with them, and I am wondering if the parents might pick up on that. I wonder if you would feel differently if you could figure out a way to reach out to them. It is*

> *possible there are some things we don't quite get about this family, and it might really help to try and understand where they are coming from.*

Refocusing on the Relationship

The supervisor may need to help her supervisee remember that whenever she identifies a worrisome behavior or have a concern about someone's actions or attitudes, these are taking place in the context of a relationship. This could be a relationship of parent and child, colleague and colleague, or teacher and child. It is always illuminating to consider this broader perspective, as illustrated in this vignette:

> *Margaret is a preschool teacher who is perplexed by Angelo's defiant behavior at circle time. She explains to her supervisor, Stephanie, that time-out just doesn't work.*
>
> ***Stephanie:*** *I wonder if the time-out makes him feel a little left out?*
>
> ***Margaret:*** *Oh no, I am very careful about it.*
>
> ***Stephanie:*** *Well, he does seem so engaged with you that I wondered if he had a little special time before circle he might have an easier time of it.*
>
> ***Margaret:*** *Well, I don't want him to think he is special.*
>
> ***Stephanie:*** *I know you have a lot of kids to think about, but I have noticed how Angelo relaxes more when you are able spend time one-on-one. I just wondered if this might be a little preventive medicine, to help him through the group time, which seems so hard for him. He may be a little boy who needs a little reassurance that he is actually cared for. That might make sense, given what we know about the recent changes at home for him.*

Reframing

Reframing occurs when supervisors help staff members broaden their perspective, or see things in a new light. In doing so, staff members can come to understand a problem, behavior, or feeling in a new way. This can be accomplished by posing a hypothesis, questioning an assumption, offering new information, or suggesting an alternative path of action.

Carissa, an early interventionist, is working with an 18-month-old child who has severe cerebral palsy. The child is developing typically in his cognitive abilities but has language and mobility problems. Until now, the child has seemed content to play with toys when the mother left the playgroup for the separate parent support group, but recently he protests plaintively each time she goes out of the room.

Carissa: *I just don't get it. She is such a good mother, and he always managed the separations so beautifully. Now he just cries and cries. I wish I could understand what is going on, so I could help her figure out what to do.*

Supervisor: *I wonder if there is any chance that he feels more powerful and assertive now in some ways, but the fact that he just can't make his body move toward her is so frustrating that he can't bear it?*

Tracking Themes

The supervisor has the opportunity and the responsibility to be the "historian" of the work she does with her staff members. She should take the time to observe and record the themes that emerge during supervisory sessions. These themes may relate to the supervisee's interventions and relationships with children and families, her interactions with colleagues and teammates, her ability to balance clinical and administrative responsibilities, and any other important aspects of her job. The supervisor needs to remember and reflect on each individual supervisee's work and should be consistent in recording her thoughts and observations regarding their work together. Then, as she reviews her notes, she will be better able to identify important issues or recurring themes. These can then be discussed and reviewed with her supervisee. In this vignette, Shanetta, the supervisor, is working with Wendy, a case manager at a domestic violence shelter. She helps Wendy to focus on an area of practice that may need some attention in the future:

Wendy: *I tell you, I am so overwhelmed with this case—the housing hasn't come through, and I am not sure that the mom can hold out much longer here. It is hard being in a place with no privacy and so much noise. I think the noise triggers her memories of the abuse.*

Shanetta: *That sounds like it might be so, and I was glad to hear she is getting some therapy there. How is the baby doing at the shelter?*

Wendy: *Oh, he seems okay. I haven't really spent much time focused on him. I've just been working so hard at making sure the housing comes through and trying to deal with the mom.*

Shanetta: I know you have done wonders with other families, helping them get settled, but I've noticed that with this family and in other cases sometimes it does seem to be hard for you to focus on the baby, given everything else that is going on.

Wendy: You're right in a way. I know I get pulled in, and if the kid seems okay, sometimes I don't bother much.

Shanetta: And…?

Wendy: I think I miss some good opportunities.

Applying Professional Use of Self

Professional use of self is central to understanding the reflective supervision model. Use of self can be thought of as an internal ability to reflect upon and examine one's own internal responses, thoughts, and feelings, and then simultaneously to imagine the thoughts, feelings, and perspectives of others. The supervisor directs her self-awareness—monitoring her own emotions, perceptions, and responses while striving to keep an open mind, stay curious, and understand the perspective of others. This awareness is essential to help the supervisor take in the endless ordinary yet rich differences in humanity and the possibly unfamiliar worldviews related to differences in education, region, gender, class, culture, age, and professional discipline. Use of self also refers to more active ways of using internal awareness while working with a supervisee or colleague. In these cases, the supervisor uses the process of monitoring but speaks thoughtfully about her own reactions and feelings to encourage her supervisee to do the same. This active use of self also models for the supervisee how engaging feelings is helpful for understanding a situation. Below are examples of how the use of self can be integrated into real-time interactions with supervisees:

Supervisor: I have found myself worrying a lot about this family but haven't wanted to question this until we had more information. I had a kind of uneasy feeling after you told me about the accident with the baby. I am wondering if you had any reactions like that. I was really quite scared for him when I heard about it.

***

Supervisor: I have been struggling with something and wanted to talk with you about it. I could be wrong, but it feels to me as if you might be uncomfortable with me coming to observe you in your classroom. Is there anything about the way I am doing my visits that is making it hard or unpleasant for you?

Containing, Exploring Limits or Boundaries, Making a Decision, and Moving Forward

The supervisor is often in a position to help contain feelings, actions, or events that threaten to obscure the larger picture and are a barrier to effective decision making. To do this, the supervisor must be able to hear and empathize with the supervisee and acknowledge her desire to help, respond, or interact in a particular way. However, at the same time, the supervisor should clearly identify priorities, possible risks or dangers, boundary concerns, and actions needed to make a plan and move forward.

Tamara: I went to the Smiths' house again, and Tommy had marks on his legs again. I could tell he had been hit or something. They were kind of raised welts. He seemed pretty happy though. I know you have said I need to bring this up, but what if I am wrong?

Supervisor: Tamara, I know that this is really hard. I get the feeling you might be worried that the family will be upset or angry.

Tamara: I am worried about that, and I just don't know if there really is a problem, or if we might really do something that would cause harm if we addressed this.

Supervisor: This is so hard, but it sounds to me like it is time to open this up a little bit with the family. I would like to ask you to bring this up with the family the next time you are there.

Tamara: What if everything looks okay?

Supervisor: This is complicated. I believe the discussion will be the right thing here. Let's see if we can figure out a way you can do this without seeming accusatory or judgmental.

Here are some questions to help supervisors explore boundary issues with their supervisees:

1. What are the costs and what are the benefits? For example, if you go to your client's birthday party, it might give the message that you are a friend. If you don't go, there may be hurt feelings.

2. What is your motivation? Help staff members consider concerns such as safety, feeling liked, or feeling appreciated.

3. What might be the parent's motivation? How might various responses be understood?

4. What is your work? What is your primary role with this client?

5. What are you committing yourself to? For example, if you bring food to the family, will this develop as an expectation for this family or for other families? Are there ways of framing what you do that make your role clearer to the family?

Holding the Supervisee or Team in Mind

A supervisor has the task of striving to help her supervisees develop the competence and confidence they will need to do the work. The reflective supervisor provides a secure base for them from which they can venture out to explore and practice new skills—knowing that their supervisor is there when needed. One way that the supervisor can communicate this availability, without encouraging overdependence, is by letting staff members know that she is thinking about them even when they are not together. If supervisees feel that they are "out of sight, out of mind," they may be less willing to try something new or difficult. Simple statements from the supervisor can be very powerful, such as: "As I was driving home last night, I was thinking about your conversation with Mrs. Brown. I was wondering if she was actually hoping we might intervene." In saying this, the supervisor lets her supervisee know that the supervisor is supporting her even when she is not present. Supervisory notes can serve the same function: The supervisor can review the notes prior to meeting with her supervisee. She can then say: "Before meeting with you today, I was looking back at my notes, and I see that you wanted to talk some more about possible resources for the Olsen family. I looked in my file and found a couple of things that might be helpful. Let's take a look." The supervisor has then communicated that their work together is important to her, that she has been thinking about it, and that she has made some efforts toward their common goals.

Regulating Oneself and Assisting Supervisees to Regulate Their Emotions and Responses

An important supervisory skill is the ability to remain calm enough to listen, be open-minded about the content being presented, and be fully present for the supervisee. This entails managing one's own emotions and reactions so as not to let them take over the situation. Each supervisor should be alert to her own responses and know herself well enough to understand what she has to do to regulate herself and stay composed. Self-care is essential. A few minutes between supervisory situations, a calm environment for supervision, breathing, looking at symbols or pictures that bring back relaxing memories, and strict personal commitment to limiting multitasking, texting, cell calls, and interruptions are examples of ways supervisors can help themselves stay calm and responsive.

Engaging the Difficult-to-Engage Supervisee

From time to time, a supervisor will encounter a staff person who seems uninterested, unwilling, or unable to become actively involved in the reflective supervisory process. This resistance or inability
is demonstrated in a number of ways, including:

- Difficulty making and keeping supervision appointments, constantly reassuring the supervisor that "Everything's just fine! Nothing to talk about today!"

- Persistently asking the supervisor to just give the answer or fix the situation.

- Seeming impatient with the supervisory process.

- Focusing on paperwork and administrative concerns, with reluctance to talk in depth about clients or families.

- Displaying overt hostility or resistance (e.g., "I don't need to talk about this. I am just fine on my own.").

The first step to addressing a difficult-to-engage supervisee is to strive to understand the possible reasons for the supervisee's apparent reluctance. These are numerous. She might not trust that the supervisor actually wants to support and help her, and, because of experiences in prior supervisory relationships, she may fear that she will be criticized or punished for any mistakes or inadequacies. She might not really understand the process and might need some clarification as to the kinds of discussion and collaborative problem solving that are the foundation of reflective supervision. She might not be comfortable with the degree of self-reflection typically involved in this supervisory model. The supervisor could lack credibility because she is not out in the field or comes from a different professional discipline. If the supervisor and supervisee have cultural, educational, racial, class, gender, or other differences, these could be unexplored barriers to the supervisory relationship. The supervisee could have a basic mistrust of those in authority and be reluctant to engage no matter how collegial and respectful the supervisor may be. It is also possible that the supervisee's professional training stressed independence and autonomy, so that the idea of reflective supervision might seem to imply a lack of competence or a threat to autonomy. The supervisee may lack confidence. Finally, it is important to consider the "goodness of fit" between supervisor and supervisee: some matches are better than others. When there seems to be a poor match, it is the supervisor's responsibility to make the extra effort to understand the needs of her supervisee and to consider the ways in which their respective vulnerabilities may make working together more difficult. Once the supervisor comes to some understanding or at least an hypothesis as to the underlying causes of her staff person's reluctance to be involved in supervision, she will be able to respond accordingly. Some strategies that can be helpful include:

1. Be responsive to any requests made by the supervisee. Meeting her expressed needs in a helpful and timely manner may make her start to trust that you really would like to be supportive. Do this even if the requests do not seem to be of the highest priority, assuming they are at least reasonable. Ask the question "How can I be most helpful to you today?" and then listen to the answer!

2. Attend to and respond positively to any slight overtures from the supervisee, even a passing comment related to an issue she might like to talk about sometime.

3. Self-assess: Are you providing a safe, respectful supervisory environment? Has anything happened that might cause the staff person to wonder about the confidentiality of supervisory conversations or to worry about being criticized for mistakes?

4. Go slowly, be patient, and follow the supervisee's lead—allow her to discover her own comfort level with the process while at the same time being persistent in the expectation that the work will be shared and discussed.

5. Find ways of asking questions that encourage reflection but that do not pressure or push.

6. Look for informal opportunities—such as when accompanying the staff person on a home visit—for talking about a particular child or family. These discussions can then be carried forward into a supervision meeting.

7. Clarify mutual expectations about supervision timing, agenda, process, and topics to be discussed.

8. Spotlight your concerns that it seems difficult to connect and engage through supervision. Ask for feedback as to how it looks and feels to the staff person. Ask if there are ways you could be more helpful.

9. Revisit the underlying rationale for reflective supervision: why it matters and how it can be helpful to the supervisee and be of ultimate benefit to the families.

Some of the most effective strategies for difficult-to-engage employees are proactive efforts, made before a staff person accepts a position and during the first weeks and months of her employment. The role of reflective supervision can be highlighted during the interview and hiring process. Applicants should be informed of the agency's commitment to the model and the fact that everyone—regardless of experience or discipline—is offered this support and is expected to participate. They can receive information about their likely supervisor (i.e., whether that person will be from the same discipline or another and what the expectations will be around individual and team meetings). Interview questions can focus on an exploration of the candidates' previous supervisory experiences and their feelings about the kind of supervision that works best for them. If an interviewee repeatedly stresses the desire to be independent and autonomous, she may not be the best fit for the position. Involvement in supervision can be included in the job description and be addressed during the performance review process. (See Appendix 5 for a sample job description/performance review form.) New employee orientation can include a discussion of reflective supervision and the implications of having a blended model in which both clinical and administrative issues are addressed.

Supervisory Pitfalls

There a few supervisory approaches that are usually ineffective. The list below is short and certainly not inclusive.

Overuse of the unexamined war story

Supervisors should usually avoid using stories of their own successes as direct service providers or parents. These anecdotes tend to be self-aggrandizing for the supervisor and at the same time can succeed in making the supervisee feel less competent by comparison. In addition, while circumstances may seem similar, the feelings and skills of the staff members, the context, and the family circumstances often do not match, and so the anecdote is of limited relevance. Before talking about her own experiences, the supervisor should first ask herself if she is responding to the supervisee's need. The supervisor should be sure she is not actually reacting to her own need to process a difficult issue or even to establish credibility with her supervisee. The supervisor can ask if it might be useful to hear an example of a strategy that the supervisor has used. If the supervisee answers yes, the supervisor should be sure to directly link her story to the current situation. A more helpful way to use a personal story is just to reference generally the feelings or insights evoked by the past event (e.g., "I once worked with a family who was in a similar situation, and I remembering feeling overwhelmed. I am wondering how this has been for you.").

Labeling or implying the feelings of others

Supervisors must be careful to use questions rather than labels when discussing the supervisee's feelings or reactions. "What was that like for you?" is better than "You must be so happy to have been there when the mom finally got him down for a nap without a fuss."

Prediction or crystal ball gazing

While listening to details of a child or family situation, supervisors can make the error of using minimal information to predict maximal outcomes:

> **Supervisee:** *The baby was born with a positive toxicology screen.*
>
> **Supervisor:** *Well no wonder there are such problems with his sleep. If you don't get this under control, this will be real trouble later. This kid should probably be getting a full evaluation right now.*

Using other staff members as examples

One supervisee may raise an issue or take an action that you, as supervisor, would like to bring up in a team meeting. No matter how brilliant that person has been, or how much you want to use her as an example, don't do it unless you have specifically asked permission to do so. A surprise announcement or statement will erode the supervisee's trust in the confidentiality and safety of supervision, as illustrated in the following example:

> *Katherine is a very conscientious member of an early intervention team who often goes the extra mile for her families. Her supervisor, Sally, wanted to encourage the rest of Katherine's teammates to be a little more forthcoming with resources for families, so she decided to share one of Katherine's recent successes with the team. Later, Katherine came to her in tears saying that she was very uncomfortable being the center of attention and worried that her team members would think she was showing off.*

SUMMARY

In this chapter, we have described the knowledge, abilities, and skills that will help supervisors provide reflective supervision to their staff members. They constitute competencies that are continually developing over the course of a lifetime. No supervisor is likely to be equally at ease in all areas. In fact, the mark of a good reflective supervisor is being fully aware of her own imperfections and shortcomings and actively seeking to do better and know more.* In this way, her quest parallels that of her staff members: Together they can strive to do their best work with children and families.

GUIDING QUESTIONS

Reflect on your own level of mastery of each of the reflective supervision skills described in this chapter.

---

*You might consider using the *Supervisor's Professional Development Guide* as presented in Appendix 1 or think about pursuing a professional endorsement that encompasses supervisory skills such as the *Michigan Association for Infant Mental Health's Competency Guidelines* or the *California Training Guidelines and Personnel Competencies for Infant Family and Early Childhood Mental Health* which has specific endorsements for reflective facilitation.

- What skills are most comfortable for you?

- Which ones would you like to target for future growth and development?

- Who could help you do this, and what resources would be available to you?

REFERENCES

Bernstein, V. (2002–2003, Winter). Standing firm against the forces of risk: Supporting home visiting and early intervention workers through reflective supervision. *IMPrint, 35*.

Edelman, L. (2009, October). *Using digital video in early care and early intervention*. Resources to accompany a preconference workshop at annual meeting of the Division for Early Childhood, Albuquerque, NM. Received April 10, 2010, from larry.edelman@ucdenver.edu

Johns, C. (2008). *Becoming a reflective practitioner* (2nd ed.). Oxford, England: Blackwell.

Lao-Tzu. (1988). *Tao te ching*. (S. Mitchell, trans.). New York: Harper Perennial.

Simpson, P., & French, R. (2006). Negative capability and the capacity to think in the present moment: Some implications for leadership practice. *Leadership, 2*(2), 245–255.

Starting Early Starting Smart. (2003). "Ordinary miracles: A training package to foster nurturing parent-child relationships," facilitator manual. Washington, DC: Casey Family Programs and the U.S. Department of Health and Human Services, Substance Abuse and Mental Health Services Administration.

Wajda-Johnston, V., Smyke, A., Nagle, G., & Larrieu, J. A. (2005). Using technology as a training, supervision, and consultation aid. In K. M. Finello (Ed.), *The handbook of training and practice in infant and preschool mental health* (pp. 357–374). San Francisco: Jossey-Bass.

Further Readings

Bertacchi, J., & Coplon, J. (1992). The professional use of self in prevention. In E. Fenichel (Ed.), *Learning through supervision and mentorship to support the development of infants, toddlers and their families: A source book* (pp. 84–90). Washington, DC: ZERO TO THREE.

Bromwich, R. (1997). *Working with families and their infants at risk. A perspective after 20 years of experience*. Austin, TX: PRO-Ed.

Foulds, B., & Curtiss, K. (2002). No longer risking myself: Assisting the supervisor through supportive consultation. In J. Shirilla & D. Weatherston (Eds.), *Case studies in infant mental health: Risk, resiliency, and relationships* (pp. 177–186). Washington, DC: ZERO TO THREE.

Hawkins, P., & Shohet, R. (2007). *Supervision in the helping professions* (3rd ed.). Maidenhead, Berkshire, England: Open University Press.

Heffron, M. C. (1999). Balance in jeopardy: Reflexive reactions vs. reflective responses in infant/family practice. *Zero to Three, 20*(1), 15–17.

Pawl, J., & St. John, M. (1998). *How you are is as important as what you do in making a positive difference for infants, toddlers and their families.* Washington, DC: ZERO TO THREE.

Senge, P., Scharmer, C. O., Jaworski, J., & Flowers, B. S. (2005). *Presence: An exploration of profound change in people, organizations, and society.* New York: Doubleday.

Shahmoon Shanok, R. (1991). The supervisory relationship: Integrator, resource and guide. *Zero to Three, 12*(2), 16–19.

Shahmoon Shanok, R., Gilkerson, L., Eggbeer, L., & Fenichel, E. (1995). *Reflective supervision: A relationship for learning.* Washington, DC: ZERO TO THREE.

CHAPTER 5

TEAMS AND GROUPS REFLECTING TOGETHER: THE WHOLE IS GREATER THAN THE SUM OF ITS PARTS

This chapter provides a brief overview of several group leadership roles, a discussion of the skills and strategies central to such roles, and vignettes of supervisory discussions using language infused with reflective principles. Although no supervisor is likely to feel she has mastered all of these skills or is equally strong in all the roles, we hope this chapter will provide guidance for supervisors seeking to further develop their practice.

THE SUPERVISOR AS TEAM LEADER

> *Julie has recently been promoted to the position of child development manager for the Healthy Families program where she has worked as a home visitor for many years. The previous manager had a reputation for being quite disorganized, and staff members had been frustrated by her apparent lack of preparation for their team meetings. It was generally felt that the meetings were a waste of time.*
>
> *As Julie prepares for the first meeting with her staff members, she realizes that she is quite anxious. The previous supervisor also tended to dominate the conversation and to allow for relatively little collaborative problem solving or open-ended discussion. Julie is determined to try to make it a more meaningful experience and wants to provide an opportunity for everyone to participate. But she feels overwhelmed by the number of administrative tasks and issues that have to be addressed. She knows that somehow she is going to have to find a balance between time spent on these duties and time for team members to help each other think about their work with individual children and families. She is not at all sure how to present herself. Should she sit at the head of the table? Should she come in with a prepared agenda? What role should she play in structuring the meeting?*

Julie is wise to be giving some careful thought to her role as a team leader and to be thinking about the many competing priorities. She is perceptive in her awareness of the possible effect of the team's previous experiences and the need for striking a balance between providing structure and guidance and protecting opportunities for reflection and open-ended exploration about the work with children and families.

Supervisors like Julie are likely to be involved with various types of teams and groups with different purposes. These include, for example, ad hoc teams that come together to support a particular child or family, teams that represent programmatic or administrative entities such as an Early Head Start or IDEA Part C, early intervention teams working with families in a defined geographic area and providing a prescribed set of services, and supervisory or consultation groups of many kinds.

Team-based work is part of a growing shift to coordinated care methods in the management of medical conditions. Coordination maximizes efficient use of both expertise and financial resources by drawing on multidisciplinary staff members and eliminating duplication of effort. These same benefits also apply to the complex work with multistressed, high-risk children and families.

Ideally, every individual practitioner will take personal responsibility for seeking out the other professionals working with a family to initiate and sustain communication, to collaborate, and to integrate information gathered and intervention provided. The special role of the supervisor in coordinated care is to make sure that the staff members make such efforts and follow through over time. The supervisor will also provide guidance and support for these coordination responsibilities.

Work with young children and families is often accomplished through a team-based approach. Staff members can learn a great deal from one another, and no one individual, profession, or discipline is likely to have all the knowledge, skills, or expertise needed to provide holistic and comprehensive services. Best practice dictates a multidisciplinary team assessment, coordinated intervention planning, and integrated service delivery. In some cases, one professional is the primary service provider and the one who carries the relationship with the child or family. The primary provider can then be supported by a number of other professionals, some providing direct service and others in a consultative position. One important function of these kinds of multidisciplinary teams is to build a coherent understanding and intervention approach from the varied assessments and input offered by team members. This can then be communicated clearly to families seeking help and support for their child. Supervisors play a central role in bringing team members together and helping them collaborate to be as effective as possible in supporting child and family health and well-being. The supervisor creates an environment for the professionals on the team to work together.

GROUP REFLECTIVE SUPERVISION

Reflective supervision can be provided in a group setting, and in some cases group supervision can be a valuable adjunct to individual supervisory work. In other cases, it will be the main source of reflective supervision. Some programs have the resources to support separate supervision meetings solely devoted to discussions of children and families; others need to manage team meetings so that administrative issues can be discussed along with consideration of the team's clinical work. Some agencies create leadership or supervisory groups that bring together supervisors from a wide variety of programs. They offer opportunities for professional development and skill building in a specific area (e.g., learning about a particular strategy or content area). They also can be used as a way of providing that leadership group with their own supervisory support.

EMBRACING THE LEADERSHIP ROLE INHERENT IN SUPERVISION

The first step for any supervisor, manager, or leader is to acknowledge that she has an important and complex responsibility. The supervisor needs to be comfortable in accepting this leadership position and to understand that in doing so she can be very helpful to a team or group. It is important not to be dismissive of the role or give mixed signals about it. This might happen when a supervisor one day acts as a leader and the next day acts as part of a group of peers.

This uneven acceptance of a leadership role can happen when a supervisor is first promoted to the position, especially if she is now responsible for the work of former peers and feels that she might lose important relationships with them if she appears to take her role too seriously.

Underlying an acceptance of the leadership role should be an understanding that the leader's job involves engagement with others, drawing out the talents and different perspectives of group members, embracing diversity of all kinds, creating a safe atmosphere, and communicating a sense of the whole so that the group has a feeling of unity and purpose. In an odd way, the supervisor must truly step up and assume her leadership role in order to step back and create the desired opportunities for reflection.

There are many ways to be an effective leader of a team or supervision group. Individuals with different temperaments will have unique challenges as they take on these roles and responsibilities. Some may need to cultivate the "taking charge" part of leadership, whereas others need to build their abilities to truly listen to others and engage them in the group process.

SKILLS SUPERVISORS NEED FOR FACILITATION OF TEAM MEETINGS AND GROUP SUPERVISION

Following is a description of some of the key skills supervisors will need for effective team facilitation. The reader will note that these closely parallel skills used in individual supervisory meetings.

Contracting and Clarifying

When any team or supervisory group begins to work together, time is needed to contract and clarify the purposes and processes of the group. This needs to happen at an administrative level and with the group itself. Recontracting and reclarifying may be necessary when members join or leave a group or when a group has lost direction and needs to get back on track. The supervisor organizes and tracks the following steps:

Doing the groundwork with agency managers and administrators to discuss the scope of work, roles, expectations, and purpose

What is this team or group supposed to do? What did it do before? How did it work? What can be improved? As conditions and needs of a group change, additional discussions at this level may be necessary.

Orienting team members about the mission of the team or supervisory group

How will the team use its time? What is the purpose of the team or supervision group? What can participants expect? What are their expressed needs and thoughts about the group?

Defining processes for how the group will work together

For example, the supervisor may hold the overall responsibility for how the group runs, but individual team members may rotate the facilitation. Some groups may want notes or minutes to track the work in a way that can be shared.

Working with the team or group to create a set of agreements particular to the team or group

Agreements about how the team or reflective supervision group will run are a basic need if it is to be productive. For example, group members should decide the beginning and ending times and how they will start their work. There should be an agreed-upon agenda, so that team members have a clear understanding of how the time will be spent. Some groups may choose to address administrative issues at the beginning of the meeting, and others may wish to save those for the end. Groups may want to develop rituals such as sharing of food, highlighting a recent success, or simply a reminder to come in the room and be present with one another. In some supervisory groups, members choose to start meetings by picking a red, yellow, or green card. A red card means that the member has an urgent concern, yellow means that the person would like to talk if possible, and green means smooth sailing and no urgent needs.

Supervisors are encouraged to explore with the group how electronic downtime may enhance the group experience and figure out how to handle text and phone use. It is better if agreements are written. Some teams or groups may want to have agreements available on laminated cards or wall posters. Agreements about confidentiality are important in early discussions.

Highlighting the value and importance of teams and groups and creating the expectation that all members will protect and respect the time to participate

Orientation for new staff members should include discussion of the ways in which group or team work is integral to their job.

Ensuring that staff members are actually afforded enough time for team meetings and group supervision

Supervisors may need to advocate for this time and should stand ready to explain ways that the groups support program quality and develop staff members' skills.

Front-loading the process by spending extra time when a new team or group is just getting together, in order to lay a solid foundation

Front-loading should always include some training and practice on how to use reflective approaches in a group and how to work effectively as a team. Staff members will learn a great deal from the way the team leader or group supervisor works, but explicit training and guidelines will move the reflective skills of the team members along exponentially.

Planning for upcoming time together

Staff members are likely to be only as prepared and committed as the supervisor. The nature of this planning depends on the purpose of the group meeting, but all groups are enhanced by a review of what happened the last time the group was together before moving on to new topics or discussions. The supervisor should keep and review notes of issues discussed, past case presentations, agreed-upon action items, and questions raised for future discussions. She should be sure to follow through on any responsibilities she has assumed.

Containing and Organizing

The supervisor has the task of promoting the well-being of the team or group as a whole, while attending to the individuals within the group itself. Although each individual member also plays a part and can have an important role in supporting fellow team members, giving feedback to others, and helping the group stay focused and true to its mission, the team leader or group supervisor ultimately has responsibility for the team's operation. If she can avoid the temptation to jump to conclusions too quickly, but instead model a calm and reflective stance, it will be easier for the team members to contain their more reactive impulses. If the supervisor hears a remark that is potentially damaging to the group or far off the mark from the group's mission, her role is to notice and comment. She must work to make sure that all team members have a chance to participate and be heard. As team leader, she helps staff members use their time most productively, balancing the need for process and exploration with the need to come to a decision and make a plan. She can summarize a discussion to help the group move on. Above all, she should monitor the group to make sure that there are no invisible members or absent voices. All this should be done in a collaborative and collegial manner, as in the following examples:

- "How much time do you think we need for this discussion?"

- "Before we start figuring out what to do, are there other things we need to know about this situation?"

- "I know the question about whether we are going to expand the geographic boundaries of our service area is on everyone's mind, but could we start by taking some time to talk about some of the recent trends with our families, so we can better forecast what our program capacity will be for next year?"

- "Christine, I appreciate your thoughts on this, but I'd like to hear from Jodi too, and she has been wanting to say something for a few minutes."

- "It sounds like some of us felt quite upset with this parent for being so hostile in the parent group, but I wonder if there is another way to understand her anger? Do you think there is anything that happened while she was here that may have added to her distress?"

- "We have been discussing this situation with Alice's new foster mom for some time. I wonder if we can move on to the questions Peter wanted to discuss, or do you think you need a few more minutes?"

The supervisor helps the team or group members keep their purpose in mind and consider what is and is not within the scope of their work. She stays attuned to the tone and mood of the group as a whole, helping it to regulate strong emotions, to focus, and to avoid a hijacking by a single vocal member, issue, or point of view. She is vigilant about "group-think," or the tendency in groups to jump on a bandwagon without fully exploring all perspectives. Here are examples of how a supervisor can keep a group meeting productive and on track:

> *Deadlines are killing everyone, and I am willing to help anyone who is struggling to meet a deadline on an individual basis, but I want to table this discussion now and return to our discussion about some of the difficulties we are having phasing new children into the center.*
>
> ***
>
> *It sounds like everyone is really upset about the changes in the Department of Health Services billing procedures. Unfortunately, there doesn't seem to be much we can do about it right away—so let's try to figure out how to minimize the effects on our program while we continue to advocate for change. If you can get me examples of how these changes are hurting children and families, I can bring this information to our meeting with the Department next month.*

In teams and group meetings, time is often needed for exploring fears, negative emotions, and concerns:

> *Jackie has been pretty clear about her worries and feelings about safety concerns in this neighborhood where the family is now living. I sense it has been upsetting to hear some of the things that have happened. I'd also like to hear from anyone else who may have had similar concerns.*
>
> ***
>
> *We have spent a lot of time exploring how painful it is for Camille to cope with this mom's depression and to watch the effect on her baby's communication development. What do others think—is there anything else that Camille could explore?*

Team members get real support by being able to talk about these kinds of strong feelings and reactions with their team. The supervisor should help create an atmosphere that supports this because so often what is shareable is bearable (Siegel, 2010). Ideally, the supervisor first gives time for the group to listen, respond, and help; however, if the mood seems to be escalating, or if staff members start "catastrophizing" (i.e., overreacting and appearing unable to pull themselves back together again), then the supervisor should step in to bring them back to a calm and constructive state. This kind of subtle pivot on the part of the reflective supervisor allows the team to reconnect, explore the situation in a more objective fashion, and, if warranted, come to a consensus and make a plan. The supervisor helps to keep the balance between the need for expression and recognizing when the team needs to move on. In making this kind of a pivot, it is crucial that the supervisor acknowledges the strong feelings and avoids giving the impression that she simply wants to avoid controversy:

I think we are all in shock that Paula has suddenly decided to move to Los Angeles, where she doesn't seem to know anyone or to be connected with any of the services that she will need to care for her baby. It is particularly upsetting since you all have worked so hard to help her get a really good service team in place here, and things seemed to finally be turning around for both of them. But since it looks like she is pretty determined to follow through with this plan, let's do some brainstorming about how to help her find the resources she will need when she gets there. And we should remind ourselves that Paula's ability to make a move on her own is a testimony to how well you have helped her become more confident in her own abilities.

Managing Change

All the skills described will be important in helping the supervisor manage change effectively. This is an issue that arises frequently for infant–family service providers because of increases or decreases in funding levels, the effect of new developments in research or standards of best practice, changes in contracts, loss or addition of staff members, or new regulatory requirements. Please see chapter 2 for a more extensive discussion of this topic.

Creating a Safe and Supportive Environment

Teams and supervisory groups work well only when group members feel safe enough to both be themselves and be part of an endeavor shared by the team or group. To achieve this sense of safety and comfort, a supervisor must encourage expression and awareness of others and insist on a respectful stance. The supervisor should communicate that differences of opinion and perspective are an asset as long as there is a willingness to hear out differing views. Supervisors can also help create a sense of safety by communicating the insight that one can be visible and included even if one's voice is not heard as often as some others. When these conditions are present, groups are more likely to be free to do their most creative thinking. They are also able to provide the highest level of support to one another.

Many of the same strategies for building a sense of safety and support in individual supervision apply to the team or group supervision setting. However, the task is more complex, because the supervisor must consider individual responses and needs as well as the team as a whole. The supervisor should start by monitoring her own behavior closely and avoiding being judgmental, critical, dismissive, or directive, or seeming to have favorites. Staff members need to trust that they will be respected and that the group will support them or at least that they will not be shamed or scolded. The supervisor should do everything possible to stay open-minded when listening to a discussion, thus encouraging the team as a whole to follow her lead. This atmosphere usually helps individual staff members feel comfortable enough to explore their own reactions, values, beliefs, and the effect these might have on their work, including situations where they may have done less than their best work.

> *Sara: This is hard for me to admit—but this mom just doesn't seem to like me. I don't know why, but I am almost tongue-tied when I am with her, and I am sure she was wishing she still had Sarah as her home visitor.*
>
> *Johan: I bet every one of us has felt that way from time to time. I am wondering how you would like the group to help you—would you like to share more details about this, or might it be helpful to hear how others have managed transfer cases?*

Supervisors can set the tone for openness and exploration by bringing up their own past mistakes and admitting to their own misgivings. With this kind of openness, team meetings and group supervision offer opportunities for learning and growth possible through sharing rough spots and mistakes.

It is critical to assure that confidentiality is maintained and that sensitive personal, client, or programmatic information shared during a team meeting stays within the group. Everyone on a team or in a supervisory group should have a chance to review and discuss the reasons why this is so important. The supervisor should clarify that if anything comes up that constitutes a danger to a child, family, team member, or the agency, then the information may need be discussed with her own supervisor or other appropriate program staff members. Team and supervisory group members need to be informed regarding any particular exceptions to confidentiality that may arise so that they understand what the next steps will be.

If there are multiple lines of supervision in an agency, these issues can be complicated and deserve clarification in initial stages of group formation. The following is an example that illustrates this complexity:

> *In her reflective supervision group, Tanya, a site supervisor for a Head Start program, asks her colleagues for help with one of her teachers who is having trouble working with parents due to her extreme shyness. Tanya has been doing the required home visits for the teacher and finds herself feeling resentful but also pressured because of the upcoming federal review. She wants the site to do well and have all requirements met. Margit, the supervisor for the group, finds herself working hard to monitor her own feelings. She is aware that the education coordinator has been explicit that all teachers must do the home visits to go over the education plans. She wonders whether the education coordinator knows that Tanya is doing*

> *this. Rather than put herself in the middle of this situation, she asks Tanya if she*
> *has talked to the education coordinator. Tanya says she hasn't, and Margit asks her*
> *whether she thinks she might be able to ask that person for assistance in addressing*
> *the teacher. Margit adds: "I think that would really help. Hiding this from the*
> *education coordinator is keeping the teacher from building her skills, and you*
> *from getting your other work done."*

Supervisors may be tempted to transport issues from individual supervision sessions to the whole group because of the learning value of a particular example. Before doing so, they should first ask permission from the supervisee, thus respecting the confidentiality of those one-on-one conversations.

Addressing Difficulties and Conflict in Group Settings

Even in well-functioning teams and groups, difficulties arise that should be addressed or responded to in some fashion. Comments are made that are hurtful, whether or not they are intentionally so, and team members behave or respond in ways that negatively affect their colleagues. A member of the team may express a prejudice toward a group or individual; another person may be tuned out throughout a meeting; a sarcastic remark or outburst of negative emotion directed at a team member may have a jarring effect. Typically a supervisor is advised to address these situations in the moment, when they happen, but often there may need to be a fuller discussion in a private meeting later on. By engaging in a direct and respectful way, the supervisor demonstrates that difficult topics can be discussed and will not go underground.

> *Valerie is a social worker who is assigned to help young children transition from*
> *foster care to permanent homes. In a recent meeting, she asks the team for help.*
> *She says that she feels it is wrong that the department is placing a little boy with*
> *two dads. She states that her religious beliefs hold that homosexuality is wrong. She*
> *says she feels she has no place to talk about this conflict. Valerie's supervisor Andi*
> *feels a surge of anger as she listens to Valerie. She then says: "This is tough. I*
> *appreciate your honesty about your beliefs. I think some of us see this differently,*
> *but I wonder if we could explore how these feelings are making it hard to help little*
> *Alex settle in to this family." Valerie says she wants to do the right thing, but it is*
> *hard to hold her beliefs separate. Some team members express that they had similar*
> *feelings in the past but think that it is important to look at the abilities of the new*
> *parents rather than their sexual orientation. This conversation seems to help*

> *Valerie relax in the team, and she asks her team members who had worked with same-sex couples for more specific ideas and help about her case.*

Finding the Teachable Moment

As represented throughout this book, reflective supervision is seen as a primary vehicle for promoting staff members' development (see chapter 2 for a discussion of some of the core concepts and content areas common to most types of infant–early childhood practice, which staff members may need support in learning or applying). Team meetings and group supervisions offer many opportunities to help staff members grow and learn as professionals. The supervisor can make a conscious effort to take advantage of these in a variety of ways. If, for example, the group has recently attended a workshop, the supervisor can watch for ways of applying the training content to a specific case discussion.

> *Molly seems to be wondering whether this baby's refusal to try pureed foods might be related to some sensory problems. Thinking back on the training we had last week about the possible sensory basis of feeding disturbances, do you think this child fits the profile?*

The supervisor can identify trends or make connections among issues that have come up for several team members, to help the group think about the underlying concepts and try to see the "big picture."

> *It seems as if the last few toddlers we discussed have teen moms who are struggling with their own independence from their mothers. Maybe we can understand their reactions to their toddlers' behavior in the context of their own challenges. Do you think this might be useful?*

The supervisor also functions as "team historian" and provides continuity for the discussions that take place from one week to the next. She can be depended on to follow up on past conversations.

> *Jorge, could you please give us an update on the Alfonso family? When we talked last week, you were just about to go with them to the school district transition*

> *meeting. We were all wondering whether the district would be receptive to our suggestions, and what information would be important to them to help with the placement decision.*

These approaches will be useful only if the supervisor is authentic in asking her questions or making her observations. Staff members will be put off by comments that seem patronizing or have an obvious hidden agenda. All questions should be statements of honest inquiry rather than disguised efforts to elicit a desired response.

Finally, the supervisor can help staff members learn that part of their job is to seek information and input from others. She can create a space for collaboration and dialogue and help staff members learn how to learn from each other.

> *In a group supervision, Elaine is discussing a toddler whose family is about to have a new baby. The supervisor asks, "Do any of you have good picture books that you would recommend to Elaine to give to this little boy? There are a lot of them out there, but it might be helpful to have some specific recommendations of ones you have found helpful."*

SUPPORTING POSITIVE TEAM AND GROUP COMMUNICATION AND INTERACTIONS

The quality of relationships and communication will directly affect team and group supervision effectiveness: The supervisor has many ways of helping to make these positive and constructive. She can be a careful and attentive listener (which may, at times, be difficult if she also feels responsible for having the group make a decision and move forward). She will then be a model for the group as a whole. She can be mindful of the need to elicit input and participation from team or group members who are more reticent and set limits for those who tend to dominate the conversation. She can reframe the discussion or ask clarifying questions when it appears that team members may not be understanding each other, and she can shine a light on areas of commonality—even when there appear to be major disagreements.

> *Sarah and Janine, I can see that you have different ideas about how we should address Mrs. Olsen's inconsistent attendance, but it seems that you both agree that a likely cause is her preoccupation with her older daughter's troubles at school. Let's*

think about what might be a realistic expectation under the circumstances and then talk about how best to approach Mrs. Olsen.

Group discussions often have a tendency to meander and lose their focus. The supervisor can use strategies such as creating a "parking lot" to keep track of questions or issues to be addressed at a later date. A list of these topics can be kept, so that no one's concerns are ignored or dismissed, but the group is still able to stay on track. At times, a subject will surface that elicits strong feelings and reactions from the group but is not strictly relevant to the topic at hand. It is helpful for the supervisor to acknowledge this and the intense emotions attached to the subject. She should assure the group members that they will have a chance to explore it more fully when they can give it the time it deserves. Likewise, the supervisor may have concerns about content or team interactions that need to be addressed, but rather than interrupting or redirecting the ongoing discussion, she may simply make a comment highlighting the issue, with a commitment to return to it later.

Inevitably, there will be times when the team or group is pulled apart either because of conflicts about specific issues or as a result of subtle but powerful disturbances in the relationships among group members. These could be related to a history of negative interactions in the past; differences in race, education, ethnicity, or class; past personal experiences; or differing assumptions about roles and scope of practice. The supervisor needs to be acutely aware of "zones of silence"—that is, topics or issues that staff members avoid and seem too uncomfortable to discuss but that have a strong presence nonetheless. The supervisor can seek ways of bringing up difficult issues in a safe and productive manner, sometimes by simply commenting on them and then stepping back. She will need to tolerate pauses when no one is speaking and resist the temptation to step in and save the day. This entails learning to ride out difficult moments and allow team members to repair the relationships within the group.

A supervisor will have to be willing to let go, to realize that she cannot be solely responsible for repairing team relationships or for ensuring that everyone is friends. She can, however, set standards of conduct and establish expectations for the ways team or group members treat each other and work together in the job setting. She can also ensure that everyone is treated equally, that no one is embarrassed in front of the group, and that they all have access to the same information. Lines of communication should be clear and open to all. If one team member treats another in a disrespectful manner during a team meeting, the supervisor has to figure out if there is a way to address the breach in the group and how to follow up in individual supervision.

*Suzy is the supervisor in a supervision group that meets to work on case formula-
tions and treatment plans for a small group of infant mental health clinicians. In a
meeting to discuss a baby who has just been placed in foster care, Carol blurts out
to her colleague Jane, "You are going on and on about the baby's diagnosis, but
you don't seem to realize the depth of what has just happened to this kid." Jane
replies in a disgusted tone, "Here we go again." Suzy takes a deep breath, working
on her own self-regulation, and says, "Carol, I think we are all worried about this
little kid, but I wonder if there is a different way we could express our feelings
rather than accusing one another of not caring." Carol then turns to Jane and
says, "I am sorry; you are just so calm, cool, and collected, and I am an emotional wreck about this." Later in individual supervision, Suzy checks in with
Carol to discuss ways she can monitor her feelings and expressions so they are
more supportive of her team members.*

ENHANCING CRITICAL THINKING—SUPPORTING EXPLORATION AND REFLECTION ON THE PART OF THE TEAM OR SUPERVISORY GROUP

A team or supervisory group will often be called on to solve a problem, collaborate on a
program development project, or work together to formulate a diagnostic impression and
intervention plan. The supervisor is in a position to facilitate the process, much as she does
during individual supervision sessions. She can help the team explore complex situations,
attend to the "big picture," and maintain their focus. The supervisor can ask clarifying
questions (e.g., "Why do you think the mom is so inconsistent in her follow-through?"),
seek additional information (e.g., "What more would we need to know about this child's
birth history?"), and remind the group to look for possible strengths or resources
(e.g., "Are there any other family members who can share the caregiving responsibilities
while mom is in the hospital?"). The supervisor can then summarize to move forward.

*It seems like most of you are feeling that it is too dangerous for Caroline to
continue to see this family at home because of the continuing domestic violence
between the mom and dad. Let's move on to think how she can continue to be
involved and also how to think about the mom and the kids.*

The supervisor should pay special attention to issues that have been left out of a discussion.
Sometimes these relate to the broader context: culture, race, class, and other areas of

diversity. Sometimes issues about the child or a key family member may have been missed. The supervisor can help the team by inserting questions or cues about omitted aspects of the discussion.

> *We have been talking a lot about this little boy, but it seems that we haven't taken into account the significance of the fact that he is placed in a classroom where he does not really know the language.*

She can identify underlying themes or trends and keep track of the group's past discussions and decisions.

> *I am a bit concerned because in the last few weeks it seems as if we have identified a large number of children as having language-processing problems. I wonder if we have been overly influenced by the conference on language disorders we attended last month. We need to step back and make sure we are considering other possibilities.*

Teams and supervisory groups have a tendency to engage in "hydroplaning" or "group-think"—that is, deciding on an interpretation and course of action without fully exploring the situation. They may not pay attention to the strong feelings associated with an issue or overlook practical details that could affect the outcome of their decision. A related phenomenon is when one team member makes a strong case for a particular point of view or plan and the others jump on the bandwagon without having thoughtfully considered the alternatives. In both instances, the supervisor can intervene and remind the group of the work they need to do before they are in a position to come to consensus and make any decisions. She can insert a pause or a subtle signal to the group that they should slow down and consider the broader implications.

> *A family support team has been asked to move their community playgroup to a new location while the current space is being renovated. One team member suggests that the group should just be suspended during the 6 months that the community center is being remodeled. Others quickly agree, stating that it would be too much work to find an alternative site and that it will give everybody a chance to catch their breath. The supervisor listens for a few minutes and then asks, "I wonder how this will be for the families who are attending the group?"*

When a staff person gives a presentation to the group about a case where she finds herself stuck and unable to make progress, her teammates will often jump in and deluge her with a multitude of suggestions and recommendations. These unsolicited quick fixes are often based on what they themselves have done in similar situations. This mountain of suggestions can overwhelm the person presenting the problem, sometimes creating feelings of incompetence. It is the supervisor's responsibility to cue the group to slow down and help the staff person fully explore the situation, discover what her own needs and concerns are, and then together think of some possible interpretations and next steps.

> *In her supervisory group, Nanae, an early interventionist, tearfully says that Devin's father had been wounded in a drive-by shooting that Devin and his mom had witnessed. Team members immediately begin to pile on suggestions: "That mom needs to get in the support group." "Be sure Devin gets referred for therapy." "You need to be careful—that family might be involved with a gang." The supervisor notes, "These are ideas worth exploring, but let's think a minute about the direction we are taking in our discussion." One team member replies, "I think this shooting makes us anxious, so we are all about problem solving and have forgotten about Nanae's feelings and needs."*

Teams and groups, like individuals, have a tendency to be influenced by the past when encountering new situations. This can, of course, be quite appropriate; the team uses what it learned and applies that knowledge to the new circumstance. However, at times, the past can exert a negative, or distorting, influence. The supervisor should be alert to this possibility and help staff members analyze the situation in an objective and open-minded manner.

> *I've heard back from everyone that they are pretty reluctant to collaborate with the Lil' Round-Up child care center for our parent–toddler playgroups. Several of you mentioned concerns about their curriculum and whether the child care staff members would be attentive to the social–emotional needs of the children. This is certainly an important consideration—who would like to go with me to visit and observe at the center? We need to keep an open mind, which is a little difficult, I know, since our experience last year at the Wee Ones center was pretty bad.*

Team or group supervisory discussions can seem fragmented and disjointed, especially when individual members focus on aspects of a situation of specific concern to them. Some team members may be more detail-oriented or concerned with the regulatory consequences of a decision, whereas others may be more interested in creating an overall vision or plan. Some may concentrate more on the affective components of their work. The supervisor can help integrate these different perspectives into a coherent whole, capitalizing on the diversity of the group rather than being paralyzed by it. She should facilitate the process by which the team can discover and articulate key issues, identify missing information, make note of strong feelings, formulate functional goals, and, if warranted, develop an integrated plan. And finally, the supervisor also can play a major role in supporting a transdisciplinary approach and promoting consideration of issues within a broader agencywide or interagency context.

STRATEGIES TO SUPPORT EFFECTIVE TEAM FUNCTIONING AND GROUP SUPERVISION

In the preceding sections of this chapter, we have described skills a supervisor needs to successfully fulfill the role of team leader or group supervisor. The following are some specific strategies the supervisor can use to help the team or group do its best work.

Forecasting

Some staff members are able to process new information quickly and generate ideas and solutions on the spot. Others need more time to think about an issue, explore their own feelings and reactions, and develop a response or proposal. It is very helpful for the supervisor to preview upcoming issues, changes, and discussion topics prior to team meetings or group supervision. This forecasting allows others time to process information, formulate their questions, and articulate an opinion before the group meets. The supervisor can identify themes for future conversations and set up a schedule for presentations that highlight particular kinds of cases. All team members can then be well prepared and will be more likely to contribute to the group.

Use of a Specific Case Presentation/Case Discussion Format

It is helpful for the team to have an agreed-upon format for their case presentations or problem-solving discussions. This framework will help slow the process down, encourage broad exploration before coming to any decisions, and provide a road map for developing an action plan. It will provide structure and a way of thinking and working together. This has many benefits: It builds a sense of safety because it is predictable, it helps staff members stay focused and organized and therefore more efficient, and it teaches critical thinking by identifying the steps needed for a thoughtful problem-solving process.

For example, the Portage Project experience-based case discussion format identifies three phases of the discussion process (Copa, Lucinski, Olsen, & Wollenburg, 1999). In the first phase, the staff members bringing the case or issue to the group "tell the story." They give basic information about the child, family, and progress of the work. They describe their thoughts and feelings as related to the issue or situation. They present the group with their initial questions or dilemmas. In the second phase, the team helps with further exploration by asking clarifying questions, trying to identify potential strengths and resources, and discovering what additional information is needed to move forward. Toward the end of this phase, the presenters are asked to restate their key questions, which by this point have often changed. In the third and final phase, interpretations are proposed, plans are made for next steps, including how to obtain the additional information needed, and the presenters are asked to summarize the discussion, including their own feelings about the process.

A discussion format such as the one described above accomplishes several important goals. It allows for a deep and broad exploration of a complex issue, drawing on the expertise of the group as a whole. It prevents premature decision making or jumping to conclusions. It acknowledges the importance of staff members' feelings and reactions and provides emotional support. It ensures adequate attention to potential strengths and resources without minimizing the very real difficulties and challenges. It results in a possible interpretation and proposal for a plan of action, with the explicit expectation that these will be revisited and very likely revised. And finally, it offers the presenter an opportunity to reflect on the process as a whole and then to move forward.

Minimize and Contain Time Spent on Administrative Issues

Unless the supervisor makes a conscious and persistent effort to limit the team or group supervisory time devoted to consideration of topics such as billing, caseloads, regulatory compliance, and other administrative concerns, these can easily come to dominate group meetings. Group time should be preserved for consideration of only those administrative issues that need to be processed and discussed by the team as a whole: simply reading and reviewing memos or other administrative guidelines should be avoided. The supervisor can commit to sending out such materials in advance of the meeting and establish an expectation that all team members will have read them prior to the meeting. Group time can then be used to address specific questions and concerns. There should be a set time on the team meeting agenda for review of administrative issues: ideally this is at the end of the meeting. This will preserve the earlier parts of the team meeting, when staff members are more likely to have energy and be creative, for consideration of important issues dealing with a child, a family, or the program.

Maximize Time Spent Talking About the Work

Groups serve many purposes, including providing a social and supportive connection. In a reflective model of group interaction and group supervision, staff members are invited to consider their own feelings and reactions. It is important for supervisors to figure out how to support and honor individual circumstances and emotional needs while avoiding the temptation to overemphasize personal issues or needs. Reflective supervisors and leaders need to acknowledge, listen, support, and help move the discussions about the individual staff member's need or family concern back into the realm of the work to be done.

Ronnie is a Healthy Families home visitor who has recently lost her own mother. She was encouraged to take more time off by her supervisor, Toby, but she insisted on coming back to work. She is having a hard time with her loss, and the group has listened to her speak about what this loss will mean. After about 20 minutes, Toby softly asks her what it is like to be with other mothers when she has lost her own. Then a group member asks if she feels her work is suffering. Ronnie says no, but she wonders how to explain to her clients why she is crying so often. One of the staff members wonders if she needs some time for herself to grieve. Another staff person wonders if families might hide their troubles and worries if they see she is fragile. At the end of the group, Ronnie asks to speak to Toby alone. She bursts out crying and asks for help arranging for a longer leave.

Maintaining a Focus on Issues of Interest or Importance to the Group as a Whole

Individual group members may bring up topics that are relevant only to one or two other members. Often, the team meeting time is one of the few opportunities they have to be together, and so there is a natural tendency to use the group time for discussion of these issues. The supervisor can respect their need to communicate with each other, while at the same time protecting the very limited meeting time by providing some mechanism for supporting these individual connections. For example, a flip chart can be positioned by the door so that, as staff members come into the meeting, they can write down who they need to talk to before leaving the meeting. The supervisor can open the meeting by asking if anyone else needs to touch base with a colleague and then adding those names to the list. This strategy also sends the clear message that team time should be saved for issues of concern to the whole group.

Monitoring Group Process

It is important for reflective supervisors to notice shifts in engagement and open a space for staff members to comment on a feeling, tone, or mood that the supervisor may not fully understand.

Sandy, the supervisor, notices during group meetings that there is often a lull in the discussions and that team members seem to be looking at their watches quite frequently. In a neutral tone, she notes that the group doesn't seem to be as lively as before and asks, "Has anything happened?" Someone replies that the new assessment forms are way too cumbersome. Sandy thanks the individual who has spoken up and asks if this is troubling others as well.

Offering Regular Opportunities for Feedback

Periodically, supervisors should check in with group members to get a broad picture of the usefulness of the group or effectiveness of the team. This feedback can be solicited during a meeting or in writing. Questions might include: How is the group useful to you? Are there ways it could be more helpful? Is there anything happening in the group that makes it hard for you to participate? Do you have any ideas about how we could improve our work together? This feedback can be used to strengthen and improve team/group processes. Common feedback for groups that are not working includes issues such as lack of clarity about purpose, members who talk too much or offend others, lack of follow-up, or an unaddressed strain among group members.

Providing Consistent Follow-Up

When the supervisor demonstrates a high level of accountability to the team or group, she helps set the standard for others to follow. Keeping notes during team meetings, sending out minutes, following through on agreed-upon tasks, and following up on discussions from previous meetings all provide a sense of continuity. These activities will underscore the importance of teamwork and the supervisor's commitment to the group. Follow-up might include sending out resources that were mentioned, thanking the team for a hard discussion, or clarifying information the group might find useful. The following are examples of brief e-mails sent out by supervisors after a team or supervisory meeting:

I appreciated our exploration of the concern about favoritism today. It was a hard discussion, but I think we took it on in a diplomatic and thoughtful way.

***

Thanks for your hard work on the field trip policies. I am hopeful that the new guidelines will help us all make these great events for kids and families. Bring in any additional thoughts so we can finish that up next week.

***

I am attaching the article on early signs of autism that I mentioned in our supervision group. I hope you can find time to read it before we meet next week. I think it will be helpful in thinking about the child of Kristy's who we were talking about yesterday.

TEAM AND GROUP CHARACTERISTICS THAT CAN INTERFERE WITH EFFECTIVE FUNCTIONING: AVOIDING THE SINKHOLES

We have all had the experience of being on a team that has difficulty accomplishing its work and where relationships among team members are poor. Although each team has its own history and individual challenges, there are some team or group characteristics that are predictable barriers to success. The supervisor should use her leadership position to prevent or counteract these barriers before they have a chance to damage the team's effectiveness or morale.

Unclear Objectives or Expectations

As noted earlier in this chapter, one of the supervisor's primary roles is to help the team or group develop a clear vision and set goals that are understood by all. For example, if child or family case staffings are part of the team's work and part of the regular agenda, it is important to clarify expectations about the purpose of the staffings and the degree of preparation required. If some staff members see these discussions as pertinent only to those team members directly involved with the child or family being discussed, they are likely to tune out and disengage from the conversation. If, however, the supervisor has made it clear that everyone is expected to provide support and thoughtful assistance, then the whole group is likely to stay engaged. The supervisor can encourage this by using the specific case discussions to highlight important themes relevant for other children and families and to make the connection between the case under consideration and others taken up in previous meetings.

A common source of difficulty on teams is misunderstanding about the role of the team in making programmatic decisions. This can lead to a good deal of frustration and even anger. The supervisor should let the team know if she is gathering input and opinions to be brought forward to agency administrators or if the team is actually in a position to make a plan or a decision on its own.

Ill-Defined Roles

Unclear roles can lead to considerable stress and distress. First of all, it is important to clarify whether there is a team leader, and if so, what her responsibilities are. Some teams may have a rotating team facilitator, while others may cast the supervisor or manager in this position. Second, if the team is made up of professionals from different disciplines, there must be a clarification of expectations regarding discipline-specific input. On a multidisciplinary or transdisciplinary team, all members are likely to contribute equally to a discussion regarding a child or family. This is done with an understanding that individual team members have expertise in particular areas but that others may have relevant observations or questions related to that area. Other kinds of teams may have less tolerance for this type of cross-disciplinary discussion and even be offended when it occurs. Finally, there needs to be a shared understanding as to each team member's responsibility for preparation and follow-up activities: who develops the agenda, who takes notes, and who carries out the agreed-upon plan. When these responsibilities are not clear, the team is unlikely to be efficient or effective.

Issues related to role clarity also arise in group supervision. For example, what happens when a group member has a supervisor who is not present for the group discussion? How do information, interpretations, and recommendations get communicated to that supervisor? There should be a clear policy regarding these lines of communication.

> *Lydia is a teacher in a child care program that is part of a large homeless shelter. She takes part in a monthly reflective supervision group with four other teachers. The reflective supervisor who leads the group is a mental health clinician in the program. At today's meeting, the teachers discuss a child who is worrisome to them. He does not eat and seems more and more lethargic. The supervisor raises a question about his health and immediately realizes that there will need to be discussion of how the information about the child's deteriorating health will be brought to the program's social worker. As this is discussed, the supervisor wonders to herself if the makeup of the group needs to be expanded to include other team members, such as the social worker.*

Lack of Boundaries

Problems related to a lack of well-defined professional boundaries arise at many levels. They can occur in relationships involving staff members and clients, supervisor and supervisees, and team or supervisory group members with each other. In some instances, a team or group may gradually come to spend more and more of its time on social activities such as birthday parties, potlucks, and holiday celebrations to the point where these interfere with the group members' ability to accomplish their work. In other instances, team members may forget to observe the standards of confidentiality that are an absolute prerequisite for developing an atmosphere of safety and trust. Or, some individuals may express strong political or religious feelings that are not shared by the group and that are inappropriate in a work setting. Sometimes team members import fund-raising or business matters into the group and create uncomfortable pressures to participate or purchase goods that are being sold. The supervisor is in a position to address these issues as they arise and to help the group maintain appropriate professional relationships.

"Us Versus Them" Mentality

There is a natural tendency for a group to develop a collective sense of being under siege from a common "enemy." Problems or difficulties are attributed to that entity (such as a regulatory agency), and much time can be spent bemoaning its shortcomings. This process does little to help the group solve its own problems, come up with constructive ideas, or move forward, and it closes the door on any attempt to understand the other entity's point of view, needs, or constraints. It also interferes with the team's ability to form any working relationships with representatives of the other group. In these situations, the supervisor must take the lead in applying the principles of relationship-based work to interactions with the "opposing" agency: wondering about the reasons for its behaving as it does, reaching out to make a connection with someone in that agency, and seeking to discover any examples when things have gone well between the two groups.

Defensive Routines

Defensive routines are analogous to bad habits that can develop in response to stressful or difficult situations. These routines are often manifested as avoidance or even as passive-aggressive behaviors. The supervisor may enable the process or, alternately, spotlight the issue and help the group find a more productive way of handling its problems.

> *The members of one team know that budget cuts mean they do not have the resources to continue to serve their traditional catchment areas. However, they cannot bear to make the hard choices about which areas they can keep and which they have to let go. As a result, they keep coming up with additional pieces of information that they need before they can finally decide. This endless information seeking has spanned several months and has allowed them to put off the final decision. In this example, the supervisor joins in and prolongs the information seeking rather than helping the group members notice their defensive routine that is keeping them from making a hard decision.*
>
> ***
>
> *The members of another team have become polarized by a personal feud between two of its members. Every issue that comes up for discussion degenerates into a contest between those two individuals, with everyone else being forced to take sides. The actual conflict is not mentioned, but the two debate the pros and cons of different treatment approaches almost as if they are reenacting World War II.*

In both these instances, supervisory leadership is needed to break through the defensive routines and allow the teams to work together effectively and respectfully.

Differences in Learning, Interaction, and Communication Styles

There are tremendous benefits to be gained from having a team or supervisory group with diverse backgrounds, training, experience, skills, and strengths. Group members will differ according to gender, class, culture, age, temperament, and many other parameters too numerous to mention. This diversity is a great strength, but it can also be a source of difficulty particularly when it relates to interpersonal styles and approaches. For example, some people think by talking through an issue, while others wait until they have fully processed and digested an issue before making a comment. Some are focused on details, while others focus on the big picture. Some are very interested in new ideas and projects, while others work better within established routines and structures. Some are quite comfortable with conflict and disagreement. Others shy away from even hints of a contest. Some use humor as a form of aggression and others as a way of smoothing the way. Some are afraid of authority, and others seek to challenge. Some thrive when they are the center of attention, but for many the spotlight is painful because they are shy or their cultural norms require them to be quiet and deferential.

These differences can be sources of difficulty or conflict and can limit the effectiveness of the team unless the supervisor finds ways to encourage appreciation, respect, patience, and tolerance. The supervisor herself must be acutely aware of her own styles, preferences, and difficulties and make sure that she is not privileging or favoring group members with whom she is the most comfortable.

Team or supervisory group functioning will be harmed when members or supervisors are judgmental, embarrass each other in public, tease or dismiss a concern, or assume and jump to conclusions without listening. Groups are also negatively affected when members or supervisors cross-examine a colleague, overlook communication style differences, or make comments related to culture, class, gender, or age that might be hurtful or offensive. Team members may not have a negative intent, but a comment can be hurtful and can cause rifts to develop in the team or supervisory group. The supervisor often has to think on her feet and decide if a remark should be addressed in the moment or at a later time. The following examples illustrate one supervisor taking a "here-and-now" approach and one scenario in which the supervisor's response is delayed:

> *In a team meeting, an English-speaking home visitor talks to the group about a family she has just started to work with. She says she has just discovered that the mother and father are bilingual but that the 18-month-old speaks only Spanish. Several members of the team state strongly that they think it is unethical for her, as an English speaker, to work with the family. They say that the agency needs to support families to use their home language with their children. The supervisor stops the discussion and acknowledges the strong feelings of the group. She reminds the group that the home visitor was asking for assistance in exploring this situation. The supervisor follows with some questions about what the parents thought about the matter, what it would mean to change providers at this point, and if there even was a Spanish-speaking staff person available for this family.*
>
> ***
>
> **Supervisee:** *I know Ana didn't mean any harm during our group yesterday, but I felt so stupid when she asked why on earth I hadn't brought up this family sooner. It makes me think I might be just better off keeping my mouth shut.*
>
> **Supervisor:** *I was wondering how you felt when she said that. I'm pretty sure she didn't actually mean to come off so critically. I was really glad you brought the family up. We have all had that experience of starting to tell about a family and realizing in the middle of our story that there is something we might have done differently. This is really what the group is for.*
>
> *What would it be like for you to talk about this with Ana? If you feel up to it, you might let Ana know that you felt kind of badly after she made her comment. That could help her realize the effect she has on others.*

There are many ways that the supervisor can help to mitigate potential problems and provide an environment in which everyone thrives and contributes. She can start by observing the following:

- Who participates, and who does not

- How team members take turns talking and handling interruptions

- Whether any member or members seem to dominate

- If there appears to be subgroups or cliques within the larger group

- What topics appear to be off-limits. Are there any "elephants" in the room?

- If silence is tolerated, and if so, for how long

On the basis of these observations, she will be able to help the team or group to develop ways of working together so that each person is respected and can contribute. She can be sure that she is fair and consistent in her treatment of each person and that she really listens to what each person is saying, demonstrates clear concern for each one, and always follows through on her commitments and responsibilities. She can step forward and directly address areas of conflict or discomfort in such a way that each person feels safe to express herself.

It may be helpful to engage in periodic team-building activities designed to heighten awareness as to each individual's style and the value of their contribution in teams and groups. For example, programs may bring in a trainer to administer a personality inventory such as the Myers-Briggs Type Indicator (MBTI; Myers & McCaulley, 1985). This tool allows individuals to discover their preferred ways of thinking and acting and how they tend to perceive the world. No traits are considered more or less positive. The trainer can guide the team to understand the underlying concepts as they apply in the work setting and then to think together about how similarities or differences among team members might affect the way they work together. So, for example, a person who is higher on the MBTI "thinking" function might be more likely to make decisions based on logic and facts. Someone who is higher on the MBTI "feeling" function might be more likely to come to a conclusion through empathy. Because both functions are vital for successful reflective work, training activities will help staff members be able to appreciate that it is valuable to have both types of individuals on a team. These activities also help all members appreciate what others bring to the group so that diversity can be understood as a source of strength rather than a source of weakness.

We have developed an exercise based on Phillip Schlechty's classic article on education reform (Schlechty, 1993). Participants are told a parable about the inhabitants of a small village on the East Coast who respond differently to rumors they hear about the wonders of the West. A few *trailblazers* like to go where no one has gone before, and they depart without maps or sufficient supplies. The *pioneers* follow in the path of the *trailblazers* because they are excited by the tales they have heard. The *settlers* in the village wait until there are roads and a functioning hotel before they venture out West, and the *stay at homes* enjoy the stories but put off the trip until they are sure there are paved streets and houses. The *saboteurs* think that the West is evil and the trip is a bad idea, and they try to find ways to keep the *pioneers, settlers,* and *stay at homes* from even considering leaving the village.

In this exercise, individuals are asked to think about which group they usually fall into in the work setting and then to meet with other members of their group to talk about why they think they fall into that category. After this first exercise, individuals are asked to list the benefits and difficulties of belonging to each group and discuss this with members of the other groups. The process can then lead to a discussion of how these differences are invaluable in a group setting.

Collective Tendency to Put Self-Interest Above the Group's Interests

While self-interest could describe an individual team member, it could also apply to the team as a whole. In these instances, each person appears to be most interested in protecting her own turf or pushing her own point of view. This can come about for a number of reasons. There may be a serious shortage of resources, and individuals may feel pushed to simply try to get the most for themselves, their families, or their program or team. Or, there may be an impression that decisions are made capriciously and that the supervisor listens to whoever advocates most forcefully. The group may lack clarity of purpose and have no clear vision or mission to guide its work.

There are various ways of addressing these problems, beginning with an identification of the possible underlying causes. As described above, it is critically important for the supervisor to give each person the same respect and consideration. Every effort should be made to have the team involved in the decision-making process and to make choices as a group. When the team is exposed to major stressors—for example, reduced funding, significant changes in regulatory demands, or loss of treasured colleagues—the supervisor can create a space for expressing the many feelings likely to be present. Only then will staff members be ready to consider their options and start to make a plan for the future.

If there is a clear vision, mission, and guiding principles, the supervisor can reference them as a way of refocusing the team members on their joint responsibilities and the meaning of their work. This will help avoid a conceptual drift away from the fundamental values and shared purpose. From time to time, the team may need to pause and reconsider these foundational concepts as a way of recalibrating and coming back together.

INDIVIDUALS WHO MAY INTERFERE WITH THE TEAM PROCESS

Most groups will include at least one or two members whose particular style or individual issues will at times be a barrier to collaborative teamwork. These difficulties may be chronic or surface only during times of stress. Following is a brief sketch of some of the more common players in the team or group drama:

- The Bully: intimidates others through actions, words, or nonverbal communication.

- The Dominator: tends to control the discussion by talking much more than other team members.

- The Yes-But... Person: consistently comes up with an objection to any idea.

- The Know-It-All: never admits to needing assistance, is not interested in learning new skills, and is quick to tell others what they should and should not do.

- The Clown: uses humor to derail the discussion, calling attention to herself while at the same time diverting attention from the issue at hand.

- The Whiner: can be depended on to complain about something, regardless of the situation, generally without offering any constructive suggestions.

- The Ostrich: keeps her head in the sand and does not want to acknowledge or deal with looming problems.

- The Challenger: may have a low tolerance for any kind of authority, is quick to present objections to any proposal, and questions the basic structure of the decision-making process.

- The Disorganizer: often has a similar effect on the group as the Clown, has difficulty staying focused and on-task, and introduces red herrings that can derail the group process.

- The Princess: sees all issues through the lens of how a decision will affect her, demands special attention and consideration, and may be quick to imagine that "my sky is falling!"

- The Apple-Polisher: is highly motivated to please the supervisor or other persons in a position of authority and goes out of her way to do special favors or to agree with whatever the supervisor says.

- The Obsessor: has a one-track mind and keeps pulling the group discussion back to the issue of primary concern to her.

Although all team members have a duty to help build a strong, well-functioning team, the supervisor has a particular responsibility for the well-being of the whole. In thinking about how to work with the range of individuals and the challenges they may bring, the supervisor can use the principles of reflective practice and relationship-based work to guide her.

One of her first steps would be to try to understand the meaning of the staff person's behavior and to develop some empathy for her by taking her perspective or point of view. The supervisor can observe that person over time and explore with her directly what she was thinking and feeling during particular interactions. It is essential that the supervisor not make any assumptions, as they may be far from the truth.

The supervisor should also take time to think about and perhaps consult with her own supervisor about the actual effect or importance of the seemingly difficult staff members' behavior. She may discover that although a staff person's communication style is irritating to her, it does not actually seem to be interfering with team functioning. In these cases, the supervisor runs a real risk of overreacting to that team member, so that the team setting no longer seems safe. In supervision, the supervisor can be helped to think about the ways she may be contributing to the behavior that is so perplexing to her. The supervisor also needs to be careful to avoid getting overly focused on one team member's reactions, behaviors, or contributions. These should be kept in perspective so as not to consume a disproportionate amount of her supervisory time and attention. It is critical that the supervisor try to maintain some balance and perspective when evaluating the situation. One way to do this is to make a conscious effort to focus on that staff person's strengths and to identify what resources she brings to the group.

Once the supervisor has observed, explored, and reflected on the challenges presented by a group member, she will need to find a way to give that person feedback in a manner that is helpful, supportive, and clear. This may be challenging with staff members who have difficulty with self-reflection and who do not respond well to observations offered to them. This must be done in private and with sensitivity so as not to make that person feel ashamed. The spotlighting techniques described in chapter 4 can be very helpful here. Through this process the supervisor articulates clearly and simply the nature of her concern, including the effect on work with the team. She then provides an opening for the supervisee to respond.

Of course, the supervisor then has to be prepared to receive feedback herself, as it is always possible that she is actually a contributor to the situation. She must keep an open mind and be prepared to accept and take responsibility for her part. Here is one example:

Helene is the most articulate member of the supervisory group. She has a few talking points that she will go on about for a very long time. People begin to fidget when she speaks, anticipating what is to come. After observing this pattern for several months, Alex, the new supervisor, finds that her more subtle ways of trying to include others have failed. So, in her individual supervision meeting, she asks Helene about the issues she is so passionate about. Together, they note their importance, and then Alex asks Helene if she is aware that sometimes she brings these up in a way that is out of context. In the discussion, Alex learns more about why these issues are so central to Helene and also gets her agreement to be more discreet and bring these up only when they really apply.

SUMMARY

In this chapter, we have discussed the importance of team and group supervisory work in infant and early childhood work, the role of the supervisor as team leader or group reflective supervisor, supervisory strategies for promoting effective team and group functioning, and some of the challenges that arise in doing this work. We close by delineating some of the characteristics of a successful team or group, and describing what it feels like when things are going well.

An effective team or supervisory group will ideally have these features:

- A clear vision, mission, guiding principles. and communication guidelines

- Well-defined roles

- Effective leadership

- An atmosphere of trust, safety, and mutual respect

- Space for strong emotions and different points of view

- Open and direct communication

- Adequate resources such as time and space

- Well-defined outcomes and a means of evaluating them

- A shared dedication to high-quality services

- Synergy among the team members

- The ability of members to get their work done effectively and efficiently

If we are lucky and work hard enough, we will each have the pleasure of being part of a successful team or group. We can recognize it when it happens. Staff members come to the meetings fully prepared and ready to participate, having left other tasks behind. They come ready to approach problems in a collaborative and constructive manner, having already started to think about possible solutions. Everyone participates. The group members are able to take the time they need to reflect and explore broadly but are also able to come to decisions and make plans in a timely manner. They do not stay stuck in repetitive cycles of frustration and inaction. Members can tolerate the ambiguity of complex situations. There is an atmosphere of calm but also an alertness and lively spirit within the group.

Team and group members know each other well and are supportive of each other. They are respectful and know how to help each other. There are no obvious zones of silence; difficult issues can be raised and discussed in a safe and respectful manner. Staff members take responsibility for their own actions and are self-reflective and able to accept and use constructive feedback. Team time is protected; everyone arrives on time and stays fully engaged.

All members take advantage of the opportunity to learn from each other. There is a creative energy that is focused appropriately on critical needs of the program. Ideas discussed in team and group meetings start to be discussed and referenced outside the meeting.

At these times, it feels like being a member of a gold-medal rowing team: Everyone is strong, they pull together, and the boat flies through the water.

GUIDING QUESTIONS

Think of a positive and a negative team experience which you have had in the past few years.

- What made them positive or negative, and how did these experiences affect you?

- What role did you play in each?

- Is there anything you might have done differently?

- Do you have any "lessons learned" from these experiences?

REFERENCES

Copa, A., Lucinski, L., Olsen, E., & Wollenburg, K. (1999). Promoting professional and organizational development: A reflective practice model. *Zero to Three, 20*(1), 3–9.

Myers, I., & McCaulley, M. (1985). *Manual: A guide to the development and use of the Myers-Briggs Type Indicator* (2nd ed.). Palo Alto, CA: Consulting Psychologists Press.

Schlechty, P. (1993). On the frontier of school reform with trailblazers, pioneers and settlers. *Journal of Staff Development, 14*(4), 46–51.

Siegel, D. (speaker) 2010. The neurobiology of "we": How relationships, the mind and the brain interact to shape who we are. (Audio recording no. ISBN 159179949x). Los Angeles: Mindsight Institute.

Further Readings

Bertacchi, J. (1996). Relationship-based organizations. *Zero to Three, 17*(2), 3–7.

Siegel, D., & Hartzell, M. (2003). *Parenting from the inside out.* New York: Tarcher.

CHAPTER 6

GOOD BEGINNINGS

This chapter describes three kinds of beginnings in reflective supervision that are basic to the development of quality program services:

• Orientation, training, and support for a new supervisor

• Formation of a new supervisory relationship with an individual or a group

• Revisiting a supervisory agreement when problems have occurred in a supervisory relationship

TRAINING FOR NEW SUPERVISORS: OFF TO A GOOD START

A new supervisor can be a recent hire or someone who has been promoted from within. Taking the time to get off to a good start will help avoid future problems and set a positive trajectory. It is prudent to assess the new supervisor's needs carefully and then provide training, orientation, and support before she is "in the thick of it" and has to assume full program responsibilities. It is tempting to take shortcuts or have new supervisors start their work right away in response to pressing program needs. This is especially true when hiring from within, as there may be an assumption that the new supervisor knows the ropes and is ready to go. After all, she has usually been chosen with care and often brings skills and knowledge that are needed right away. However, this "throw them off the dock" approach is usually problematic.

A training and orientation period for a new supervisor provides opportunities to learn about the agency culture: This is important even for someone who is promoted from within, because being in a supervisory position involves looking at the agency from a different perspective. It also allows time for relationship building with her own supervisor and other colleagues. This is an essential part of the orientation process and helps the new supervisor build a sense of her own support systems within the agency. During this time, the new supervisor can contract and clarify with her supervisor about the specific details of her job expectations. A new supervisor will be able to build a conceptual framework regarding overall job responsibilities—the big picture—while having the chance to start learning and practicing key skills. During this period, as the new supervisor learns more about her position, she can begin the process of self-assessment, which will help her to prioritize ongoing professional development needs.

Training for a new supervisor must have a strong interactive and experiential component, so that she can begin to have firsthand experience of reflective and relationship-based practice. Having the experience of learning to listen, slow down, step back, look for the big picture, take the perspective of others, explore, and attend to one's own reactions will help the new supervisor begin to internalize these core principles. Trainers should be sure to consistently point out the parallels between the supervisor's experiences in training and what she will seek to provide for her own staff members during supervision. These include multiple opportunities for critical thinking, reflection, exploration, and attending to their own feelings and reactions. Trainers can extend this thinking to help supervisors learn more about the ways supervision provides a kind of laboratory experience for staff members to learn to interact reflectively with parents, children, and colleagues.

The goal for any orientation and training process is for the new staff person to feel confident in a basic understanding of her position and assured that the program will provide the support needed to flourish in that role. However, each new supervisor will have different training needs, and so an assessment should be made of her current skills and competencies so that an individualized orientation can be designed. In supervisory training, one size will not fit all. In chapters 2 and 4, we identified five key supervisory roles, along with the knowledge, skills, and competencies needed to carry them out. These should be the foundation for supervisory training. A new supervisor and her own supervisor can review an inventory of knowledge, skills, and competencies for each key role and determine individual needs and priorities. This same inventory, or supervisory assessment tool, can be used later during ongoing supervision and referred to as a resource whenever there are job performance concerns. (See Appendix 1 Supervisors' Professional Development Guide for a sample assessment tool.)

Training for a new supervisor can be informal or formal, depending on the needs and number of staff members involved and the availability of training resources. Even in the most informal orientation and training situation, the time should be thoughtfully planned out with careful preparation of agendas, goals, and materials. Time to process information and training processes should be built into the agenda for each day.

Involving a variety of key people from the agency in the training will also help in the acculturation and relationship building that are needed for someone to move into a new position successfully. The message to the new supervisor should be that she will be exposed through the orientation and training to much of what she needs to know, but it is expected that it will take a much longer time to master the information and skills presented. The following is an outline of a basic agenda for new supervisor training covering five essential training content areas. We have used several vignettes to show how this basic agenda can be adapted to the particular needs of a new supervisor and her agency.

Training New Supervisors: Basic Agenda

In reality, much of the material in the introductory supervisory training will constitute an initial exposure and orientation to key concepts. Most participants are unlikely to remember all of the details shared, but if the training agenda is well developed, new supervisors will emerge with a kind of mental outline, a well-organized collection of orientation material, and a sense of being welcomed and linked to an organization that values reflection, dialogue, and transparency. It is important that the training be planned so there is enough time for the participants to digest the material a bit, ask questions, and begin to link the pieces presented together into a cohesive whole. In this section, we have listed categories of training topics and possible content under each. Organizations will need to think carefully about what materials and information will be most useful to the incoming supervisors. In some cases, there will be enough new supervisors to form a training group, but in many situations material will be covered during a series of one-on-one supervision meetings and observations. Staff members will be given materials for review and plenty of time for dialogue. However, no matter how informal the training may seem, it is important for there to be an agenda, goals, and a clear sequence to help the new supervisor understand both what is expected of her in her job and what she is expected to learn over time.

Learning the lay of the land

- Where am I? What kind of organization am I in, and what are its vision, mission, and history? Where does my program fit in the organizational picture?

- Who are my future supervisees, and what is their training? Where does this program fit in the system of care for young children in the community?

- What is the governance of the agency? Are there a board and advisory groups?

- What is the agency culture? Is this an agency that has many levels of authority and responsibility? How do people relate to one another?

- What are the funding streams and supports for the program?

- What are the expectations for a supervisor, and what levels of responsibility does a new supervisor assume?

- How are supervisors seen and valued?

- What is the place of supervision in the overall program structure?

- What are the specific licensure or training requirements needed to provide super-vision under the new supervisor's license or credential?

Learning the nuts and bolts

- What procedures are used, and what records are kept in the program? How are these used, and what is expected of the supervisor in terms of training others to do this, ensuring quality, and monitoring services?

- What staff training and support processes are in place for supervisees?

- In what ways are direct work with families similar to or parallel to reflective supervision? How are the similarities reflected in agency policies, processes, and culture?

- What are the human resource roles and responsibilities of the new supervisor? Often these include hiring, performance review, documentation, tracking time, vacation/sick policies, Family and Medical Leave Act benefits, and the Americans With Disabilities Act and Office of Economic Opportunity regulations. It is important that these administrative parts of the work be introduced at the same time as the training, technical assistance, mentoring, and support functions. It is essential that these topics be presented in a way that is reflective and relationship-based and that models the blended supervisory model right from the beginning.

- What administrative responsibilities will the new supervisor have? These could include such things as yearly evaluations of assigned supervisees, quality assurance for service reports, and logs of activities.

- What are the most important collaborating organizations, services, and referral sources for areas such as housing, adult health, literacy, and immigration services?

Articulating the reflective supervision model used in the agency

- Review of the service model in the program and agency

- Clear articulation of the conceptual model of supervision used, with appropriate handouts, outlines, schematics, and supplementary reading

- If a blended model of supervision is used, how is this operationalized? (see chapter 2)

- If a blended model is not used, how and by whom are quality assurance issues and performance evaluated?

- Roles of the reflective supervisor (see chapter 2)

- Key skills and competencies (see chapter 4)

- Engaging new supervisees and talking about how supervision happens

- Use of a supervision agreement (see Appendix 2) as a way of contracting and clarifying

- Review of team meetings and support processes that will involve the new supervisor

Building reflective supervision skills

- Core skills. The roles and basic competencies needed for reflective supervision are outlined in chapters 2 and 4. Mastery of these skills takes time, but it is essential for new supervisors to have at least a crash course of 1–2 days to think about the basics and learn about the supervisory model aspired to by the agency.

- Overview of common supervisory dilemmas (see chapter 8). This will assist supervisory trainees to preview challenges that may arise and provide some beginning guidance for how to address them.

Plan for supervision of the supervisor, future support, and development

During the orientation and training period, a new supervisor should be given opportunities to figure out with her supervisor the kinds of things that she will need to learn and how they can go about doing this. The areas of potential growth and development are described in chapters 2 and 4. A self-assessment form based on the supervisory roles described in chapter 2 is provided in Appendix 1. Having a road map to chart next steps in professional development can be reassuring to a new supervisor who, through orientation and training, begins to realize the magnitude of the supervisory role.

Other questions for discussion include:

- Who has the new supervisor been as a professional and what will a move to a supervisory position mean? What are the key experiences the new supervisor may have had with past supervisors?

- What kinds of support and supervision will the supervisor receive?

- What sorts of professional training opportunities are available?

- What are the priority needs for training as well as longer term needs of the new supervisor?

- What are the career paths for a supervisor in the agency and the broader community?

Each of the vignettes below provides an example illustrating how training in the five essential content areas can be provided in different settings.

Newly Hired Supervisory Staff Members in a Small Agency

Tanisha, an experienced infant mental health therapist, has moved into a position as a supervisor to a group of social workers, child care teachers, mental health providers, family advocates, and health aides working in a domestic violence shelter. Although Tanisha has had some exposure to traumatized children and families and training in treating families exposed to trauma, she does not know the laws, practices, and concerns related to women who were victims of domestic violence and their children. She also has no experience or understanding of what it takes to run a domestic violence shelter and the kinds of safeguards that must be in place. Tanisha has never supervised others but has received excellent supervision throughout her career. The agency wants Tanisha to jump right in because their needs are so great. Wisely, Tanisha requests a training period, and the director concedes that this will be necessary for her success. The plan below is jointly constructed by Tanisha and the director.

Learning the lay of the land

The agency that hired Tanisha does not have much time or energy to train her. She has been chosen for her knowledge of children and families, her compassion, and her clinical skills and flexibility. She is expected to supervise staff members, consult on cases, train new staff members and volunteers, write grants, and provide a small amount of direct service. Tanisha is given a three-page written orientation outline and schedule that guides her to different aspects of the program during a 5-day period. There are guiding questions under each section, and she also meets staff members responsible for different areas of the program. She observes as new clients come in, as clients participate in the child care or support groups, and as family advocates and clinicians work with clients. She also reads procedure manuals. The director of the program asks Tanisha to list questions about these materials and observations. The director sets aside an hour in the morning and in the afternoon to meet with Tanisha to discuss, ask and answer questions, and help her identify areas where she needs more information or more intensive training.

Learning the nuts and bolts

On Day 2 of her training, Tanisha is provided with materials including intake forms, a list of referring agencies, family action plans, and documentation requirements. On the following days, she continues her observations but uses the organizing documents to get a sense of what is required in different parts of the program. The forms are used as organizers to help Tanisha understand different aspects of the work in which she will play a vital part. In her discussion time, the director brings in other staff members such as child care teachers, family advocates, and the facilities manager so she can discuss their roles and their current needs for support. Hearing about current concerns directly from staff members is particularly helpful.

Articulating the reflective supervision model

On Day 2, Tanisha meets with the director for an hour to discuss how supervision has occurred in the past in the agency. The director notes that the previous supervisor had gotten swept up in the clinical work herself and had not been very available to staff members. Together, Tanisha and the director wonder how they might create a better balance, given that Tanisha will also be expected to do some direct clinical work. The director is clear with Tanisha that supervision must be reflective of the blended model and include attention to clinical issues as well as providing administrative oversight. She explains that she has to keep things funded and will rely on Tanisha to make sure that the records reflect the services accurately. At the same time, Tanisha will need to model a clinical approach that helps the staff members remain supportive and empathic with the high-risk families who come to their center exhausted and frightened. Children in the child care are often very dysregulated, which is difficult for the teachers. The director provides Tanisha with materials to read on reflective supervision.

Building reflective supervision skills

The director realizes that Tanisha will need instruction and mentoring in reflective supervision. She spends a half day with her, reviewing materials Tanisha has read and discussing how the principles of reflective supervision might play out in the setting. She locates a community training session on reflective supervision for Tanisha to attend as well. The director also offers to send Tanisha to a regular community-based reflective supervision support group where she can receive consultation that will supplement her regular meetings with the director.

Plan for supervision of the supervisor, future support, and development

After reviewing the supervisory self-assessment checklist, Tanisha feels that a first priority for her is to get acquainted with the laws by attending a court hearing for a domestic violence case, walking through what it takes to get a restraining order, and understanding the special regulations affecting undocumented immigrants. She follows this up by shadowing other workers during intake. To refresh her knowledge of how trauma affects young children, she reads materials recommended by shelter staff members. She notes that a future need of her own staff members will be to learn more about treatment for the kinds of trauma associated with domestic violence. She begins to think about learning specific vocabulary related to the kinds of work that she will be doing. She starts to feel at home and is comfortable enough to tell her supervisor that she feels she may have overestimated her own skills as a supervisor given the needs of the program. The director makes an agreement to meet with Tanisha for 2 hours of supervision a week for several months to become more comfortable with her job requirements.

The director also arranges for a time for staff members to get to know Tanisha informally at a luncheon and meeting. The program newsletter welcomes Tanisha, and her picture goes up on the bulletin board for staff members and parents.

New Supervisors Hired Because of Program Expansion: Applying Skills in Little Rapids

The city of Little Rapids has recently been granted funds to expand an Early Head Start program to start four new teams that will implement center and home visiting programs in an urban area. Each team has a supervisor; the program has selected four experienced Early Head Start staff members from their other programs for these new positions. Their job descriptions will include hiring and training their own teams. None of them has any experience with supervision, but all were chosen for their child development knowledge, familiarity with the program and agency, and leadership potential. The director works with a local consultant to develop and implement this training plan for the four new staff members.

Learning the lay of the land

On Day 1, the new supervisors get to meet their supervisor and the program director, and they learn about their job descriptions and their new responsibilities. They are given time to reflect on the role shift that they are undertaking and given support in exploring their thoughts about becoming supervisors. The individuals are given time to think carefully about what skills they are bringing from their old positions, what personal qualities they feel will be useful, and what things they will be learning to do that are new to them. The director also uses team-building activities to help them develop as a group, as she believes that this new group will benefit from a strong sense of collegiality.

At the end of the first day, the director carries out an exercise called "ghosts of supervisors past" in which the participants identify qualities and actions of supervisors from their own past that had helped them and those that had hindered their skill development. The new supervisors are asked to think about qualities of these past supervisors and think about those they want to cultivate.

Learning the nuts and bolts

On Day 2, the supervisory trainees review the kinds of documentation and monitoring for which they will be responsible, as well as the agency's evaluation structure. They meet with the supervisor and director of the current Early Head Start program and look at videos of home- and center-based activities. They participate in discussions about how to support staff members to use the Early Head Start program model. The national Early Head Start reporting and monitoring standards are reviewed.

Because the supervisors will be involved in hiring new staff members, the human resources director spends time with them reviewing interview procedures.

Articulating the reflective supervision model

On Day 3, the trainees are introduced to the blended model of reflective supervision in a training session conducted by the director and an outside trainer. The participants receive information on their various roles and on the skills needed to implement these roles. Particular attention is paid to the ways that reflective supervision is related to the service approaches outlined in the Early Head Start performance standards.

Building reflective supervision skills

This training day focuses on specific skills related to the supervisory contract with staff members, skills needed to address sensitive issues, and ways to integrate cultural and contextual sensitivity into their work. Participants are given more examples and practice with reflective supervision skills. Video clips of program activities are provided for discussion and role play.

Plan for supervision of the supervisor, future support, and development

On Day 5, participants are briefed on their own one-to-one supervisory structure and their regular supervisory team meetings. The trainees complete self- and group assessments related to the skills, knowledge, and support that they will need as supervisors. The individuals, and the group as a whole, prioritize their training and support needs. Individual and group plans are made to address these needs in the first 6 months.

The new supervisors learn about their own evaluation process and more about the structure of individual and group supervision. Trainees are told about the twice-yearly agency supervision training for all agency supervisors. Supervisory trainees also are given time to discuss structures for supporting one another.

A Direct Service Provider Becomes a Supervisor Within the Same Program: Ella Gets a Promotion

Ella is a home visitor in a community-based program for new parents and their babies. She has 10 years of experience and the deep respect of her peers. She has recently been promoted and will be replacing a supervisor who left the agency. Ella's agency values reflective supervision. There is little staff development money for outside training at this point, but experienced supervisors and the director come up with the following training plan for Ella.

Learning the lay of the land

Ella is very familiar with all aspects of the program, the job of a home visitor, and the community where she works. She has never been a supervisor, and her director spends a long time with her helping her think what it will mean for her to have this promotion. They discuss friendships that Ella has with people who are on the team she will now be supervising and ways she can create boundaries that will help her do her job. She is also helped to examine the feelings she has and the possibilities that others will feel slighted, envious, or annoyed that she has now gotten a different job and will be supervising the work that she has been doing for so long.

Learning the nuts and bolts

Ella spends Day 1 learning about the managerial aspects of her job, such as time sheets, payroll reports, and data systems. She learns about her job, her lines of support, and what she should do when she needs help with different kinds of problems.

Articulating the reflective supervision model

Prior to the training and orientation period, Ella is given many materials on the blended model of reflective supervision. After reviewing these materials, Ella meets with another supervisor to talk about ways that the reflective aspects of supervision are blended in with the administrative role. The experienced supervisor shows videos of her supervisory sessions to provide concrete examples for discussion. In these sessions, Ella is invited to think about what might be difficult for her in her new role. Later in the day, she discusses what she has learned and talks about things she might want to do in her new role to make supervision as effective as possible.

Building reflective supervision skills

Using case examples from her own work, Ella works with an agency supervisory trainer and identifies issues and concerns that have been hard for her in her role as a home visitor.

Using these examples, the trainer introduces core reflective supervision skills and allows Ella to practice. Later in the day, Ella and the trainer videotape a practice role play, with Ella playing the supervisor. The trainer points out ways she is attuned to the "home visitor." The trainer discusses the role play, pointing out skills, identifying alternative approaches, and asking Ella to reflect on what she has done in the exercise.

Plan for supervision of the supervisor, future support, and development

During her self-assessment, Ella rates herself on supervisory skills and competencies. Her director works with her to complete a year-long plan in which she will attend certain agency trainings, meet with other agency supervisors to learn from them, and work on her time management skills.

A plan is set up for regular supervision with the director as well as ongoing participation in the agency supervisory meetings. One of the supervisory trainers from the agency is assigned to Ella as a mentor, and the frequency and purpose of these meetings are discussed.

BEGINNING A NEW SUPERVISORY RELATIONSHIP: BEYOND GHOSTS TO A GOOD START

Beginning a new relationship between a supervisor and supervisee can mean many things for each partner. For the supervisee, a new supervisor may bring a welcome change or conversely trigger feelings of mourning for the loss of a beloved former supervisor. Many staff members will have "ghosts" from their supervisory past that will tend to shape their expectations of the next supervisory relationship. These may be benign or even idealized figures, or they may be harsh, punitive, or neglectful.

New supervisors may be worried about beginning work with a staff person whom they do not know or whom other supervisors have described as difficult. Supervisors themselves will have their own ghosts created from supervision they have received or memories of supervisory relationships in which they may not have been effective. Brand new supervisors may be anxious in spite of solid training and ongoing support.

Each new supervisory relationship offers an opportunity for a supervisor—whether new or experienced—to reassess her skills and start afresh to build a clear and supportive relationship. These new beginnings also offer a possibility for staff members who may have had difficulties at work to partner with someone else to help them deepen their skills and abilities to do a job more effectively. It is essential that this concept of a new beginning be conveyed at the outset of any new supervisory relationship.

Even for experienced employees it is essential to work through basic agreements and beyond assumptions before plunging into the world of work. Here is a list of topics that should be discussed over the course of several conversations. Talking about these before beginning the real-time work sets the stage for how the work will be done. Clear expectations elaborated up front make it easier to resolve problems that arise after the work has begun.

1. *Explore what has worked in the past.* What kinds of things has the supervisee found useful in working with past supervisors? These can include activities specific to a particular work setting, for example in a home-based setting, having the supervisor come along on home visits, setting up a regular check-in time after a difficult home visit, or having the supervisor introduce the home visitor to new community partners before starting a collaboration project.

2. *Request feedback.* What kinds of things in supervisory relationships have not worked so well or have made it harder for the supervisee to do her work? When supervisees share information, thank them for their candor and encourage them to let you know if you ever act in a way that that is uncomfortable or not helpful for them. If the new supervisee does not share this kind of information, explain that there may be times when the work together gets rocky, and if so, you will appreciate being able to stop and talk about what might be getting in the way of an effective supervisory relationship.

3. *Clarify expectations for feedback.* Supervisors should be clear that they will provide direct feedback about staff members' performance in a way that they hope will be helpful. Supervisor and supervisee may see things differently, and these conversations about different points of view are often enriching for both parties. Supervisees can be reassured that their supervisor will always speak to them directly and promptly about any concerns, rather than waiting to address an issue at the time of the performance review. The supervisor can also say that, in her experience, these discussions generally lead to a better understanding of the situation for the supervisor and the supervisee.

4. *Talk directly about differences—convey openness to thinking and talking about differences.* The supervisor should invite discussion about ways in which differences in race, class, gender, age, religion, disciplinary training, and other factors may affect their work together. When these conversations are conducted up front, it often makes it easier to bring up areas of friction or misunderstanding that may be related to points of difference. Here is an example of how to introduce this discussion.

> **Supervisor:** *As we work together, I want to acknowledge that there may be ways that our different experiences affect our observations and approaches to the work we will be discussing. We have some generational differences, but I also realize that my experiences as a Latina immigrant who went to school in a different country may affect some of my feelings, responses, and even the way I phrase*

> *things. I imagine there will be things that come up for you as well, and I hope we can talk about this as things emerge. Is there anything you would anticipate we should talk about beforehand or that might arise for us?*

5. *Establish mutual expectations.* Conversations about what is expected on both sides of a supervisory relationship are essential. Here is a list of important topics:

- Frequency of meetings

- Circumstances that warrant canceling supervision

- Participation in team meetings and being part of a team

- Preferred means of communication with one another

- How to manage work emergencies

- Expectations about times when the supervisor can be available outside of supervision and emergency contact information

- Evaluation procedures and ways that the supervisor will let the staff members know about any concerns. It is essential that this process be reviewed in detail, including frequency of performance review, performance review forms, and an orientation to the idea that the evaluation is merely a way to organize and document the things that have been discussed in an ongoing way.

- How will the supervisor and the supervisee assess training needs? Formal and informal ways should be previewed.

- How often will the supervisor review any written work?

- How does the supervisor prepare for meetings? For example, will the supervisor read any reports or notes that the supervisee has prepared in advance? Supervisors are also advised to review notes from prior supervisions so that follow-up questions can be asked.

- Expectation that supervisees will prepare for supervision. This can be done by encouraging them to bring in questions they have, topics they wish to discuss, or concerns that have arisen for them about their work.

- Confidentiality and its limits should be discussed in detail. Supervisees should be assured that what is discussed in supervision will not be shared outside of the room without their permission unless there is something that is a grave concern to the program or to an individual child or family. Examples of this might be a home visitor who has witnessed a crime in the community or a staff person who has broken a critical safety rule.

• What happens in supervision? Even experienced supervisees who work in an agency where reflective supervision is the norm should discuss what is meant by reflective supervision. Supervisees should understand that they are invited to bring in their feelings, questions, and responses to situations so they can be discussed and understood more fully. Supervisors should emphasize that they will not see these questions as evidence of weakness or vulnerability but rather as an expression of the person's desire to do her work well. Supervisees should understand that the supervisor will need to ask questions and explore, and that together they will try to come up with a deeper understanding or an intervention that is best for the child or family. Supervisees should expect that, at times, the supervisor will provide them with information, help them seek additional consultation, or suggest a course of action, but that in the end the goal is that supervision is a time for thinking together and co-creation of an approach to the supervisee's work.

• The supervisor will also bring in topics that she would like to discuss. Supervisee and supervisor should mutually negotiate the supervisory agenda.

6. *Clarify the purpose of supervision time.* Supervisors must explain to new supervisees that asking about feelings and responses to the work is a part of reflective supervision and that these responses are an important source of information about a family or child. Supervisees should be reminded that practitioners often react to people and events at an unconscious level. Supervision provides opportunities to pay attention to these responses more deliberately so a situation can be better understood at a more conscious level. In addition, practitioners need opportunities to examine how previous experiences, values, and culture may affect the way families and children are perceived and related to. Exploration in supervision develops the ability to view any situation from a variety of perspectives.

The supervisor can acknowledge that the discussion of feelings and personal responses can be confusing at times. When supervisees choose to discuss how feelings about the work are related to their personal concerns or vulnerabilities, there may be an expectation that the supervisor will be a support for their own needs beyond the scope of the supervisory work. Listening to the personal concerns of a supervisee can lure supervisors into the arena of personal counseling. Because of these possibilities, it is vital that a supervisor clarify right from the start that reflective supervision in the infant–family field is devoted to promoting high-quality services for children and families and not to addressing the personal needs of the supervisee. Understanding the ways that a particular supervisee is affected by work with a child or family can be essential to the work of supervision, and in exploring these concerns a supervisor will also learn a great deal about an individual supervisee's personal struggles. However, it is important for all to know that supervision is not therapy! At times the supervisor may observe or hear that a supervisee needs more time to explore a personal issue in a way that is not related directly to the work of the agency. In these cases, the supervisor should approach this situation with empathy and compassion and do what is possible to help the supervisee find an outside support to meet her personal needs.

7. Talk about style. It is useful for supervisors to talk about their own style and quirks with an eye to modeling openness and self-awareness. For example, tell the supervisee, "I want you to know that at times I may have a tendency to jump to conclusions when I hear about a struggle you describe. I have been working on this, but if you catch me moving too quickly, please feel free to let me know."

8. Model partnership and collaboration. Supervisors should stress that they are partners in the work of serving young children and families. Although the supervisory role has specific responsibilities for evaluation and accountability, the responsibility to work collaboratively is highly valued. Creating collaboration with a supervisee who is not used to working in this manner takes time and patience. Answers such as: "I don't know" or "What do you think?" may reflect a lack of experience with a collaborative approach to supervision and not necessarily a lack of ideas or observations. It may also indicate a lack of trust; the new supervisee will need to learn over time that it is safe to share concerns and vulnerabilities with the supervisor.

9. Communicate a worldview. Conveying belief in the value and importance of the supervisee's work is essential at the outset of a new relationship. Rather than telling a new supervisee about this, it is helpful to ask how she values the work. Framing work with young children and families and the importance of supervision through the lens of a relationship-based approach will help establish a common sense of purpose.

A sample supervision agreement that lists most of these points is provided in Appendix 2. The value of such an agreement is in the full and open discussion of the key ideas. This requires not only time but also openness to beginning a new relationship that will support the work of the agency and the growth of the supervisee.

BEGINNING AGAIN: RUPTURE AND REPAIR IN THE SUPERVISION PROCESS

A supervision relationship, like any other professional or personal connection, is vulnerable to miscommunication, missteps, or breaches of confidentiality that may require a new beginning to move forward. The process of creating a new beginning in an existing relationship can take many forms. Consider the following vignette:

Hedy is a teacher in an Early Head Start classroom who is supervised by Sara, the site manager. At one point, it comes to Sara's attention that Hedy has been late to work several days in a row. Rather than address this directly, Sara announces in a staff meeting that she would like to be notified if staff members are going to be late so she can be sure that there is adequate coverage. Hedy feels singled out by this announcement and cancels her regular bimonthly supervision meeting with Sara. She also talks to other staff members, telling them that Sara seems out to get her.

Sara feels annoyed with Hedy and seeks help from her own supervisor about how to approach the situation. After reviewing her own feelings and exploring why Hedy might have responded so strongly, Sara calls Hedy into her office.

Sara says: "Hedy, I realize that you are very upset with me, and I hope we can talk this through so we can get back on track with our work. I value your skill with children and families and want to make sure that you feel you have my support. I have thought a lot about what happened and realize that it would have been better if I had talked to you privately, rather than making that announcement in the staff meeting. But I am also not sure if there might be other things I may have done that have made you upset."

Hedy replies that she really worried about being late because her car had been in the shop. Sara wonders if there was a reason she hadn't asked for help. Hedy shakes her head and says that she had been taught to be a responsible person and not rely on others.

Sara replies that she values Hedy's willingness to take responsibility but wishes Hedy would have turned to the team for support. She reminds Hedy that they all have a shared responsibility to the children and families and that they have often worked together to help each other out. Sara says she is pretty sure that Hedy would help out one of her team members and that she too deserves support. At the end of the session, Sara has learned something important about Hedy, and Hedy has learned that it is better to express a need than to try to do the impossible. Sara finishes the session by appreciating Hedy's willingness to talk about this issue and to make a fresh start in their relationship.

The following are steps to consider in repairing a rift and making a new beginning in a supervisory relationship:

1. As the supervisor, consider your own feelings about the situation and ways that you may have contributed to miscommunications or friction in the relationship.

2. Try to consider the other person's point of view and speculate about her perceptions or worries that might be driving the rupture in the relationship.

3. Take time to consider specifically how the rupture has affected program services or could do so. This will tend to make the discord less personal and take it into a professional realm.

4. Set a time to talk about what has happened and how it is affecting supervision and the work.

5. Be open to hearing the other person's point of view and position. Acknowledge your contribution to the situation and your hope that you can both move beyond this so that you can focus on the work you are doing together.

6. Acknowledge, explore, and contain feelings. Focus on what you can each do differently to avoid ruptures or miscommunication in the future.

Most of the time, this kind of a conversation will get supervision back on track. Sometimes a third party may need to get involved. Please note that there are additional steps and considerations when addressing a job performance concern with a supervisee. At those times, it is critical to actually spotlight the concern, clarify the expectations, and agree on a course of action.

GUIDING QUESTIONS

Consider the agency/program where you work now or have worked recently.

- When a new supervisor comes to the agency, or when someone is promoted to a supervisory position, how are the components of the "Basic Agenda" addressed?

- Are there components which might benefit from more attention?

- What might be some first steps in improving your program's support for new supervisors?

FURTHER READINGS

Bertacchi, J., & Norman-Murch T. (1999). Implementing reflective supervision in non-clinical settings: Challenges to practice. *Zero to Three, 20*(1), 18–23.

Gilkerson, L., & Shahmoon-Shanok, R. (2000). Relationships for growth: Cultivating reflective practice in infant, toddler, and preschool programs. In J. D. Osofsky & H. E. Fitzgerald (Eds.), *WAIMH handbook of infant mental health: Vol. 2. Early intervention, evaluation, and assessment* (pp. 38–76). New York: Wiley.

Keyes, A. W., Cavanaugh, A. E., & Scott Heller, S. (2009). How do I, as a reflective
supervisor, repair ruptures in the supervisory relationship? In S. Scott Heller & L. Gilkerson (Eds.),
A practical guide to reflective supervision (pp. 99–119). Washington, DC: ZERO TO THREE.

Weston, D. R. (2005). Training in infant mental health: Educating the reflective practitioner.
Infants & Young Children, 18, 337–348.

CHAPTER 7

GROWING AND LEARNING AS A SUPERVISOR

Reflective supervisors need to seek out ongoing opportunities for professional growth and development in a number of different areas.

All supervisors, regardless of their training or experience, will benefit from ongoing attention to developing their supervisory skills and competencies (as outlined in chapter 4). Because reflective supervision is a blended model, this would include working on improving administrative and program development skills as well as striving to remain attuned and reflective in the face of internal and external pressures. As the supervisor takes on additional responsibilities, she may need to expand her expertise in training, leadership, grant writing, or data management. Supervisors whose positions change may find new challenges, such as supervising others who are supervisors or involvement in the start-up of new teams, models, or programs.

In addition, it is essential for supervisors to stay up-to-date about advances and standards of best practice in their particular field. Supervisors should remain current about evolving theories, research, related fields of study, and effective methods of service delivery. They should also seek out information about changing community needs or new regulations that affect services, new models of intervention, or evaluation studies related to the infant–early childhood field.

ONGOING SUPERVISION FOR REFLECTIVE SUPERVISORS

All reflective supervisors should have their own agency supervisor who works with them on enhancing their supervisory skills, addressing dilemmas, handling management issues, and setting priorities. Supervisors need opportunities to recognize and deal with the places where they are stuck, their blind spots, and their vulnerabilities with a supportive supervisor of their own. For beginning supervisors, regular weekly meetings are recommended for at least 6 months or until the supervisor finds her "sea legs" and gets her bearings. All supervisors should have regular supervision or consultation available to them at a minimum of once a month. As with any supervision, regularity is essential. For new supervisors, the ability to contact their own supervisor to check in and ask questions as needed is particularly important.

Because participation in reflective supervision is the best way to refine one's own supervision skills, some have found it helpful to seek consultation outside their agency.

This is in addition to their regular supervision and is especially helpful if their own supervision is not sufficiently challenging to meet their needs and grow their skills. Before pursuing this option, it is essential to discuss the possibility with the agency supervisor and to establish clear guidelines regarding confidentiality around agency families and internal agency affairs.

Supervisors who are providing a blended model of supervision, incorporating all five of the supervisory roles outlined in chapter 2, need their own supervisor who understands and supports this model. If no one is available within the agency to provide this support, the new reflective supervisor should consider how her supervision needs can be met.

> *Ruby is a new supervisor at a family shelter serving homeless families. Ruby feels comfortable with the direct work with families and children but has never been a supervisor. She is willing to read and attend outside training that the director has located for her. Ruby's supervisor, the director of the shelter, encourages Ruby to develop a supportive atmosphere for the staff members, incorporating reflective supervision at their team meetings. She also wants Ruby to be on top of admissions and discharges from the shelter. The director feels that she could help Ruby with the administrative parts of the job but has no training in reflective supervision. She arranges for Ruby to meet weekly with a skilled supervisor from a nearby agency to help her learn the ropes of reflective supervision.*

REAL-TIME OBSERVATION OF SUPERVISION AS A PATH TO CONTINUED GROWTH

For both new and experienced supervisors to continue their professional growth, it is essential that their own supervisors not only hear about their work but also have chances to observe in real time or via video/audiotaped sessions. Supervisors can also sit in on team meetings facilitated by the supervisee. This real-time observation of supervision activities facilitates discussion of the subtle details of the work. Victor Bernstein, in his work with the Ounce of Prevention Fund and his involvement in the Developmental Training and Support Program, designed a strong supervision model in which supervisors regularly review videotapes of home visit sessions with supervisees (Bernstein, 2002–2003). Training tapes available from this project also show supervision sessions in which these videos are being reviewed by the supervisee and supervisor.

ONGOING NEEDS: REVISITING BASIC REFLECTIVE SUPERVISION APPROACHES

After new supervisors have had a few months on the job, they will benefit from another day or two of basic supervision training. At this point, they will have had their own experiences, which will add another layer of meaning when they revisit fundamental skills, concepts, and dilemmas. More experienced supervisors will also benefit from this kind of refresher training and can serve as a resource to their less experienced peers.

This revisiting of basic reflective supervision approaches can be in mixed training groups with supervisors from other agencies or in internal groups of supervisors from different programs within an agency. Training that focuses on supervisory dilemmas and allows for supported practice through observation of supervision videos, role plays, and guided discussions will be more effective than a more didactic review of skills and concepts.

SPECIAL TOPICS IN REFLECTIVE SUPERVISION

Reflective supervisors will also benefit from having ongoing training opportunities that focus more narrowly on specific topics. Department or agency managers can use formal or informal surveys to discover areas of special interest and need for the supervisors.

The following is a list of topics for ongoing training that will be of interest to supervisors with a wide range of supervisory experience:

- Integrating culture and context into reflective supervision

- Helping supervisees negotiate appropriate boundaries

- Addressing job performance issues

- Developing supervision agreements

- Addressing legal and ethical issues in supervision

- Balancing mentoring and monitoring responsibilities

- Helping staff members avoid triangulation of conflicts and difficulties

- Working with "difficult to engage" staff members

- Handling change and helping staff members handle programmatic stress

- Being an effective team leader

SUPERVISORY TEAM MEETINGS

Most agencies or programs have regular staff meetings for supervisors. Some agenda items will most likely be administrative. However, if the time is well planned, these meetings can be an opportunity to practice reflectively in a group, to promote use of one another as supports, and to use a group process for collaborative problem solving. The confidentiality and professionalism of these meetings must be ensured, but frank discussions of supervisory issues with supportive colleagues can be very helpful. They give less experienced supervisors the opportunity to grow by observing more experienced peers and by providing practice opportunities for reflective approaches in a safe environment.

SUPERVISORY LEARNING AND SUPPORT GROUPS

Reflective supervision learning and support groups can help supervisors deepen their understanding and increase their competence. These groups can be valuable for supervisors whose agencies do not have the resources to provide ongoing, in-depth support for individual skill development.

One model is for a number of supervisors to attend 1 or 2 days of training that outlines elements of reflective supervision theory and skills. Those individuals then agree to participate in follow-up groups that give them an opportunity to explore their own work. These group discussions are facilitated by an experienced supervisor who anchors the discussions in a reflective approach and draws on the ideas and skills covered in the training workshop. Over time, participants develop a common language of reflective supervision that helps them solidify their skills and call on reflective approaches when their work becomes complex or difficult. These kinds of groups are suited to larger agencies and to communities where several agencies are working together to improve reflective supervision skills. The success of these groups rests on assurance that all material discussed is confidential and that actual names of supervisees are not used in the discussions. A strong focus on the professional use of self helps participants concentrate on the supervisory skills in question rather than on the individual staff members or situations being discussed by the group.

This group format helps supervisors learn to hold theories and principles in mind while grappling with day-to-day programmatic dilemmas. Members of the group are also receiving support and encouragement from their peers and the facilitator to more fully integrate these skills and approaches into the complexities of everyday practice. It is ideal if these support groups can be held twice a month or monthly.

SUPERVISORY COMPETENCY

Some communities and professional groups have study groups or courses that are useful for supervisors who wish to expand their professional competencies. For example California's Infant, Preschool, and Family Mental Health Initiative developed training guidelines and recommended personnel competencies (*California Infant-Family and Early Childhood Mental Health Workforce Competencies*, n.d.) that include a specific set of competencies and an endorsement pathway for supervisors. The Michigan Association for Infant Mental Health (2007) sponsors a well-developed system that also addresses reflective supervision competencies. Other states have adopted the Michigan competencies and guidelines as a support for supervisors who are looking to build their skills.

Continually Putting the Needs of Others First—A Common Pitfall

Supervisors can often feel that there is so much to do—so many people to hold, nurture, and organize—that their own needs for support, learning, containment, and growth are secondary. The failure to keep growing or to renew through ongoing professional sustenance often leads to reduced effectiveness, mistakes, boredom, or chronic irritability. All supervisors need and deserve both training and their own supervision so they can remain open, receptive, and available to others. An exhausted, overworked supervisor who fails to care for herself will not be able to be fully present or engaged when tough supervisory problems arise.

Growing as a supervisor entails creating or sometimes demanding space for regular self-assessment and reflection about what is challenging in the supervision role. This kind of assessment often entails discussions with supervisors, mentors, and colleagues who can provide feedback and raise questions to initiate this process. These mindful efforts are used to examine successes as well as the times and places where things did not go well. They can lead to fruitful discussions as well as concrete efforts to seek out new knowledge and skills that will sustain the supervisor for the long haul.

Failure to Use Supervision or Consultation

The reflective supervisor's failure to take time to reflect about her work is a bit like driving without a license. The supervisor can do it for a long time and maybe even get away with it, but when she is "caught," or stuck, the consequences can be very serious. Everyone needs and deserves support from a skilled partner in supervision or consultation. The following is an example of a reflective supervisor stuck in an agency dilemma:

> *Evelyn is a supervisor of a community resource center that provides a variety of parent education groups and a series of parent–child developmental playgroups for infants and toddlers. Evelyn works hard to provide reflective supervision to her staff members and is considered an excellent employee by her agency. Evelyn has also been a little reluctant to seek assistance from the director of the program because she wants to be seen as deserving of her reputation as competent. However, over the past 6 months, a new member of the team has demonstrated*

a pattern of rudeness toward fellow workers and sometimes toward parents in the center. In supervision sessions, the new worker has dismissed these observations about her rudeness as cultural differences between herself and the others in the program. Evelyn has felt very conflicted because this new worker is also reliable and supportive of the center in many ways. As time goes by, Evelyn notices that other staff members come to her frequently to complain about the new worker. Because of this, Evelyn conducts some training sessions about cultural differences in communication and urges the staff members to talk directly to one another to sort out difficulties.

When Evelyn finally approaches her director to review her struggles with the new employee, the director helps her sort out her complicated feelings about how to address this situation. In the conversation, Evelyn realizes that her ability to address issues related to the cultural and linguistic differences between staff members is being complicated by her worries about appearing unfair because of her own ethnicity. She also realizes that she is pulled in two directions. She does not want to lose the new employee, nor can she tolerate the current and worsening atmosphere in her program. Together, Evelyn and the director sort out how these worries have kept Evelyn from being effective in her attempts to manage this situation. In the discussion, the director realizes that she has made a huge mistake by not having regular supervision meetings with this competent young supervisor. Meeting more frequently might have prevented the situation from worsening despite Evelyn's sincere attempts to make it better.

Very busy supervisors will sometimes skimp on their own supervision or consultation even when it is available, if they feel too pressed or exhausted to stop, step back, and reflect. In some cases, organizational support for the supervisor in the form of reflective supervision is nonexistent or minimal. These organizations sometimes consider achieving the status of supervisor as analogous to obtaining a merit badge of the highest order, with no further maintenance needed. Some agencies fully embrace reflective supervision and the needs of their supervisors to refuel through their own reflective time, but the agencies skimp on these basics when resources shrink or crises arise.

Supervision for supervisors is a shared responsibility. For agency and program directors, it is important that regular supervision meetings are built into supervisors' job descriptions and expectations. The program director must ensure that these meetings do happen and communicate the fact that they are not optional. At the same time, supervisors must take responsibility for having reflective time for themselves. If reflective supervision is not available on a regular basis, supervisors are advised to self-advocate for it as a professional development and program quality necessity. If reflective supervision opportunities are available, the supervisor must prioritize her time so as to be able to take advantage of them. She should actively seek out the support that is so richly deserved and universally needed in this demanding position.

GUIDING QUESTIONS

Look at the "Special Topics in Reflective Supervision" section of this chapter (p. 159).

- Are there one or two that are of particular interest to you?

- If so, why?

- What resources might you draw on to help you build your skills in this area?

As a supervisor/manager, consider whether you have regular reflective supervisory support.

- If not, what resources are available to you?

- What would be an important first step in securing your own reflective supervision?

REFERENCES

Bernstein, V. (2002–2003, Winter). Standing firm against the forces of risk: Supporting home visiting and early intervention workers through reflective supervision. *IMPrint, 35.*

California Infant-Family and Early Childhood Mental Health Workforce Competencies. (n.d.). Retrieved April 19, 2010, from www.ecmhtraining-ca.org

Michigan Association for Infant Mental Health. (2007). *Best practice guidelines for reflective supervision/consultation.* Retrieved April 17, 2010, from www.miaimh.org/documents/20100204_bpgrsc.pdf

FURTHER READINGS

Bernstein, V., Campbell, S., & Ajers, A. (2001). Caring for the caregivers: Supporting the well-being of at-risk parents and children through supporting the well-being of the programs that serve them. In J. Hughes, J. Close, & A. La Greca (Eds.), *Handbook of psychological services for children and adolescents* (pp. 107–131). New York: Oxford University Press.

Heffron, M. C., Ivins, B., & Weston, D. R. (2005). Finding an authentic voice—Use of self: Essential learning processes for relationship-based work. *Infants & Young Children, 18,* 323–336.

Samuels, M., & Betts, J. (2007). Crossing the threshold from description to deconstruction and reconstruction: Using self-assessment to deepen reflection. *Reflective Practice, 8,* 269–283.

Schafer, W. (2007). Models and domains of supervision and their relationship to professional development. *Zero to Three, 28*(2), 10–17.

Shahmoon-Shanok, R., & Geller, E. (2009). Embracing complexity across disciplines: Reflective supervision and postdegree training integrate mental health concepts with speech-language therapy and graduate education. *Infant Mental Health Journal, 30,* 591–620.

CHAPTER 8

Supervisory Dilemmas

Supervision often uncovers complex dilemmas that are difficult to sort out and resolve. The supervisor may find herself pulled in different directions: "Should I or shouldn't I comment on and explore what I have just heard or read?" "Is X or Y the best option right now?" "Is this my issue, or is it truly a concern for the quality of services?" "Am I, as the supervisor, missing something? Could I have hit a blind spot where I am too sure about my own perspective or focusing too little on something?"

These dilemmas are to be expected: They are part of the work. The challenge is how to think, feel, and talk about them in ways that are honest and productive and that protect the supervisory relationship. The supervisor will have to try hard to interact with her supervisee in a way that does not arouse feelings of shame or denial or cause her supervisee to become defensive or dismissive. The alternative to reflection and discussion with the supervisee is for the supervisor to "let it be." In some cases, this might be the right path, but unexamined or unexplored dilemmas often pose a risk to the growth of the individual supervisee, to supervisory effectiveness, and to the quality of the work or the integrity of the program.

In this chapter, we describe and discuss common supervisory dilemmas through presentation of vignettes that are composites of experiences we ourselves have encountered. These dilemmas are offered so as to provide examples of supervisory thinking and language. They do not prescribe a definitive "right answer" or a final resolution. These vignettes are intended as jumping-off points for training groups, teams, and individuals who are working to expand and refine their supervisory skills. In discussing and thinking about these dilemmas, we encourage a reflective approach, considering the exploration of many possibilities.

We have included questions after each dilemma to help illuminate the issues raised in the vignette. These dilemmas are also useful material for informal role plays: Supervisors can explore the language, pacing, and approaches they might want to use in opening up a dialogue about the situation. We have used these in group supervision or training meetings and have found it useful to have someone read the vignette aloud before the group proceeds to discuss the situations and questions raised. This reading aloud seems to bring the situations to life and stimulate lively conversations.

A vignette summary is included after the questions. This summary is meant to touch on main points but not to limit the possibilities for learning and exploration. The summary is intended for trainers. If individual readers wish to use the summaries, they should first wait until they have had opportunities to reflect on the questions presented.

1. "To Go or Not to Go...": How to Support Without Taking Over

Bonnie, a young home visitor in an Early Head Start program, returns from an initial visit with a family who recently enrolled in the program. She approaches her supervisor with an anxious look and a plea: "I can't handle this case. Can you transfer it to somebody else?" Natalie, the supervisor, listens intently as Bonnie describes a homeless family living in a transitional shelter with little hope of permanent housing in the near future. The family has two prematurely born children less than 2 years old. Both parents have mental and physical health challenges. The parents verbally attacked one another in front of Bonnie, each apparently attempting to get her to see the other as the problem. She was unable to stop them. Her fleeting descriptions of the 21-month-old toddler are worrisome; the 4-month-old baby had cried incessantly during the visit and was not offered comfort by either parent. Food and diapers were in short supply. Bonnie breaks down crying at this point, questioning her competence and her ability to assess the degree of danger to the children.

As she listens, Natalie feels herself simultaneously wanting to rescue Bonnie and at the same time to scold her for being so reactive. In her mind, she begins to question the hiring committee who recently selected Bonnie from a large pool of qualified applicants. She wonders how the seemingly competent home visitor has been reduced to such a state. She asks Bonnie, "What was the hardest part of being there?" Bonnie replies, "I just felt helpless in the face of so many problems. I couldn't get a handle on anything." Natalie responds, "You became paralyzed just like they are by these overwhelming obstacles. I am glad you are asking for help. Tell me a little bit more about what you know about this family."

As she gathers more information, Natalie begins to think about her choices. She could go with Bonnie on the next home visit and see how accurate the reports had been, or she could explore some more and attempt to help Bonnie find her way solo. She continues to question herself: *If I go with Bonnie, what message might this give to the newly hired home visitor? Would my direct support undermine Bonnie's confidence? If I go, would I discover that the family's troubles are indeed overwhelming? Would I leave as distressed as Bonnie? Would Bonnie develop a pattern of not being able to cope with the distress common among the population served by our program? What if these children are really in danger?* After further discussion, Natalie and Bonnie make a decision to go together on a home visit as soon as possible.

At the start of the visit, Natalie introduces herself as Bonnie's supervisor and someone who is familiar with resources for preemies. They learn more about the parents' difficulties, including information about the father's severe seizure disorder. The visit is calm, and the family seems eager for all the help they can get with their babies and their own relationships with them.

On the way back to the office, Bonnie volunteers that, on the first visit, she had been frightened by the father's aggressive words to the mother. She wonders if his epilepsy affected his emotions. Natalie says that it might have, and she asks if Bonnie thinks she can remember the tone of this visit if things get rough again. Bonnie says she can, and she agrees that it might help her regulate her own fears to remember that this family seemed calm and capable of using her support at least some of the time. Bonnie remarks that it has been helpful to see Natalie in action. Natalie comments on several helpful interventions Bonnie had made. She also says: "This visit will be useful for me as your supervisor. Now I really have a picture of this family."

Reflective Questions

1. What feelings does this situation bring up for you as a supervisor?

2. What are the strengths, resources, and elements in this situation that a supervisor could build on?

3. What questions do you have? What would you like to know more about?

4. What are the key areas of concern?

5. What is the supervisory dilemma?

6. Which supervisory roles are called into play in this situation?

7. What core principles and key skills of reflective supervision might be helpful in this situation?

8. As the supervisor, how might you proceed? Keep in mind how the various possibilities might play out over time.

Summary

Natalie's concerns about the effect of her direct support on Bonnie's sense of competence were important. Natalie considered her role as a supervisory partner with Bonnie and her responsibility for the services to these children. Natalie realized that she felt worried about the safety of these two vulnerable children and their parents. Natalie's dilemma was that she wanted to build Bonnie's sense of competence and her own confidence in Bonnie's assessments. Yet, she did not feel she could wait to figure out whether the children were really in danger or whether Bonnie was simply thrown off kilter by her lack of skills. Natalie was at a disadvantage because Bonnie was a relatively new employee whom she did not know well. She felt she could not adequately judge Bonnie's reactions and decided that the possibility that the children were in danger was significant enough that she should accompany Bonnie on the next visit.

2. "CRYBABY": ADDRESSING PERFORMANCE ISSUES

Lucy is an experienced Head Start teacher. She is reliable, and her reports are always on time. Her classroom is well organized, and there is considerable attention given to setting up appropriate materials. Lucy's teaching style is quite directive. Elena is her supervisor, and she places a high value on comforting and supporting children when they are distressed.

When a child is obviously upset, Lucy's style is to give the child space. She does not usually move to comfort the child, nor does she include other children in the process of comforting. Other staff members have complained to Elena that they have heard Lucy tease a child, labeling him a "crybaby."

Lucy has received a lot of training about the importance of warmth and nurturing. Elena has brought up her concerns about both her directive teaching style and her belief in not being too nurturing when children are upset. Lucy has responded that it is important for children to learn to cope and that coddling them only makes them more dependent on adult help. Elena wondered if these strong feelings were in part due to cultural differences between her and Lucy (they are from different cultural backgrounds). She wasn't sure how to address these at the time. Instead, Elena has tried very hard to be warm, nurturing, and supportive to Lucy, hoping that this would translate into a more responsive approach to children who are upset. So far this has not worked, and Elena is struggling to find a way to address her concern again. Elena's dilemma is how to address the importance of nurturing the children in a way that Lucy will hear and will translate into behavioral change. Elena wants to open up the area of cultural differences but is not sure how to do this or whether this will make Lucy even more dismissive of the idea of nurturing and comforting.

Reflective Questions

1. What feelings does this situation bring up for you as a supervisor?

2. What are the strengths, resources, and elements in this situation that a supervisor could build on?

3. What questions do you have? What would you like to know more about?

4. What are the key areas of concern?

5. What is the supervisory dilemma?

6. Which supervisory roles are called into play in this situation?

7. What core principles and key skills of reflective supervision might be helpful in this situation?

8. As the supervisor, how might you proceed? Keep in mind how the various possibilities might play out over time.

Summary

Lucy has not taken in key information that has been presented on multiple occasions through training and supervision. Elena wonders if this focus on nurturing may conflict with Lucy's own core beliefs about what children need. Recent reports from staff members about Lucy's lack of nurturing are threatening to cause a split in this classroom. Elena's dilemma is how to bring up an issue that can no longer be ignored in a way that will be heard. Should this be presented clearly as a performance issue? Should she try to explore Lucy's beliefs about coping to see if she can help her see the perspective of the child more clearly? Will highlighting differences in beliefs bring up cultural and racial differences that will create tensions?

3. "MAD AS HELL": WHAT TO DO WHEN A SUPERVISEE HAS STRONG NEGATIVE FEELINGS ABOUT A CLIENT

Candy, an experienced family support worker, is furious with her client and wants to talk about it right away. She comes into the supervisor's office and flops into a chair. She tells the supervisor, Priscilla: "I am so mad that I simply cannot see this woman. The way she is treating her baby is a crime. She went for 6 days without filling a prescription for her baby and told me that she didn't want to spend her own money. I should have called Children's Protective Services, but I knew that they wouldn't do anything." The supervisee recounts more case details. It seems as if she is stuck in a state of rage and agitation.

Near tears, Candy tells Priscilla that she cannot believe some of the things she has found herself doing. She is giving direct advice and has even gone so far as to threaten and shame the client—saying things like "they're going to take this baby away from you." She was surprised to hear what was coming out of her mouth. However, as if to justify her words, she reports that the other staff members and residents in the treatment center feel the very same way about the woman. Priscilla finds herself wanting to tell Candy to calm down. This is a strong feeling, and for a moment she worries that she would not be able to contain Candy's rage. However, instead of telling Candy to calm down, she says, "I get the feeling that it is hard to watch this baby suffer." She listens to more details about the mother's deplorable care of the baby. She notes that Candy's rage has diminished a little. In time, she revisits the detail that the other staff members and parents in the program are mad at the mother as well. She wonders with Candy how it must be to have everybody so mad at you. She wonders with Candy how the mother might respond if she were asked what it was like to have so many people mad at her all the time. Or what it felt like to be criticized openly, in addition to receiving the critical looks and side comments of others.

Reflective Questions

1. What feelings does this situation bring up for you as a supervisor?

2. What are the strengths, resources, and elements in this situation that a supervisor could build on?

3. What questions do you have? What would you like to know more about?

4. What are the key areas of concern?

5. What is the supervisory dilemma?

6. Which supervisory roles are called into play in this situation?

7. What core principles and key skills of reflective supervision might be helpful in this situation?

8. As the supervisor, how might you proceed? Keep in mind how the various possibilities might play out over time.

Summary

In this vignette, the supervisor's dilemma is how to find her empathy for Candy, so that Candy could feel heard, which would help her calm down and find a way in with this mother. Priscilla felt a strong urge to correct and criticize Candy while listening to her, but she hoped to find some empathy for her supervisee by focusing on Candy's caring for the infant. Candy's feelings of outrage at the mother are toxic and threaten her services to mother and baby, so the supervisor needs to find a way to help Candy see the bigger picture. The supervisor chooses to take the mother's perspective and invites Candy to imagine what it would be like to have everybody mad at you. Through this discussion, Candy eventually discovers that she has made a very frequent home visitor error. She has been so protective of the baby that she has completely lost her sense of empathy for the mother. This loss of empathy and critical approach has perhaps decreased the mother's ability to function and follow through. At the same time, both Candy and Priscilla have to find a way to keep the baby's safety and well-being in mind.

4. "STAND BY ME": MAINTAINING THE DISTINCTION BETWEEN SUPERVISION AND THERAPY

Lilly is a manager in an early intervention program. She is also a licensed mental health therapist with a strong background in child development. Each staff person in the program receives monthly one-to-one supervision with Lilly. In addition, there is a weekly staff meeting. Occasionally, the supervisor can arrange additional individual time. Marty, a child development specialist, has requested an extra one-to-one supervision meeting. She begins talking about a child with mild delays who has been referred to her. As Marty describes the child and the parents' interactions with the child, she becomes tearful and quiet. The supervisor comments gently that this case seems hard for her. Marty responds that this family reminds her so much of her own situation that she can hardly stand to go to the home. As Lilly works to understand these circumstances, it becomes clear that Marty's marriage is on the rocks and that she is unclear how to proceed with her husband. The supervisor notes to herself that she is strongly pulled to help Marty with her marital problems. Lilly thoughts begin to wander, and she thinks about offering Marty another meeting time to just talk about this personal issue. She even considers calling a friend who has a private counseling practice and seeing whether she will see Marty pro bono in that practice. Lilly finally is able to find the words she wants to say to Marty : "I feel so sad that your marriage is in trouble, and in a way I feel pulled to talk more about this, but I think you deserve more support than I can give since our time here is really about your work with the families. This particular family seems to bring up your own pain, and we can continue to figure out how best to address this, but I wonder if you have considered getting some support specifically for yourself?" Marty replies that she trusts the supervisor and didn't know who else to turn to. Marty continues that she feels embarrassed about this and doesn't know where to find help because they live in such a small community. Lilly concludes the session by discussing some places where Marty could get support and where her confidentiality would be assured. Later, Lilly wonders if she should follow up and ask Marty if she has been able to obtain the counseling services.

Reflective Questions

1. What feelings does this situation bring up for you as a supervisor?

2. What are the strengths, resources, and elements in this situation that a supervisor could build on?

3. What questions do you have? What would you like to know more about?

4. What are the key areas of concern?

5. What is the supervisory dilemma?

6. Which supervisory roles are called into play in this situation?

7. What core principles and key skills of reflective supervision might be helpful in this situation?

8. As the supervisor, how might you proceed? Keep in mind how the various possibilities might play out over time.

Summary

In this vignette, Marty wants and needs somebody to help her, and the supervision session seems like the right place. Lilly's dilemma is how to contain her own empathy, which is leading her to want to help Marty with her personal problems. If she follows her heart, the work with the troubled family will be forgotten. If she dismisses Marty's needs, she risks increasing the pain and despair that Marty is expressing. Lilly skillfully contains Marty's pain and distress about her marriage and how the work with the family brings this all up for her. At the same time, she clarifies the boundary issues in an empathic way, stating that the supervision time must be protected as a space to focus on the work with the family, not on Marty's marital concerns. Although most of the session gets taken up with the discussion about Marty's pain, Lilly manages to make it clear that the time and space are for discussion of the families and children who are her clients. Yet, even with her clear boundaries, Lilly is empathic and helpful in finding a resource that can be accessed in this small community. As the supervisor, Lilly wants to follow up with this discussion but needs to do so carefully to make it clear to Marty that the supervision time cannot be used to regularly address her personal needs.

5. "IT'S JUST A FEW PAIRS OF JEANS": CLARIFYING BOUNDARIES

Elvia is the director of an infant care center that primarily serves recently arrived immigrant families. During a supervision session, Elvia's supervisor, Harry, asks her about her newest family and their young son Hector. Elvia replies, "He is so adorable—he is just 6 months younger than my boy Paul and is so much like him that it feels like he is a cousin." Harry hesitates and says, "I am not sure I know what you mean." Harry notices that Elvia seems uncomfortable, and he says, "Is this something you'd like to talk about?" Elvia quietly says no and continues talking about Hector's progress and his parents' delight in his new words. Harry senses that there is something else on Elvia's mind. He asks her what it is like having a baby in the center that reminds her of her own son. Elvia says that it is sad because she sees how Hector has so little and Paul has so much more. As Elvia continues, she reveals that she thinks she has made a big mistake. She lets Harry know that she has been giving Hector's family all of Paul's outgrown jeans and toys. She says she is worried that Hector's mom resents her for having so much that she can just give it away. Harry senses Elvia's confusion, pain, and worry about what she has done. Right away, he lets Elvia know that this confusion is understandable but that she is right, that it was not a good idea. Rather than tell her why, he asks her what she thought might be a problem. Elvia says that she may have offended the family or implied that they could not take care of their own child. Harry asks if this would fit with what Elvia understands about the family's culture and values, and Elvia nods that the family is very hard-working and does not want to be seen as weak. She adds that her family is like that too. She also worries that they might expect her to keep bringing things, and in fact the mom has asked her when she will bring some more jeans for Hector. Elvia admits that the family's poverty brings back memories of her own childhood when she had to wear hand-me-down clothes. Elvia then adds, "but this kid really needs the clothes." Harry says he admires Elvia's generosity in sharing her own child's things, but he wonders if there was another way to do this without the family knowing that the items formerly belonged to her own child. Elvia says quietly, "I could just put them in the clothes exchange the way I used to do it." Harry concurs and says to Elvia, "I am sure it was very hard for you to see Hector dressed so poorly, and it felt like the right thing at the time. I am glad you brought this up." Leaving supervision, Harry realizes that this dilemma is not really solved. He knows that Elvia has temporarily regained her sense of her own boundaries with this family. As he walks down the hall, Harry worries about whether and how to talk to Elvia about the distress she feels when working with families whose circumstances remind her of her own childhood in such painful ways. He also wonders if he has been missing other boundary issues that are troubling for Elvia or for the center.

Reflective Questions

1. What feelings does this situation bring up for you as a supervisor?

2. What are the strengths, resources, and elements in this situation that a supervisor could build on?

3. What questions do you have? What would you like to know more about?

4. What are the key areas of concern?

5. What is the supervisory dilemma?

6. Which supervisory roles are called into play in this situation?

7. What core principles and key skills of reflective supervision might be helpful in this situation?

8. As the supervisor, how might you proceed? Keep in mind how the various possibilities might play out over time.

Summary

Harry's dilemma in this case is how to let Elvia uncover and discuss her own boundary issues and confused feelings about Hector and his family. Earlier discussion with Harry might have helped Elvia figure out ways to manage her feelings and her charitable impulses in a way that would not have unintended consequences. This vignette illustrates how certain kinds of situations can cause interventionists to remember their own experiences and to react without considering the consequences. This case is especially poignant because the two little boys are so close in age. Elvia seems to feel somewhat guilty about her own son's experience of growing up in a family with more resources, and she sets about in her own way to alleviate her guilt by passing on her son's clothes and toys.

6. "STILL WATERS—DO THEY RUN DEEP?": THE SUPERVISEE IN HIDING

Kim is the director of a rural early care and education center. Donna has been supervising Kim for 6 months. Donna has done a good job of clarifying and contracting the purpose of the sessions, but each session drags with shallow conversations that do not seem to be helpful to Kim. By report, she is an effective leader in her program, but Donna dreads the twice-a-month sessions with Kim because she senses that Kim is present with great reluctance. Kim dutifully reports that things are going well or tells her about problems that she has solved in a competent manner.

At the end of one session, Kim asks if they can cut down to once a month. Donna, feeling a little dismissed, somehow finds a way to say that she has been wondering about how Kim feels the sessions are going. She asks Kim if they could wait a little to talk about frequency and instead talk more generally about how their meetings together are going.

Later, as things unfold, Donna uncovers that Kim does not feel really seen or supported because Donna does not observe much in the center. When Donna offers to observe a half hour before each supervision, Kim seems to feel more comfortable bringing in real concerns about issues that she is having trouble addressing.

Reflective Questions

1. What feelings does this situation bring up for you as a supervisor?

2. What are the strengths, resources, and elements in this situation that a supervisor could build on?

3. What questions do you have? What would you like to know more about?

4. What are the key areas of concern?

5. What is the supervisory dilemma?

6. Which supervisory roles are called into play in this situation?

7. What core principles and key skills of reflective supervision might be helpful in this situation?

8. As the supervisor, how might you proceed? Keep in mind how the various possibilities might play out over time.

Summary

This dilemma represents what some supervisors call the "doldrums." The supervisee is hard to engage. Things feel stuck, there is little exploration, no breezes blowing, and the time does not feel well used. In this vignette, the supervisee's request for fewer sessions is the port of entry for a discussion of the supervisory experience and relationship. Kim does not explicitly complain about supervision, but her request opens a door for exploration. In this case, you may wonder why Donna did not address the lack of engagement earlier on and in a more direct way. It is very easy to "blame" the supervisee for poor use of time or think of possible explanations (e.g., she has never had supervision before; she is so effective as a worker that supervision makes her feel unfairly micromanaged; she interprets supervision as an indication that she does not know how to do her job; or she resents having a supervisor with less classroom experience than she has).

Donna could have probably opened up the work more effectively if she had addressed the problem more directly, perhaps saying something like "Sometimes I feel as if our supervision meetings don't have a lot of energy and that we don't have a chance to get into real conversations about your work with your families. I wonder how they seem to you. Is there anything I can do to make them more helpful to you?"

7. "You Just Don't Get It": Addressing Issues of Race, Class, and Power in Group Supervision

Markita is an African American social worker with a wide range of experiences and training in infant mental health and case management. She has recently been hired as a supervisor and team leader in a community neonatal intensive care follow-up program staffed by nurses, case managers, and early interventionists. There is often tension in the team meetings when staff members describe how clients don't always follow up with the appointments for their medically fragile babies. There are no overtly racial remarks, but Markita has picked up on the critical tone in the room as parents are discussed. She is sensitive about this, as she feels that some of the clients may be feeling looked down on or worse, and that some of the staff members just don't get what it means to be Black and poor. She finds herself a little angry at her staff members and begins to blame them for their insensitivity to the diverse low-income population of the program. Given how they talk at the center, she wonders what is conveyed nonverbally by the staff members to these families. However, she just can't find the words that will express her questions and worries. Despite her flare of strong emotion, she wants to support reflection, not reaction. She is worried about shutting down the discussion because missing these appointments is a real problem for the program. After a few deep breaths, Markita asks the group whether they have ideas on how they could increase the rate of attendance at the critical follow-up medical appointments. She takes a position by the flip chart, ready to record their ideas.

This intervention focuses the group on solutions, but the tone of criticism and low expectations continues. Markita finds her voice and says: "I know how hard you all work and how much you care about the babies, but as I listen I wonder if we are missing something with the parents. What we are saying somehow is so critical of these families. I wonder if we have talked with them about their experiences at these appointments and why they might be hard." The subsequent conversation becomes more aligned with the struggles of the parents. The staff members recount that parents had told them that at times they had felt blamed for their babies' conditions, had struggled with insurance issues, had felt that they couldn't get the attention of the doctors, and had to cope with long bus rides to get to the offices. Many parents dreaded the visits because they might mean more bad news and an implication that they were bad parents. Markita comments that sometimes we get swept up in worries about the kids and forget what the parents are going through. She says, "I am happy we are remembering this. They need our help so much."

Reflective Questions

1. What feelings does this situation bring up for you as a supervisor?

2. What are the strengths, resources, and elements in this situation that a supervisor could build on?

3. What questions do you have? What would you like to know more about?

4. What are the key areas of concern?

5. What is the supervisory dilemma?

6. Which supervisory roles are called into play in this situation?

7. What core principles and key skills of reflective supervision might be helpful in this situation?

8. As the supervisor, how might you proceed? Keep in mind how the various possibilities might play out over time.

Summary

Issues of race and class often are present in unspoken ways in team meetings and supervision. In this case, Markita struggles to pull herself together so she does not become overtly critical of her mainly White staff members for not "getting it." Markita skillfully engages the staff members in thinking about what she is worried about. She finds that their remarks allow her to frame her concerns in a way that strongly aligns with the philosophy of the program and the underlying intent of the staff members. As she does this, she is able to clarify that the intent of the program is to help parents understand, through support and dialogue, what their babies need. At the same time, she shines a light on the parents' struggles. Her nagging concerns about the staff members not getting it are somewhat contained, but undoubtedly these discussions will need to continue. She will need to work toward building more awareness in the staff members about their effect on families. Markita's awareness of herself has helped her find a way, as a supervisor and leader, to engage her staff members in conversations about differences in circumstances in class and race without disrupting team processes or relationships.

8. "NEXT...": MAINTAINING A REFLECTIVE FRAMEWORK FOR TEAM MEETINGS

Jolene is a family advocate in a Healthy Families program. At a team meeting, she innocently asks how many visits a family has to miss before the family is dropped from the program. Teammates ask Jolene a few questions about the family and then urge her to drop the family, as there is a waiting list. Some contribute anecdotes about families they have dropped from the caseload. Donna, the supervisor, is tracking the conversation and asks Jolene what she thinks it would mean to the family if they were no longer receiving the services of the program. This question seems to shift the tone of the team meeting, and someone asks Jolene how she has followed up on the missed visits.

Reflective Questions

1. What feelings does this situation bring up for you as a supervisor?

2. What are the strengths, resources, and elements in this situation that a supervisor could build on?

3. What questions do you have? What would you like to know more about?

4. What are the key areas of concern?

5. What is the supervisory dilemma?

6. Which supervisory roles are called into play in this situation?

7. What core principles and key skills of reflective supervision might be helpful in this situation?

8. As the supervisor, how might you proceed? Keep in mind how the various possibilities might play out over time.

Summary

This vignette illustrates the tendency of a team to function reactively, especially when the topic at hand stirs up uncomfortable feelings. It also demonstrates the strength of a well-formed question to change the tide, allowing more reflective approaches to flow into the discussion.

9. "NOT SO FAST...": CONTAINING AND REFRAMING

Emma is a new teacher in the Wee Care Child Development Program. She is in supervision with the site manager, Serena, who has come at her request to talk about a child who Emma feels should not be at Wee Care. Emma explains to Serena that little Sam, age 3½ years, has many behaviors that show he is on the way to becoming a juvenile delinquent. For example, he stole money from a jacket hanging in a cubby next to his. He also gets into fights and is disruptive during any group activity. Emma explains to Serena that she thinks it is time to consider a referral to the local therapeutic preschool where he can get the help he needs before it is too late.

Emma reports that she has spoken to Sam's mother about his worrisome behavior but that this has not been helpful. The mother is in her last month of pregnancy and ended the conversation in tears, saying to Emma that she just couldn't take this information in right now because she is so tired.

Reflective Questions

1. What feelings does this situation bring up for you as a supervisor?

2. What are the strengths, resources, and elements in this situation that a supervisor could build on?

3. What questions do you have? What would you like to know more about?

4. What are the key areas of concern?

5. Which is the supervisory dilemma?

6. Which supervisory roles are called into play in this situation?

7. What core principles and key skills of reflective supervision might be helpful in this situation?

8. As the supervisor, how might you proceed? Keep in mind how the various possibilities might play out over time.

Summary

Serena's job in this supervision session is to help Emma broaden her perspective about Sam and to think about his behavior in a developmental context. This should, in turn, lead Emma to be able to consider some new approaches to supporting him. However, before Serena can start these discussions with Emma, it will be important for her to take some time to listen and hear what it has been like for Emma to come into the program and be confronted with a little boy who is so difficult. Providing an empathic, open approach to Emma may help Emma contain her feelings so that she is able to reframe her view of Sam with more understanding and compassion.

10. "TUNNEL VISION": DEALING WITH CONCEPTUAL DRIFT

New Beginnings is a comprehensive community-based program for children from birth to 3 years old and their families. The program serves children who are at risk because of social issues, medical issues, or both. Staff members work closely with local child care and public health nursing groups. Services include home visitation, playgroups, parent support groups, and consultation to child care programs requesting help related to developmental, infant mental health, or other behavioral concerns. The New Beginnings staff members come from diverse backgrounds. They are all committed to a relationship-based approach to their work.

Each month, the staff members meet for a case presentation that is facilitated by the program supervisor, who also sees each staff person in individual supervision. Staff members are expected to prepare for the presentations by gathering comprehensive information about the child and the issues at hand. In this month's presentation, an infant specialist is discussing a family whom she has seen as part of a developmental consultation. The director of the infant care program has joined the New Beginnings team for the case presentation. The baby has some neurological problems, and the physician has stated that a shunt may be necessary. The infant specialist who has been consulting on this baby speaks at length about the family background and circumstances. In particular, she focuses on her worries about the mother's persistent depression and the father's disregard of his wife's needs. The supervisor notices that nothing has been said about the status of the baby, his medical problems, or his participation in the infant care site other than in the introduction. The director of the infant care program looks annoyed but stays silent the whole time. The staff members are animated and full of advice and suggestions that are directed at how to get the mother into mental health treatment and how to prod the father into greater awareness about his wife's mental health needs.

Reflective Questions

1. What feelings does this situation bring up for you as a supervisor?

2. What are the strengths, resources, and elements in this situation that a supervisor could build on?

3. What questions do you have? What would you like to know more about?

4. What are the key areas of concern?

5. Which is the supervisory dilemma?

6. Which supervisory roles are called into play in this situation?

7. What core principles and key skills of reflective supervision might be helpful in this situation?

8. As the supervisor, how might you proceed? Keep in mind how the various possibilities might play out over time.

Summary

This infant specialist's case presentation does not reflect the program's core philosophy of relationship-based, collaborative work within a holistic (or ecological) framework. The presenter has had a narrow focus on the family dynamics and has ignored the baby, his medical condition, and the work being done by the child care staff members. These omissions raise questions about the infant specialist's understanding of her role, as well as the team's commitment to the agreed-upon preparation and format for the presentations. The supervisor has a lot of work ahead in guiding her staff members back to an approach that is more reflective of their basic principles. This will need to occur at the individual and team level. At the same time, she has some repair work to do with the director of the infant care program.

11. "TROUBLE IN PARADISE": CAUGHT IN THE MIDDLE

Alisa is a new supervisor for an Early Head Start program. She is getting to know her job and figuring out ways she can support the teachers, family advocates, and coordinators who work at the site. One day, she decides to observe the outdoor play area. Several toddlers play contentedly with water toys in a large basin, and two teachers are nearby engaging the children and facilitating the play. Alisa feels happy that she is working in a program that values teacher–child interaction so much. However, about 5 minutes into the observation, Tina, one of the teachers, moves to the back of the patio and pulls a cell phone out of her pocket. She turns her back as if to gaze over to the building, but Alisa can see she is making a phone call, an activity Alisa knows to be against the rules of the center. Alisa notices that the other teacher, Molly, needs some assistance with one of the toddlers, who is crying. She moves closer and asks Molly if she can be of any help. Molly nods yes and gestures toward the basin of water while she takes the crying child. She comments to Alisa, "I hate it when I get left like this." Alisa asks, "What's the deal?" and Molly replies, "She's got a lot going on with her own family. I am just glad you are here now, but best not to mention this to the others." Alisa says, "The others?" and Molly replies, "You know, the big cheese, the director, the education coordinator too. They would freak out."

Reflective Questions

1. What feelings does this situation bring up for you as a supervisor?

2. What are the strengths, resources, and elements in this situation that a supervisor could build on?

3. What questions do you have? What would you like to know more about?

4. What are the key areas of concern?

5. What is the supervisory dilemma?

6. Which supervisory roles are called into play in this situation?

7. What core principles and key skills of reflective supervision might be helpful in this situation?

8. As the supervisor, how might you proceed? Keep in mind how the various possibilities might play out over time.

Summary

This vignette raises many dilemmas for Alisa the new supervisor. She is being asked in an indirect way to collude with Molly to protect a teacher who is breaking a rule about cell phones. Alisa wants to build supportive relationships with the staff members. Molly's request not to address the rule violation feels like a kind of a test. Alisa also wants to be seen as a supervisor who can develop relationships but also ensure quality and compliance with regulations and rules.

12. "CAN'T I JUST DO MY WORK?": SYSTEMS THINKING IN SUPERVISION

Wilma has provided 8 months of infant–parent psychotherapy to Billy, an 18-month-old, and his mom, Betty, who has just successfully completed 6 months of drug treatment. Billy is living with foster parents, although the case is now in the family reunification process. Billy's foster parents hope to adopt him if things don't work out for Betty. Wilma also works with the foster parents and Billy and feels a deep commitment to this little boy's well-being. The therapy has worked well to help Billy with transitions during visitations with his mom and to help Betty establish a strong relationship with her child. Yet, Wilma's supervisor, Raquelle, has noticed that, at times, Wilma feels uncertain about Betty's sobriety and worried about her abilities to provide what Billy needs. Recently Wilma has received a request from the social worker to "report to the judge" about Billy and Betty. She asks Raquelle to help her figure out a way to tell the social worker she can't do this right now or else to write the report so she doesn't have to look like the bad guy. She is reluctant to say that she still has a few worries about Betty's abilities to parent effectively in the long term. She is also worried that reporting to the judge will destroy her alliance with Betty.

Reflective Questions

1. What feelings does this situation bring up for you as a supervisor?

2. What are the strengths, resources, and elements in this situation that a supervisor could build on?

3. What questions do you have? What would you like to know more about?

4. What are the key areas of concern?

5. What is the supervisory dilemma?

6. Which supervisory roles are called into play in this situation?

7. What core principles and key skills of reflective supervision might be helpful in this situation?

8. As the supervisor, how might you proceed? Keep in mind how the various possibilities might play out over time.

Summary

Raquelle has several dilemmas in this situation. She feels a desire to rescue Wilma from the responsibilities of report writing and momentarily considers just doing it herself and sparing Wilma the agony of developing a careful report. Wilma's reluctance to report about her work to the judge is understandable given the tenuous nature of the situation. However, she does feel a commitment to this little boy's well-being, and not reporting her findings could withhold a piece of information that is critical for making decisions about Billy's future. Raquelle, the supervisor, has a pivotal role in slowing down the process, involving the social worker to fully comprehend the nature of the request, and trying to reach a better understanding of the therapist's choices regarding what information to provide.

Raquelle will also need to work with Wilma to sort out her observations, feelings, and case notes in order to provide helpful information to the court about Billy, Betty, and their work together. Raquelle will want to speak with Wilma regarding how to talk with Betty about the request for information from the court. If a report is required, Wilma and Raquelle will need to figure out how to discuss the content with Betty in a way that will not harm the working relationship. In any case, Raquelle will want to understand what kinds of discussions Wilma has had with Betty about her involvement with the child welfare system and potential requests for information. It would also be important to know what kinds of conversations Wilma and Betty have had with the social worker on these topics.

13. STAYING OPEN-MINDED AND TAKING RESPONSIBILITY

Sophia is the supervisor of a team that provides training for social work trainees who are doing infant–parent psychotherapy and case management services. Jeannie, a skilled social worker, had provided supervision to one of the social work interns but had been pulled off the team because of a conflict with the trainee that could not be resolved. Sophia had tried to resolve the conflict and felt eventually that she had no choice but to assign another supervisor. Jeannie was devastated and felt that Sophia had not done enough to support her during the discussions with the intern. She felt that Sophia had just caved in to the demands. About a year later, Jeannie asks to be reconsidered for the supervision position, and Sophia agrees to meet with Jeannie to talk about it. In that meeting, Jeannie acknowledges that she had made some mistakes but feels that she had not gotten the supervision and guidance she needed—especially given that it was her first time working with trainees. Sophia admits, with some difficulty, that Jeannie has a good point. Sophia is then faced with the dilemma of whether to give Jeannie another chance to try her wings as a supervisor.

Reflective Questions

1. What feelings does this situation bring up for you as a supervisor?

2. What are the strengths, resources, and elements in this situation that a supervisor could build on?

3. What questions do you have? What would you like to know more about?

4. What are the key areas of concern?

5. What is the supervisory dilemma?

6. Which supervisory roles are called into play in this situation?

7. What core principles and key skills of reflective supervision might be helpful in this situation?

8. As the supervisor, how might you proceed? Keep in mind how the various possibilities might play out over time.

Summary

Sophia has to grapple with the possibility that her own blind spot—that is, her inadequate supervision for Jeannie—had really been a contributing factor to Jeannie's poor performance in the past. She wonders whether things would have been significantly different if she had provided Jeannie with more support. Sophia is initially uncertain as to what would be the best decision, but after consultation with her own supervisor, she decides to give Jeannie another chance.

The authors acknowledge the contribution of Judith Bertacchi in the development of a number of these vignettes. She is an invaluable colleague and gifted teacher who provides guidance and insight into the practice of reflective supervision.

This generic supervisory self-assessment tool is to be used as a guide for the supervisor's professional development and own supervisory needs. It presents core skills, with exemplars of each skill ("Elements to Consider"). These exemplars are not all-inclusive but are offered as concrete examples of how a supervisor might demonstrate each particular standard.

I. ABILITY TO ASSESS STAFF MEMBERS' SKILLS

Standard

A. The supervisor is able to assess staff members' knowledge and skills in the areas of observing and assessing parent–child interactions, family self-sufficiency, healthy lifestyle environment, child safety, child development, disabilities, assessment, service provision, domestic violence, drug and alcohol abuse, and mental illness.

Elements to Consider

The supervisor:

- Gathers information about staff members' formal training, workshops, and course work in these areas, making use of training logs as appropriate.

- Gathers information about staff members' past work experience.

- Conducts regular family progress reviews with staff members; these reviews include a description of parent–child interactions, the child's development, consideration of disabilities if present, issues that affect the relationship of the parents to the child, social supports, and family assessments.

- Accompanies each staff member a minimum of twice per quarter on home visits to observe and discuss how well the staff member engages the family, connects all service delivery to the needs of the infant, and builds on family competencies.

- Reviews developmental screenings and assessments, progress notes, contact logs, Individual Family Service Plans (IFSPs), and other relevant documentation.

Standard

B. The supervisor is able to assess staff members' ability to develop effective working relationships with families, with special attention to the use of collaborative, partnering strategies; inclusion of family priorities, resources, and concerns; incorporation of family routines and activities; and use of strength-based approaches such as building on parental competencies and sharing concerns in a nonjudgmental manner.

Elements to Consider

The supervisor:

- Conducts regular family progress reviews with staff members: These include a description and discussion of interactions, trust building, and engagement with families.

- Accompanies each staff person a minimum of twice per quarter on home visits, and once per quarter with staff members on Parent Survey visits.

- Reviews assessments, screenings, progress notes, contact logs, and IFSPs.

- Conducts and reviews parent satisfaction surveys and written questionnaires.

Standard

C. The supervisor is able to help staff members increase their knowledge of parent–child interaction, child development, family functioning, motivational interviewing, the use of assessment tools, and service provision.

Elements to Consider

The supervisor:

- Observes staff members during team meetings, IFSPs, and other collegial interactions, with attention to active participation and positive contribution.

- Assesses staff members' ability to deal with conflict and other difficult situations through observation of team interactions and individual supervision.

- Assesses staff members' efforts to maintain good communication with team members and professional colleagues. This can be done through observation of team meetings, observed day-to-day interactions, and review of progress notes and daily logs, as well as during individual supervision.

- Solicits feedback from team members and professional colleagues via satisfaction surveys or evaluations.

- Conducts team-building activities to develop professional norms of interaction between team members, thereby encouraging shared goals, values, and methods of communication.

II. ABILITY TO SUPPORT STAFF MEMBERS' GROWTH AND DEVELOPMENT

Standard

A. The supervisor is able to help staff members increase their knowledge of child development, family functioning, motivational interviewing, the use of assessment tools, and service provision.

Elements to Consider

The supervisor:

- Uses supervision and observation to help the home visitor develop an understanding of the relationship between the parent and child and the dynamics of the home visit that may affect the outcome of child development and service delivery. This information will be synthesized through the process of reflective supervision.

- Clarifies and explores with the home visitor the underlying meanings of the relationship dynamics that occur between the caregiver and the infant and between the home visitor and the caregiver.

- Assesses and trains the home visitor regarding increased recognition of environmental, cultural, and caretaker strengths and risks that are affecting the infant and the family as a whole.

- Encourages critical thinking related to recent research and best practices through regular discussion of articles in team meetings, supervisory sessions, or both, and applies this information to the home visitor's direct work with families.

- Ensures that staff members build their competencies of observation and assessment in the areas of substance abuse, domestic violence, and mental illness. This can be done through training, motivational interviewing, and formal assessments, as well as by using consultants.

Standard

B. The supervisor is able to support staff members in (a) developing observation and assessment skills in the areas of child development, parent–child interaction, family self-sufficiency, and healthy lifestyle environment, and (b) ensuring child safety, particularly when there is evidence of domestic violence, drug or alcohol abuse, and mental illness.

Elements to Consider

The supervisor:

- Assists the home visitor in the development of observation skills by comparing observations following a home visit and discussing how accurately the home visitor assesses what she sees and what reactions or feelings she may have.

- Ensures home visitor's ability to articulate the different individual perspectives of each member of the family through training and supervision.

- Uses video reviews to focus staff members' attention on qualitative aspects of parent–child interaction and relationships both in individual supervision and team meetings.

Standard

C. The supervisor is able to help staff members increase their skills in using assessments in planning for families who have experienced attachment issues or other early childhood trauma.

Elements to Consider

The supervisor:

- Regularly reviews the parent survey and all other assessments with staff members to collaborate on identifying areas to address during home visits and assists staff members in understanding how the identified risk factors can potentially affect the parent–child relationship and child development. This also includes assisting staff members with which strategies to use based on the relationships that the staff members and families have formed.

- Anchors all challenges in the family by supporting the home visitor in understanding how brain development and the early years affect adult–child interactions patterns for the parents participating in services.

- Reviews each family's parent–child relationship through interactions and supports staff members in identifying and building on parental competencies.

- Develops with the home visitor a conceptual framework which ensures that all strengths and challenges are considered in line with child development, family functioning, domestic violence, substance abuse, mental illness, family self-sufficiency, attachment skills, traumas, and cultural implications.

- Identifies with the home visitor competencies that lead to change and that help families move forward and accept counseling or referrals to counseling or therapy.

- Ensures that the home visitor understands the power of the relationship she has with the parents and family. This involves witnessing the parent's ability to make changes and succeed and then celebrating that success. The supervisor can do this by identifying when this occurs in the home visit and discussing how the home visitor's interventions supported the family in achieving the change.

Standard

D. The supervisor is able to use information gathered during the outcome evaluations of program services to incorporate best-practice research into program activities and to assist staff members in seeing services from a program perspective.

Elements to Consider

The supervisor:

- Regularly reviews assessment/evaluation tools to plan for families; these tools include the IFSP, the Healthy Families Parenting Inventory, safety checklists, and family retention information.

- Discusses with staff members useful information from professional journals and other sources of research and how to use this information in their individual practice.

- Uses the data provided during semiannual site visits from the program specialist team to provide inservice or other training for continuous quality improvement.

Standard

E. The supervisor is able to assist staff members in increasing their level of self-awareness in regard to the ways in which their beliefs, values, attitudes, and past experiences may be affecting their work with children and families.

Elements to Consider

The supervisor:

- Supports and arranges for training to increase self-awareness of individual staff members and teams.

- Asks questions in supervision that help staff members reflect on the effects that their beliefs, values, attitudes, and past experiences have on their work.

- Uses facilitator role in team meetings and group experiences to gain insights from peers related to the effects of beliefs, values, attitudes, and past experiences on the work.

- Takes on the role of "historian" during supervision to document and refer back to related experiences with other families or the same family. Does this to help staff members gain a greater understanding and get a different perspective on a current situation.

- Uses own experiences and self-disclosure appropriately during supervision to help staff members understand their own work with families.

- Establishes atmosphere of safety that allows for exploration of staff members' beliefs, values, attitudes, and past experiences. Does this by maintaining confidentiality and providing a nonjudgmental approach to problem solving.

Standard

F. The supervisor is able to assist staff members in improving their collaborative partnership with families using relationship-based, reflective intervention strategies.

Elements to Consider

The supervisor:

- Provides training so that staff members have resources and tools for reflection, such as trust-building techniques, a standardized case discussion format, partnering communication strategies, and regular attention to strengths and resources.

- Provides training related to community and agency resources.

- Provides regular opportunities for family case discussion in team meetings and in regular supervision.

- Uses role play and video review for reflection on work with children and families.

- Uses parallel process in supervision and team meetings to model collaborative problem-solving strategies.

Standard

G. The supervisor is able to assist staff members to become more effective in their professional use of self. In particular, staff members are assisted in understanding issues related to ethics, transference, and professional boundaries.

Elements to Consider

The supervisor:

- Provides training and facilitates discussion related to these topics.

- Adopts an agreed-upon framework for addressing boundary issues that helps staff members consider the costs, benefits, and consequences of individual decisions. This is presented during staff training and reviewed in supervision.

- Focuses on boundary and transference issues in supervision and team meetings. Supports staff members in maintaining a healthy relationship with families and recognizes when staff members are sharing a healthy relationship with families and when they are not.

Standard

H. The supervisor is able to help staff members learn new ways of partnering with families and establishing a therapeutic alliance with them.

Elements to Consider

The supervisor:

- Provides training on partnering strategies, trust building, and qualities of a therapeutic relationship.

- Uses role play, family case discussion, and video review in team meetings and individual supervision to help staff members learn and practice new approaches, as well as to think about the costs and benefits of one approach or another. Helps staff members learn to appreciate the effects that their choice of words, partnering strategies, and tone of voice have on the work with families.

- Provides training and support in defining staff members' role with individual families. This includes issues related to working with multistressed or difficult-to-engage families, setting priorities and establishing reasonable expectations, and identifying the appropriate scope of practice.

III. ABILITY TO PROVIDE PROGRAM LEADERSHIP

Standard

A. The supervisor is able to maintain a primary focus on the program mission, program goals, and critical elements.

Elements to Consider

The supervisor:

- Can articulate the program mission and goals within the community and within the agency.

- Makes decisions and sets priorities so as to explicitly reflect the program's mission, goals, and critical elements.

- Continuously reviews with staff members the goals of the program to ensure understanding of why they do what they do.

- Demonstrates mastery of the applicable regulatory, credentialing, and best-practice standards.

Standard

B. The supervisor maintains open communication at all levels.

Elements to Consider

The supervisor:

- Holds regular team meetings. These are used for open discussion of program development, administrative issues, key concerns, and team building and are opportunities for staff members to give input into the decision-making process.

- Ensures that all staff members have equal access to program information and to a supervisor or designee for any issues.

- Establishes an atmosphere of mutuality, safety, trust, and respect that facilitates open communication.

Standard

C. The supervisor is able to inspire and motivate staff members.

Elements to Consider

The supervisor:

- Leads by example—that is, joins in doing the work (e.g., by going on home visits and attending parent meetings).

- Gives recognition to staff members' strengths, achievements, accomplishments, and progress.

- Demonstrates sensitivity to the context of the individual staff person's work (i.e., the specific stresses and challenges of being involved with families).

- Gives staff members opportunities to learn new skills and take on additional responsibilities and provides adequate support for new endeavors.

Standard

D. The supervisor encourages and supports the process of team development.

Elements to Consider

The supervisor:

- Is able to facilitate the efficient and effective development of the team even as members change.

- Creates an atmosphere within the team that promotes appreciation for individual strengths and differences and encourages open dialogue.

- Regularly defines and clarifies how the team works together to fulfill program goals.

- Develops high-performance teams by establishing a spirit of cooperation, acknowledging contributions, and cohesion for achieving goals.

- Identifies and addresses issues that negatively affect the team by modeling and encouraging team members to resolve issues constructively.

- Allocates decision making and other responsibilities to the appropriate individuals to mentor leadership within the team, and allows for consensus when possible.

- Models and promotes positive partnerships beyond the team (such as within the agency or community).

Standard

E. The supervisor is able to manage change effectively.

Elements to Consider

The supervisor:

- Communicates the nature of change to staff members through supervision, training, and team meetings.

- Builds the infrastructure needed to support change by instituting realistic time frames, adjusting caseloads, and providing needed resources.

- Articulates to families and other community partners the reasons for changes in services, policies, procedures, and staff members.

- Helps staff members understand and work through how changes affect them by setting realistic expectations for change, establishing priorities, and celebrating successes as individuals and as a team.

Standard

F. The supervisor is able to support and facilitate development in the community.

Elements to Consider

The supervisor:

- Participates in local and statewide committees and work groups related to policy development and best practice.

- Collaborates with community partners to share resources, coordinate referrals, and develop services.

- Encourages and supports staff members in their participation in both agency and community committees and work groups.

IV. ABILITY TO MAINTAIN PROGRAM STANDARDS AND ENSURE PROGRAM QUALITY

Standard

A. The supervisor is able to hire staff members on the basis of their education, experiences, and ability to develop positive relationships. The supervisor ensures the quality of staff members through recruitment, hiring, and training practices.

Elements to Consider

The supervisor:

- Makes intensive efforts to recruit staff members who reflect the cultural diversity of the population and community served.

- Ensures that job descriptions clearly reflect the mission and values of the program as well as the key skills and qualifications needed to do the job, including understanding of relationship-based work and reflective practice.

- Conducts interviews that focus on key skills, including relationship-based reflective practice. Uses techniques such as asking for specific examples from the candidate's personal experience, role play, and written responses to case scenarios.

- Asks candidate's references questions related to the candidate's understanding of relationship-based work and reflective practice.

- Provides orientation for new staff members that focuses on program and values, as well as key skills for the job.

- Provides support for ongoing professional development through workshops, inservice training, and team meeting discussions.

Standard

B. The supervisor is able to develop effective staff retention strategies.

Elements to Consider

The supervisor:

- Provides regular, reflective, and collaborative supervision.

- Ensures consistent availability of supervisory support outside of regularly scheduled supervisory meetings.

- Provides opportunities for professional development and advancement.

- Surveys staff members who leave in order to understand the reasons for their decision.

- Develops an annual staff retention plan.

Standard

C. The supervisor takes responsibility for ensuring that the program meets all applicable regulatory and procedural standards.

Elements to Consider

The supervisor:

- Previews and reviews all standards and policies with staff members to ensure that they have been understood.

- Partners with staff members to ensure compliance with processes and procedures related to the credentialing standards, policies and procedures, and contractual requirements.

- Partners with the program specialist to assist staff members in meeting best-practice standards related to credentialing, policies and procedures, and contractual requirements.

- Conducts regular file and caseload reviews.

- Regularly accompanies staff members on home visits and to parent meetings.

- Solicits feedback from clients via telephone surveys and parent questionnaires.

- Participates in all monitoring and evaluation processes. Helps staff members prepare for these activities.

- Works with staff members to follow up on identified areas of program need and address any compliance issues.

- Attends and participates in mandated program meetings and trainings.

- Is able to balance attention to administrative and child/family concerns.

Standard

D. The supervisor conducts performance reviews, gives staff members ongoing feedback in a manner that reflects the program's mission and values, and carries out disciplinary actions as needed.

Elements to Consider

The supervisor:

- Provides staff members with regular feedback related to the quality of their work performance.

- Is able to address difficult issues with staff members such as concerns regarding interpersonal skills, alliance building with families, and dealing with team conflicts.

- Conducts a formal performance review on an annual (or more frequent) basis.

- Ensures that performance reviews are based on the job description and ongoing supervisory discussions.

- Conducts performance reviews that are collaborative, reflective, and respectful.

- Ensures that concerns related to performance have been addressed in regular supervisory sessions so that they are not being presented for the first time during the performance review.

- Works with staff members to develop a personal development plan that is based on the performance review and ongoing supervisory discussions.

- Provides opportunity for staff members to give feedback regarding the quality of the supervisor's work with them.

- Carries out disciplinary actions, including termination of employment, in accordance with agency policy and legal process.

Standard

E. The supervisor solicits parent/family participation in all aspects of program development and quality assurance.

Elements to Consider

The supervisor:

- Supports parent participation in program activities such as planning parent meetings, review of program materials, and serving as board members.

- Is responsive to the content of family satisfaction questionnaires.

Standard

F. The supervisor uses information gathered during the evaluation of program outcomes as well as up-to-date research regarding evidence-based practice for continuous program improvement activities.

Elements to Consider

The supervisor:

- Reviews with staff members the aggregate information gathered from program evaluation/assessment tools to improve services for families.

- Reviews with staff members recent research regarding best practice and discusses with them ways of implementing this in the program.

- Reviews with staff members any available program evaluation report for site-specific information and discusses implications for service delivery.

- Uses the data provided during the semiannual visits from the program specialist or other evaluator to provide inservice or other training for continuous program quality improvement.

Source: Southwest Human Development, Phoenix, AZ. Used with permission.

REFLECTIVE SUPERVISION AGREEMENT

This sample supervisory contract is to be used when beginning a new supervisory relationship. It should be reviewed periodically, especially when difficulties arise.

REFLECTIVE SUPERVISION CONTRACT: EARLY CHILDHOOD MENTAL HEALTH PROGRAM

- Reflective supervision is a blended model of supervision. Supervisors are responsible for providing opportunities for supervisees to learn new information, reflect and consider work they are doing, review administrative details of work such as billing and treatment plans, make decisions together regarding legal and ethical issues, and communicate in an open, reflective way with other colleagues.

- The reflective supervisor is responsible for the supervisee's yearly evaluation. The reflective supervisor will review this document with the supervisee and will bring any concerns to the supervisee's attention as they occur. The reflective supervisor–supervisee relationship is seen as a collaboration to support the growth of the supervisee in the program and the quality of the services provided to families. As the final evaluation is completed, the reflective supervisor will also solicit feedback from others involved with the supervisee.

- Each supervisor and supervisee brings her own set of experiences and beliefs into the supervisory relationship. It is important that these different points of view and sociocultural differences are explored fully.

- Ideally, the supervisor–supervisee relationship is open and accepting. Areas of difference or conflict should be brought up and explored by both parties. If mediation on these differences is needed, the supervisor's supervisor or the program manager will be consulted by either party.

- Reflective supervision occurs on a regularly scheduled basis. The reflective supervisor is responsible for keeping a log of the scheduled visits and notes about themes and content.

I have read and understood these points: _____Supervisee

_____Supervisor

*Source: Children's Hospital and Research Center Oakland, Early Childhood Mental Health Program, Oakland, CA.
Used with permission.*

APPENDIX 3
SUPERVISORY LOG FORM

This is a sample of a generic supervision log form. The form should be done on carbonless paper with a copy for the supervisor and the supervisee.

NAME:

_____

Professional Development Plan reviewed/updated?   ☐ Yes ☐ No

FOLLOW-UP FROM LAST MEETING:

SUMMARY OF TODAY'S MEETING (issues raised, topics/families discussed, etc.):

THINGS SUPERVISOR/SUPERVISEE WILL DO...

OTHER:

_____   _____   _____
Supervisee's signature   Supervisor's signature   Date

Source: Southwest Human Development, Phoenix, AZ. Used with permission.

*This sample job description of a supervisory position includes key roles,
skills, and competencies described in chapters 2 and 4.*

POSITION:

EARLY INTERVENTION PROGRAM MANAGER/SUPERVISOR

CLASSIFICATION:

EXEMPT

DEPARTMENT:

SERVICES TO CHILDREN WITH DISABILITIES

SUPERVISOR:

DIRECTOR

JOB SUMMARY:

Supervises assigned early intervention staff members in the planning and implementation of early intervention (birth to 3) services. These services include screening, evaluation, assessment, eligibility determination, Individualized Family Service Plan (IFSP) development, intervention planning, implementation of intervention, and transition planning and implementation. As assigned, monitors status of the various early intervention programs and contracts, including issues related to family-centered practice, cultural/linguistic sensitivity, use of the team-based model, team functioning, curriculum, billing, caseloads, reporting, and the transition process. Ensures compliance with state and federal regulatory, quality assurance, and data collection requirements. Ensures collaboration and integration of early intervention program services with both inter- and intra-agency services. Provides regular, reflective, collaborative supervision to assigned staff members and teams. Oversees functioning of assigned core teams. Supports lifelong learning and professional development. Assists director in planning, developing, and monitoring program services, policies, and procedures. Represents agency in the community and at councils. Works under general direction, according to the agency mission, philosophy, core values, codes of ethics, and goals.

Listed below are the essential functions of this job.

ESSENTIAL JOB FUNCTIONS:

1. **Oversees the implementation and monitors the delivery and quality of services.**

   a. Reviews records and documentation, according to department schedule or as needed, and observes directly the delivery of services to ensure that:

   - Services are delivered in a developmentally appropriate, family-responsive, and culturally and linguistically sensitive manner.

   - Individual child outcomes and strategies are developed collaboratively with families, are functional in nature, and are related to ongoing family routines and daily activities.

   - Intervention/therapy services are developmentally appropriate and integrated into home/family routines.

   - Testing procedures are carried out accurately and reliably, and in a manner that is culturally, linguistically, and developmentally appropriate.

   - Required paperwork is maintained appropriately and in a timely manner.

   - Timelines are met, and state and federal regulations and procedures are upheld.

   - Team planning meetings are held according to the agreed-upon schedule, and teams function in a respectful and collaborative manner.

   b. As assigned, monitors caseloads, billings, enrollment, progress and assessment/evaluation reports, IFSPs, and the transition process.

   c. Uses independent judgment and discretion in setting daily priorities to complete tasks.

- Maintains established work schedule, is punctual, keeps appointments, is willing to adapt schedule to meet unexpected needs and changes, and uses time effectively.

- Performs duties in an organized, efficient, and timely manner.

d. Takes corrective action to ensure delivery and quality of services.

e. In collaboration with director and program staff members, develops policies and procedures that clearly detail the specific tasks and steps required of all staff members to implement program service goals and objectives.

f. As assigned, ensures staff members' awareness of and compliance with program, agency, and state policies (e.g., regarding restraint, referral to child protective services, and health and safety standards).

g. Operates within the budget and adheres to established guidelines for expenditures, billing, and documentation. Ensures that data are correct for accurate and timely billing.

i. Develops, maintains, and uses a comprehensive record-keeping system to monitor the delivery and documentation of services, progress and performance of staff members, and other ongoing job responsibilities.

j. Uses data to enhance knowledge and understanding of trends and changes at the program and community level.

k. Analyzes program, participant, and community data to recommend program services and activities that best meet the interest and needs of the participants.

l. Ensures maintenance, cleanliness, effective utilization, and safety of the physical facility and equipment. Monitors and requests supplies and services, as appropriate.

m. Demonstrates sensitivity to linguistic, cultural, social, economic, individual, and role differences among persons and families served.

n. Adheres to the agency core values and the codes of ethics of the National Association of Social Workers and National Association for the Education of Young Children.

2. Participates in long-term planning and program development activities.

a. Participates in long-range planning activities and follows through with agreed-upon tasks.

b. Helps with the development of new programs to meet identified community needs and with the identification of resources to support them.

c. Coordinates with staff members from other agency departments, local school districts, and the state early intervention program, as well as contract therapists.

d. Helps design and implement staff training.

e. Actively participates in community meetings, agency and community committees, and associations/organizations that affect the program's services and participants.

f. Makes presentations to staff members and community about the program.

3. Provides reflective supervision in support of relationship-based work.

a. Provides supervision that is regular, reflective, and collaborative in nature.

b. Designs supervision so as to identify areas of mastery and areas targeted for growth and development. Uses supervision to promote staff members' growth and development. Assists staff members in the creation of an individualized and ongoing professional development plan.

c. Promotes staff members' awareness of their own values, beliefs, and experiences and the potential effect of these on their work with children and families.

d. Responds quickly and effectively to staff members' concerns, notifying the department director in a timely manner of any issues requiring her attention.

e. Documents supervision session according to required standards.

f. Interviews, hires, and trains program staff members.

g. Carries out staff members' performance reviews according to designated schedule and according to the principles of reflective practice.

4. Provides program leadership.

a. Encourages and supports the process of team development. Is proactive in working to ensure positive and effective team functioning, and to address any issues that may interfere with a constructive team process.

b. Facilitates and participates in integrated team process. Works to promote interdepartmental and interagency collaboration in support of "One Family, One Team, One Plan."

c. Manages change effectively and positively.

d. Provides staff members with motivation and support to do their work.

e. Facilitates open and clear communication among team members.

f. Supports decisions of the director and management team to staff members, participants, and the community.

5. Communicates accurately, clearly, and professionally.

a. Communicates in a positive, respectful, and courteous manner.

b. Practices active listening skills and uses partnering communication strategies to engage staff members in collaborative problem-solving process.

c. Interacts with coworkers and the community to build productive and collaborative relationships to support the achievement of agency and program goals.

d. Understands and maintains private and sensitive information within the confines of need-to-know parameters.

e. Demonstrates good presentation and public speaking skills and techniques.

f. Composes written communication including letters, memos, minutes, forms, procedure and policy statements, and other documents, using various writing styles and formats to produce documents that effectively communicate the purpose and intent.

g. Submits accurate and complete reports, forms, and other written information as required in accordance with department and program standards and schedule.

h. Proofs and revises work for correct grammar, spelling, and format.

6. Uses supervision effectively, takes initiative to secure professional development opportunities, and applies relevant information in the work setting.

a. Actively participates in supervision that is regular, reflective, and collaborative in nature. As appropriate, takes the initiative to seek supervisory input.

b. Accurately identifies areas of mastery and areas targeted for personal growth and development. Seeks assistance and guidance when needed.

c. Incorporates constructive direction from supervisor to improve job performance.

d. Accepts responsibility for the quality of job performance and makes changes as needed.

e. Maintains awareness of current professional information in the fields of activity, undertakes regular and ongoing efforts to maintain competencies in the skills used, and incorporates new knowledge and skills on the job.

f. Shares pertinent information with supervisor about work progress, barriers, successes, concerns, and other issues that may have an effect on the department's services.

Source: Southwest Human Development, Phoenix, AZ. Used with permission.

This is an excerpt from a sample performance review form for a program supervisor/manager. Note that this parallels the job description provided as Appendix 4. This is only a partial form: The complete performance review form would include all essential job functions as listed in the job description. It is helpful for the job description, performance review, and professional development plan to parallel each other and provide a consistent picture of key roles, responsibilities, and necessary skills.

SERVICES TO CHILDREN WITH DISABILITIES ANNUAL PERFORMANCE REVIEW

POSITION: EARLY INTERVENTION PROGRAM MANAGER/SUPERVISOR

NAME: _____

SUPERVISOR(S): _____

DATE OF REVIEW: _____

ESSENTIAL JOB FUNCTIONS:

1. Provides reflective supervision in support of relationship-based work.

 a. Provides supervision that is regular, reflective, and collaborative in nature.

 b. Designs supervision so as to identify areas of mastery and areas targeted for growth and development. Uses supervision to promote staff members' growth and development. Assists staff members in the creation of an individualized and ongoing professional development plan.

 c. Promotes staff members' awareness of their own values, beliefs, and experiences and the potential effect of these on their work with children and families.

d. Responds quickly and effectively to staff members' concerns, notifying the department director in a timely manner of any issues requiring her attention.

e. Documents supervision session according to required standards.

f. Interviews, hires, and trains program staff members.

g. Carries out staff members' performance reviews according to designated schedule and according to the principles of reflective practice.

Has mastered:

_____

_____

_____

_____

In the coming year, should work toward:

_____

_____

_____

_____

2. Provides program leadership.

a. Encourages and supports the process of team development. Is proactive in working to ensure positive and effective team functioning and to address any issues that may interfere with a constructive team process.

b. Facilitates and participates in integrated team process. Works to promote interdepartmental and interagency collaboration in support of "One Family, One Team, One Plan."

c. Manages change effectively and positively.

d. Provides staff members with motivation and support to do their work.

e. Facilitates open and clear communication among team members.

f. Supports decisions of the director and management team to staff members, participants, and the community.

Has mastered:

_____

_____

_____

_____

In the coming year, should work toward:

_____

_____

_____

_____

3. Communicates accurately, clearly, and professionally.

a. Communicates in a positive, respectful, and courteous manner.

b. Practices active listening skills and uses partnering communication strategies to engage staff members in collaborative problem-solving process.

c. Interacts with coworkers and the community to build productive and collaborative relationships to support the achievement of agency and program goals.

d. Understands and maintains private and sensitive information within the confines of need-to-know parameters.

e. Demonstrates good presentation and public speaking skills and techniques.

f. Composes written communication including letters, memos, minutes, forms, procedure and policy statements, and other documents, using various writing styles and formats to produce documents that effectively communicate the purpose and intent.

g. Submits accurate and complete reports, forms, and other written information as required in accordance with department and program standards and schedule.

h. Proofs and revises work for correct grammar, spelling, and format.

Has mastered:

_____

_____

_____

_____

In the coming year, should work toward:

_____

_____

_____

_____

_____   _____

Employee's signature   Date

_____   _____

Supervisor's signature   Date

Source: Southwest Human Development, Phoenix, AZ. Used with permission.

Appendix 6
Professional Development Plan Form

This is a sample of a professional development plan. The form should be used as a summary after completion of the performance review. Supervisees will typically develop at least three or four goals.

POSITION: _____

NAME: _____

SUPERVISOR(S): _____

DATE OF REVIEW: _____

GOAL 1: _____

_____

Implementation date for Goal 1: _____

Activities/steps necessary to accomplish Goal 1 with dates for achievement indicated:

1. _____

2. _____

3. _____

Key individuals or resources to help achieve this goal:

_____

_____

I will know that my goal has been achieved when:

_____

_____

GOAL 2: _____

_____

Implementation date for Goal 2: _____

Activities/steps necessary to accomplish Goal 2 with dates for achievement indicated:

  1. _____
  2. _____
  3. _____

Key individuals or resources to help achieve this goal:

_____

_____

I will know that my goal has been achieved when:

_____

_____

_____

Employee's signature

_____

Supervisor's signature

Source: Southwest Human Development, Phoenix, AZ. Used with permission.

Feedback for: [Name of supervisor]_____

Rating Scale:

1. Please rank the following statements on a scale with 1 being the lowest and 5 being the highest:

Job expectations are clear.	1	2	3	4	5
I am free to make appropriate decisions in my day-to-day work activities.	1	2	3	4	5
I have adequate support from my supervisor to be able to do so.	1	2	3	4	5
I am kept informed and up-to-date about issues related to my work.	1	2	3	4	5
My supervisor encourages my input and respects my ideas.	1	2	3	4	5
My supervisor is responsive to me.	1	2	3	4	5
My supervisor is knowledgeable about the specific work I do (e.g., issues related to individual classrooms, families, and children).	1	2	3	4	5

2. What does your supervisor do that helps you succeed?

_____

_____

3. Are there other things your supervisor could do that would help you in your job?

_____

_____

4. Does your supervisor do anything that makes it more difficult for you to succeed?

_____

_____

5. Please rank the following traits for your supervisor on a scale with 1 being the lowest and 5 being the highest:

Positive attitude	1	2	3	4	5
Team player/inclusivity of decision making	1	2	3	4	5
Approachability	1	2	3	4	5
Patience	1	2	3	4	5
Understanding and empathy	1	2	3	4	5
Ability to set boundaries	1	2	3	4	5
Respectfulness	1	2	3	4	5
Supportive advocate for staff	1	2	3	4	5
Appreciative of individual skills, needs, and interests	1	2	3	4	5

Accessible   1   2   3   4   5

Helps me solve problems and get information   1   2   3   4   5

6. I believe my supervisor's greatest strengths are:

_____

_____

7. I believe my supervisor could continue growing/improve in these areas:

_____

_____

8. Overall, I feel this way about working with my supervisor:

_____

_____

As you have filled out this form, you may have identified some areas of concern related to the support you are receiving from your supervisor. Are there areas that you think you could address directly with your supervisor?

_____

_____

Are there any other areas that you would not feel comfortable addressing with your supervisor?

_____

_____

Any other comments?

_____

_____

_____

_____

Source: Adapted by Southwest Human Development, Phoenix, AZ. Used with permission.

EVALUATION OF THE SUPERVISOR
BY THE SUPERVISEE—SAMPLE B

Please rank the following competencies 1–5, or select N/A if you have no experience observing the competency:

The ranking is defined as:

- 1: Serious Issue—a pressing need to address.

- 2: Weakness—results have fallen short in this area.

- 3: Skilled/OK—the manager does what is expected and is about the same as most others.

- 4: Talented—notable strength in this area; manager is better than most and could be a coach in this area.

- 5: Towering Strength—manager is outstanding in this area and is a role model.

The surveys are anonymous and confidential. The results will help your supervisor deepen these skills. Please feel free to share the results directly with your supervisor.

1. **Listening: 1   2   3   4   5   N/A**

   Practices attentive and active listening. Has patience to hear people out.
   Can accurately restate the opinions of other even when not in agreement.

2. **Organization Agility: 1   2   3   4   5   N/A**

   Knowledgeable about how organizations work. Knows how to get things done through both formal and informal channels. Understands the origin and reasoning behind key policies and practices.

3. **Composure: 1   2   3   4   5   N/A**

   Is cool under pressure. Does not become defensive or irritated when times are tough. Is considered mature. Can be counted on to hold things together during tough times. Can handle stress. Is not knocked off balance by the unexpected. Is a settling influence in a crisis.

4. Decision-Making Ability: 1   2   3   4   5   N/A

Makes good decisions based on a mixture of analysis, wisdom, experience, and judgment. Most solutions or suggestions turn out to be correct and accurate. Sought out by others for advice.

5. Sociocultural Diversity: 1   2   3   4   5   N/A

Deals effectively with all races, nationalities, cultures, disabilities, and ages, and both sexes. Supports fair and equal treatment for all. Is aware of sociocultural issues and their effect on clients and colleagues. Makes room for sociocultural discussion in team discussions.

6. Knowledge Base: 1   2   3   4   5   N/A

Has mastery of the content of early childhood development and early childhood mental health. Knows how to engage families and is effective at intervention strategies. Is a resource for other team members. Shares knowledge readily and effectively.

7. Assessment Ability: 1   2   3   4   5   N/A

Knows how to plan, conduct, and summarize assessment information. Understands and uses a variety of assessment tools. Works to include clinician in assessment. Engages parent as a partner in assessment activities. Summarizes assessment information in parent-useful ways. Completes assessments in a timely fashion. Provides useful written information to therapists and families. Works well with children and families.

8. Negotiating/Advocating: 1   2   3   4   5   N/A

Can negotiate skillfully in tough situations both internally and externally. Advocates for team members when appropriate.

9. Priority Setting: 1   2   3   4   5   N/A

Spends own time and the time of others on what's important. Quickly zeros in on the critical few and puts the trivial aside. Can quickly sense what will help or hinder accomplishing a goal. Eliminates roadblocks. Creates focus.

10. Conflict Management: 1   2   3   4   5   N/A

Steps up to conflicts, seeing them as opportunities. Reads situations quickly. Can hammer through tough agreements and settle disputes equitably. Can find the common ground and get cooperation with minimal noise.

11. Peer Relationships: 1 2 3 4 5 N/A

Can quickly find common ground and solve problems for the good of all. Can represent own interests and yet be fair to other groups. Can solve problems with peers. Is seen as a team player and is cooperative. Encourages collaboration. Is candid with peers.

12. Planning: 1 2 3 4 5 N/A

Accurately scopes out the length and difficulty of tasks and projects. Sets objectives and goals. Breaks down work into the process steps. Develops schedules and assignments. Anticipates and adjusts for problems and roadblocks. Measures performance against goals. Evaluates results.

13. Directing/Supervising Others: 1 2 3 4 5 N/A

Is good at establishing clear guidelines. Sets stretch goals. Distributes workload appropriately. Lays out work in a well-planned manner. Maintains two-way dialogue. Brings out the best in people. Is a clear communicator. Provides support as needed. Helps others meet their goals.

14. Informing: 1 2 3 4 5 N/A

Provides the information people need to know to do their jobs and feel good about being a member of the team. Provides individuals with information so that they can make accurate decisions. Is timely with information.

15. Motivating Others: 1 2 3 4 5 N/A

Knows what motivates others or how to do it. People who work with the supervisor want to do their best. Empowers others. Many people want to work for this leader. Is a good reader of others. Motivates others.

16. Building Effective Teams: 1 2 3 4 5 N/A

Assembles, builds, or manages in a team fashion. Creates a common mind-set or common challenge. Rewards and compliments the team members. Builds team morale and energy. Allows the team members space to get their jobs done.

17. Training Ability: 1 2 3 4 5 N/A

Conceptualizes and organizes ideas for effective learning. Balances content and process in training. Is able to create training materials that are helpful to others. Is able to present ideas to a diverse group. Is well prepared. Facilitates training well.

Please list the two priority areas you would like to see the supervisor address in the upcoming year:

_____

_____

_____

_____

Thanks for your time. Please return by _____. It can be returned without
                                                Date
your name for confidentiality.

Source: Children's Hospital and Research Center Oakland, Early Childhood Mental Health Program, Oakland, CA. Used with permission.

Appendix 9
Intra-Agency Staffing Form

This form can be used to guide the discussion when providers from different programs who work with the same child and family meet for a staffing.

☐Mental Health   ☐Preschool Head Start ☐Family Reunification
☐Early Intervention   ☐NICU Follow-up   ☐Parent Aide
☐Healthy Families   ☐Kinship Care   ☐Behavioral Health Services
☐Early Head Start   ☐Family Preservation

Child _____

Family _____

Team Lead _____

Date_____

(Each of these topics should be covered, at least briefly, during each staffing.)

- **Review of child's developmental status—all areas of development, including social/emotional (age-appropriate? recent progress? qualitative concerns?)**

  _____

  _____

- **Review of family status—recent events, current stressors, available resources**

  _____

  _____

- **Review of plan outcomes (all team members should bring their program-specific plans, including outcomes, goals, and strategies; e.g., an Individualized Family Service Plan or Family Partnership Agreement)**

  _____

  _____

- Review of intervention—focus of treatment and discussion of specific strategies

  _____

  _____

- How can we reinforce and support each other's work? (Be specific!)

  _____

  _____

- What is our current joint formulation of the child and family's needs and priorities?

  _____

  _____

- What questions do we have? For each, what information do we need and how could it be obtained? Who will be responsible to follow up on it?

  _____

  _____

- Are there avenues or approaches that have been successful that could be shared with other team members? Are there specific roadblocks that would be beneficial to share with the other team members?

  _____

  _____

- Next Steps:

  _____

  _____

- Next Meeting:_____

Source: Southwest Human Development, Phoenix, AZ. Used with permission.

APPENDIX 10
QUESTIONS THAT ENCOURAGE REFLECTION
AND PROBLEM SOLVING

Choose questions carefully based on attuned listening. When using questions, less is usually more.

1. Questions that raise alternatives	What are the possibilities? If you had your choice, what would you do? What are the possible solutions? What if you do … and what if you don't?
2. Questions that encourage additional thinking and perspective taking	How do you feel about it? What do you think is best? What do you think would be best for the baby? What are some other ways of looking at this? How do you suppose X sees this?
3. Questions that encourage looking at the total picture	What led up to this? What have you tried so far? What do you make of all this? When does this usually happen?
4. Questions that lead to clarification	In what way does this make sense to you? What is confusing to you about this? Can you explain what you mean by that? If you had to explain this to somebody who didn't know you, where would you start?
5. Questions that encourage description	What was it like? Can you tell me about it? How is this different from other experiences you have had with this kind of situation? What does this remind you of or make you think of?

6. Questions that encourage exploration	Why do you suppose people do things like that? How could a person handle a problem like that? If you had your choice, what would you prefer to do?
7. Questions to identify issues	What seems to be the trouble? In what ways does this bother you? What do you consider the most troublesome part?
8. Questions that encourage the use of information	What information do you need before you decide? What do you know about it now? How do you suppose you can find out more about it?
9. Questions that encourage planning	What do you see as the first thing you have to do? What are you going to do about it? Where do you go from here? What are your next steps? Where do you think this will lead? If this doesn't work, then what are you going go do? What are some other options available to you?

Source: Mary Claire Heffron, from the Consultation and Training Team, Child Development Center, Children's Hospital Oakland, CA. Used with permission.

ABOUT THE AUTHORS

Mary Claire Heffron, PhD, is the clinical director at the Early Childhood Mental Health Program at Children's Hospital and Research Center Oakland and a ZERO TO THREE Graduate Fellow. She directs the Irving B. Harris Early Childhood Mental Health Training Program which provides relationship-based training to staff working across disciplines in a variety of service delivery settings. She also directs several other projects including the Fussy Baby Program.

She has had extensive experience with infants, young children, and families including clinical work, supervision, program development, and training. She has a variety of interests within her field including development of services and professional support that address issues of culture, class, and difference. Her interest in neuroscience has helped to shape her approach to working with families and with her colleagues. She has been involved for many years in providing reflective supervision and consulting with agencies on how to set up reflective supervision services.

She is a frequent presenter at conferences in the early childhood field and has published a number of articles on supervision and reflective practice.

Trudi Murch, PhD, CCC-SLP, is director of Services for Children with Disabilities at Easter Seals Southwest Human Development, a community-based human service agency serving young children and families in the Greater Phoenix area.

She has had extensive experience in pediatric clinical work and program development in early intervention and preschool disabilities services. An area of special interest is the design and implementation of the reflective supervision model in non-mental health settings. She has provided supervision training and consultation to a wide range of programs around the U.S., including Head Start and Early Head Start, early intervention, Healthy Families, school district personnel, and state and national speech/language pathology associations. She has published in the area of reflective supervision in *Zero to Three* and *Infants and Young Children*.